Europe's

Jewish

Quarters

Europe's

Jewish

Quarters

Matthew Reisz

SIMON & SCHUSTER

LONDON·SYDNEY·NEW YORK·TOKYO·SINGAPORE·TORONTO

First published in Great Britain by
Simon & Schuster Ltd in 1991
A Paramount Communications Company

Simon & Schuster Ltd
West Garden Place
Kendal Street
London W2 2AQ

Simon & Schuster of Australia Pty Ltd
Sydney

A CIP catalogue record for this book is
available from the British Library
ISBN 0–671–71022–2

Typeset in 10.5/13.5pt Bembo by
Falcon Typographic Art Ltd, Edinburgh & London
Illustrations reproduced by Gilchrist Brothers Ltd
Printed and bound in Great Britain by
HarperCollinsManufacturing, Glasgow

CONTENTS

To Françoise and Julian,
with much love

ACKNOWLEDGEMENTS

Many people contributed help of different kinds to this book, often well beyond the call of duty, and I am most grateful to them all. Valerie Chazan had the painful task of going through all the marvellous photographs taken by her daughter Sharon, who was tragically murdered during an East End project at the age of 24. Joelle Sintes went to take photographs in the Jewish quarter of Marseilles, at a time of considerable tension during the Gulf War; she also invited my family and me to stay at her flat in Aix-in-Provence. Anne Cowen kindly provided me with a postcard from her collection and some of the original magazines which she and her husband had included in their lovely book on *Victorian Jews through British Eyes* (Oxford University Press, 1986). Linda Falter of Facsimile Editions in London loaned me a photograph taken for their forthcoming facsimile of the *Barcelona Haggadah*.

Professor William Fishman took me on an eye-opening tour of the East End. Mark Eisler, Vera Neuroth, Tim O'Brien and Brigitte Timmermann all gave useful assistance in Vienna, and Finn Jensen much advice about Copenhagen. Steven Beller shared with me some of his deep knowledge about nineteenth- and early twentieth-century Jewish life in Prague and Vienna. Harvey Kaplan of the Scottish Jewish Archive Centre carried out picture research for me quickly and efficiently, and Brad Sabin Hill of the British Library gave me useful information and material from his personal collection. My brother Barney and Lucia Alvarez de Toledo brought back documents from Venice before my own visit. Simon Cobley of the Weidenfeld Archive and many individuals in museums all over Europe were unfailingly helpful.

Although I would like to single out Eugen Dhont of Antwerp and Jan Laybourn of Copenhagen, the London and local staff of the Austrian, Belgian, Czech, Dutch, French, Scottish and Spanish tourist boards all offered much-needed help with accommodation, transport, contacts, information and photographs. The travel editors of the *Guardian, European, Independent on Sunday, Jewish Chronicle* and *New York Times* commissioned me to write general tourist articles which I was able to combine with research for this book. For the chapters on Paris, Prague and Rome, accommodation was kindly provided by Sebastian and Evelyne Goodchild, Katya Kostarova and her husband, and Titina Maselli.

Both private individuals and officials of the different Jewish communities were willing to talk to me at length, often with little or no notice, and sometimes about tragic personal or family histories. They included some wonderfully entertaining people, like Dr Ezra Golombok of the Glasgow *Jewish Echo*, but whether or not they are mentioned by name in the text, their contribution was vital. Concierges waived tight security restrictions in allowing me to visit some of the most beautiful synagogues in Europe. Ronnie Landau's classes in 'Modern Jewish History' at London's City Lit. were a major source of inspiration.

My agent, Hilary Rubenstein of A. P. Watt, was encouraging and helpful throughout; I would also like to thank his colleague Imogen Parker. My bank manager, Kevin Brown, was extremely forbearing. My parents and step-mother provided much assistance. Most of all, however, my wife and son remained deeply supportive despite all the absences, moodiness and financial pressures. It is only right that this book should be dedicated to them.

Matthew Reisz
London, June 1991

INTRODUCTION

T HE GREAT JEWISH centres today are in Israel and the United
States; Europe is just a sideshow. But what a sideshow! It
was on European soil that the bulk of world Jewry lived
until the Holocaust, on European soil that Maimonides wrote his
Guide for the Perplexed, on European soil that Zionism was forged,
on European soil that the great Jewish thinkers and artists of Paris,
Vienna and the Weimar Republic largely created the modern agenda
in music, physics, psychoanalysis and many of the arts . . . It is true
that many of the great periods of Jewish civilization or of creative
Jewish-gentile fusion ended tragically, but that is no reason to read
history backwards. If the golden age in medieval Spain, for example,
lasted close to 800 years, that is long enough for most lifetimes; why
should we believe it was doomed to disaster from the start? It is far
better to appreciate the glorious remnants of such eras for what they
are, rather than to patronize the past by assuming that all the hopes
invested in them were naïve. It is as one-sided to regard European
history as nothing but pogroms, Crusades, forced conversions and gas
chambers as to see in it a glorious steady progress towards prosperity
and the good life.

Throughout European history, however, and despite the crucial
transformations of the Enlightenment and French Revolution, it is safe
to say that Jews have been treated as a minority. This is obviously not
the case in Israel, nor, arguably, in the United States. (It is sometimes
said that the creation of the State of Israel made American Jews
more like other Americans – the Polish-Americans, Irish-Americans,
Italian-Americans, Ukrainian-Americans and so on – most of whom
feel some sort of loyalty to an 'old country' elsewhere. In a nation
of minorities, Jews obviously have a different position from that in

states with a strong dominant culture.) It might be suggested that Jews rarely feel totally at home in Europe, particularly since the Second World War, and that their lives are often characterized by caution, ambivalence and divided loyalties. If so, these complexities and tensions have their own fascination, power and creative possibilities.

Yet, quite apart from these general points, for people from backgrounds like my own, different parts of Europe are inextricably bound up with their family history. In writing this book, I visited places like Terezín, the ghetto where the paternal grandparents I never met were held, before being transported to the death camps. At Westerbork Camp in Holland, I was shown the series of slab-like books published by the Dutch government which list the people deported from Dutch soil or killed during the German occupation. A large proportion, inevitably, were Jewish. Several of my relatives were on the list – the same relatives whom my father saw for the last time as a twelve-year-old boy, passing through Holland on the *kindertransport* which brought him to safety in England.

In preparing this book it was marvellous to look at some of the most appealing and written-about places in the world from an unusual perspective. Yet I also had far deeper motives: although my mother is not Jewish, the book was produced partly as a search for my own roots, in sympathy and celebration and with a far more than professional interest. I have set out to describe the Jewish aspects of twelve major European cities, striking a balance between history, monuments and reportage on current life styles and attitudes but always basing what I have to say on *what exists today*.

There is room for argument about the choice of cities, although some were unavoidable. I have included the numerically most significant Jewish centres of today's Western Europe (Paris, London, Marseilles) and the places with Jewish monuments which count as major tourist attractions by any standards (Prague, Toledo, Venice and, to a lesser extent, Amsterdam). Although it is impossible to compress the Jewish history of Europe into the stories of selected cities, it would also have been absurd to omit consideration of certain key themes: the start of the Diaspora (Rome), the almost unparalleled cultural explosion of 'Vienna 1900', the great exemplary episode of gentile assistance to suffering Jews (Copenhagen), the single European centre of ultra-Orthodoxy which ranks with New York and Jerusalem (Antwerp). Glasgow is both a fascinating 'second city' in a land which was spared persecution in the 1940s – and, since Scotland is very different from England, a city with its own piquancy, style and endlessly entertaining inhabitants.

I have not, however, included any cities in either Germany or Poland – what one might call the heartlands of the Holocaust. This is partly out of residual superstition about setting foot there, partly because some excellent books have already been written on this theme, and also because I have tried to avoid places where there is little to say except: here there was once rich and vital Jewish life – and now there is nothing. With the single exception of Toledo (since it was essential to say something about the extraordinary riches of pre-Reconquest Spain – and the synagogues there are unforgettable), I have only included towns with a living Jewish presence today. In omitting such 'ghost towns', I am aware, the book in a sense presents a falsely optimistic picture. I certainly had moments of despair and paranoia (and a feeling that the Jews in the 1930s and '40s were not nearly paranoid enough), times when I felt that Europe is first and foremost one huge Jewish cemetery, that plans for European unification are terrifying, that talk about European 'civilization' is vacuous, offensive, perhaps even antisemitic. . . .

Yet it would have been dishonest as well as dull to dwell on such feelings. This is not only because I had a wonderful time, exhilarated by the adventure and complexity of European history, captivated by the extraordinary beauty and charm of the cities, and it would have been utterly phony to write largely about the awfulness of Europe. It also seemed rewarding and more unusual, without playing down the persecution and suffering, to put at least as much stress on how the different Jewish communities have revived in the post-War world. This is in many ways little short of miraculous. Particularly in Paris, Marseilles and Prague, I often felt a thrilling sense of re-birth which I have tried to reflect in this text.

Together with this stress on survival and reconstruction goes a celebration of the differences between communities faced with different problems, environments and opportunities. Certain themes inevitably recur. The immense dislocations of populations in the Sephardi diaspora of 1492 (and subsequent decades), after the pogroms of the 1880s and in the tragic upheavals of Hitler's (and Mussolini's) Europe; the changed intellectual horizons introduced by the Enlightenment, the French Revolution and Napoleonic conquests; the overarching power of the Habsburg Empire and Catholic Church – these were crucial almost everywhere. Parallel problems are also widespread today: sheer shortages of numbers and finance, unsympathetic attitudes towards Israel in the Western media, and so on.

Yet who really wants to read about the similarities between Copenhagen and Toledo, Venice and Vienna, or even Antwerp and Amsterdam? Each has its own fascination and spirit of place, and the same applies to the specifically Jewish aspects. It would also involve a good deal of violence to the facts. My first point of call was Antwerp, where I was struck by the good humour, religious intensity and self-sufficiency of the Hasidic diamond traders. Not long afterwards, I heard about the display of sexy Israeli swimwear which was organized for the Glasgow Garden Festival as a way of promoting Israel! Both seem perfectly legitimate expressions of Jewish identity, but they are hardly expressions of the same (or even compatible) values and life-styles.

I have not, however, felt any need to pass judgement. Although I have written often on Jewish themes, I am not really part of the London Jewish community (and have written a chapter on London which reflects this). This has certain disadvantages, but it also means that I do not have an internalized model of how Jews ought to behave. It would be ludicrous for me to start giving the individual communities marks out of ten in accordance with some standard I had dreamt up. Besides, while some of the cities are a good deal more pleasant than others, I found the communal representatives and Jews I stopped in the street almost without exception helpful and understanding.

The writing of this book has coincided with some extraordinary events: the end of Communist domination in Eastern Europe, the great influx of Soviet Jews into Israel, the changing balance of power in the Middle East created by the Gulf War. If I had written the chapter on Prague a year earlier, it would have been utterly different – and, it is worth remembering, far more depressing. On a more personal note, I should also mention that the writing of this book coincided with the birth of my nephew, since Jewish survival in Europe is tied up emotionally for me with feelings about the survival of my family despite all the odds. (My father was on the fifth of six *kindertransporten* which left Prague for London in 1939; the British declaration of war meant that the last train never departed . . .) Together, my son and nephew should assure the continuation of my grandparents' surname into a new, fourth generation.

My father came from Czechoslovakia (although not from Prague), but I am a life-long Londoner. My wife, who is French and not Jewish, comes from Marseilles; at her birth, her grandmother and another more modern midwife had a ferocious quarrel about delivery techniques. The latter was a Jewish woman whom my mother-in-law has referred to ever since as '*cette Juive au grand coeur*' ('that good-hearted Jewess') – just like a character from some nineteenth-century melodrama! In all these places, I have been influenced by my personal background and experience. In all the other cities, I write merely as a sympathetic outsider.

1

ROME

GREAT EMPIRES SELDOM express much sorrow for their victims. Hints of compassion are tempered by swaggering superiority. Yet when Jerusalem fell to the Romans in CE/AD 70, some very touching coins were minted. One side depicts a Roman soldier with the legend 'Judea capta' ('Judea has been captured'); the obverse shows a Jewish woman crying beneath a palm-tree. Even this small sign of the suffering inflicted is absent from the greatest monument to the Roman victory over the Jews, the Arch of Titus near the Forum.

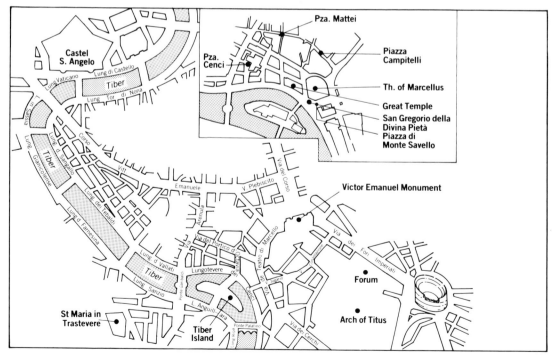

Jewish slaves depicted in the relief on the Arch of Titus: the fall of Jerusalem in CE/AD 70 marked the start of the Diaspora (Weidenfeld Archive)

A famous relief shows Jewish slaves carrying the *menorah* into exile from the Temple in Jerusalem. These were not the first Jews to live in Rome, but as they were led there in triumph, the Diaspora began. To anyone watching that procession, Roman power must have seemed eternal, the Jews just another defeated sect.

In reality, of course, the opposite has proved true. Jews have returned to Jerusalem. (Reproductions of the Arch's relief are movingly used to frame the story of Exile and Return in Tel Aviv's marvellous Museum of the Diaspora.) The religious traditions of the Hebrew slaves have been handed down directly to today's Jewish community, but the heirs of the Caesars have just become an indistinguishable strain in the Italian stock. The *menorah* remains a living symbol of the State of Israel, and is clearly visible on the façade of Rome's Great Temple (and in the name of a nearby bookshop); the symbols of the Roman Empire may have been resurrected briefly in Mussolini's cheap parody, but now they are utterly hollow. Roman *influence* – in architecture, administration, law and the Romance languages – is still a central feature of Western civilization. Chunks of Roman masonry incorporated into later buildings can be found in the Eternal City wherever one looks. But the 'empire without end' which Virgil sang of, destined 'to spare the vanquished and war down the proud', has been consigned to history.

The Jews of Rome often drop casual remarks like 'We've been here for twenty centuries, we certainly know how to survive . . .' They have indeed survived the often hostile and always arbitrary rule of the Roman Emperors, the Fascist regime, the brief but terrible German occupation towards the end of the Second World War – and the centuries of Papal authority. The Vatican remains a formidable and not always benevolent presence, even if the literal answer to Stalin's famous question – 'How many divisions has the Pope?' – is that his 'army' consists solely of the picturesque toy-soldiers of the Swiss Guard. Nonetheless, the Jews have clearly survived the darkest days of Papal prestige; and the Vatican is no longer a temporal power in the ordinary sense, nor even a major source of antisemitic propaganda.

All this makes Rome an obvious place to start an exploration of Jewish Europe. Italy represents the first country of the Diaspora and the Jews of southern Italy still employ a distinct 'Italian' religious ritual and pronunciation which may well be closer to the original usages of the Temple in Jerusalem than either the Ashkenazi or Sephardi forms. In a more general sense, too, the history of the Roman Jews is exemplary. For if Jewish life in Europe is a story of survival against all the odds – survival despite all the regimes, empires, organizations and certainties which seemed far more permanent, which should have survived instead but have not – then it is in Rome that the pattern appears at its clearest.

Paris has two islands anchored mid-stream in the centre of town, but Rome has only one. Their flavour could hardly be more different. Instead of the architectural riches of the Ile de la Cité, the aristocratic exclusiveness of the Ile St Louis, the much smaller Isola Tiberina has a very Roman sort of shabby grandeur. Instead of Notre Dame, there is a small orange chapel attached to a hospital, set back on a terrace behind trees which could almost be a café. Instead of crowds clicking cameras, huge rats scuttle across or lie dead on the path surrounding the island. Two minuscule waterfalls provide a little welcome movement to the Tiber. The Broken Bridge or Ponte Emilio stretches pathetically halfway across the river. Two complete short bridges link the Isola to the main section of the city and to Trastevere, the marvellous network of cobbled streets 'beyond the Tiber'. Both areas have important Jewish links. From the greatest days of the Roman Empire to the terrible round-ups in 1943 (and beyond), Trastevere has been a major Jewish centre; a former synagogue, identifiable by a Hebrew inscription, survives from the Middle Ages. There is also a new cultural centre hidden away in a charming courtyard in the Via Arco de' Tolomei. This contains an archive and library and provides concerts, conferences, courses and exhibitions on themes like the history of the Rome ghetto and the Jewish role in the Italian resistance. There are also occasional plays performed in the traditional Judaico-Romanesque dialect, which uses Italian constructions and word endings tacked on to Hebrew roots.

This was the language of the historic ghetto, once located on the other side of the Tiber. The nearby bridge is now called the Ponte Fabricio, but as early as the Middle Ages it was known as the Jews' Bridge. (It was later called the Ponte Quatro Capi or Bridge of the Four Heads after the simplified and much battered statues of Janus which can still be seen on the parapet.) The most evocative view, neatly summing up the history of Rome, is from the Garibaldi Bridge, which looks down on the 'nose' of the Isola. Below, like a symbol of the exuberance of today's Rome, is a riot of colourful graffiti: Christian slogans, girls' names, paired lovers' names, a giant tooth, the façade of a fanciful building, a frenzied high-heeled dancer in a green dress. On the skyline can be seen the Capitoline hill from ancient times and the winged charioteer on the Victor Emanuel monument, built to celebrate the birth of a united modern Italy in 1870. In the foreground stands Rome's remarkable main synagogue, the Great Temple; just behind are the cramped streets which once formed the old ghetto.

The building is certainly worthy of the Jews' tenacious presence in the city. The Jewish heritage of Venice will be explored in a later chapter; Florence has a huge domed synagogue in Moorish style; Leghorn (or Livorno), another major area of Jewish settlement from at least the sixteenth century, has a strange and rather creepy modern synagogue which looks a bit like a brown beetle or a slug from the outside. The Temple in Rome is at once the grandest and most charming of all; from a distance, it could almost be an opera house.

Before I consider the Temple in more detail, it is worth going back almost two thousand years, to a time when Italian synagogues were neither so grand nor so conveniently placed near the centre of town. One of the great archaeological sites is Ostia Antica, the main port of Rome in the early centuries of the Common Era. The actual wharfs are now located close to and within the grounds of Rome's main Leonardo da Vinci airport at Fiumicino. Yet much of the city itself has been dug out of the ground and now occupies an area of about 340,000 square metres. Few other places give such a strong sense of the everyday life of the ancient world.

Many of the major public buildings have been largely reconstructed: the Firemen's Barracks and the Baths of Neptune, with mosaics of the god triumphant, sea monsters and twining human-headed sea-snakes tapping on a sort of tambourine; the huge semi-circular theatre (used for aquatic events when flooded with water), where gaping masks are on display at the back; the grand staircase leading up to the enclosure which formed a temple of Jupiter, Juno and Minerva; the Christian basilica, grand residences and ancient equivalent of a shopping precinct which probably specialized in jewellery. No less fascinating are the indications of humbler existences in the smaller dwellings, the cheap taverns and at least one brothel, as revealed by graffiti and wall paintings.

The extraordinary early synagogue also counts among the humbler buildings of the town. It is located beyond the Marine Gate and dramatic broken columns which once formed a great arched window in the cold room of the Baths of the Marciana, on the far side of a field. No other building is further from the town centre, although it was once easily accessible from the main coastal artery known as the Via Severiana. Today, few visitors bother to clamber over masonry, lizards and lonely little paths to reach it. Yet this is a great pity: if Ostia Antica is marvellously evocative of a functioning Roman town, its synagogue brings back to life its Jewish community.

At first glance it looks like just a maze of low walls and unrelated columns, yet although some of the details are slightly unusual, all the different sections of a synagogue are clearly visible. One attached room with benches round the walls must have been a meeting hall, another houses a marble slab and oven used for making unleavened bread. Less easy to identify is a separate building with seats set into the walls, although it may possibly be a rabbinic court or Beth Din. The entrance to the synagogue proper leads past a well, a *mikveh* and a raised area reserved for women, then through a sort of vestibule surrounded by four columns into the main hall. Opposite the door, a podium (either the *bimah* or seating for notable members of the community) is clearly visible, and the stairs and semicircular niche for the Ark are still in place. The pillars on each side support architraves carved with the symbols of the *shofar*, palm branch and citron. While these are slightly difficult to decipher, the two *menorot* are crystal clear.

The synagogue was only discovered in 1961–62, during the building of a main road to the airport; but what is its significance? It takes up an area of about 350 square metres and obviously reveals the existence of an important community, perhaps of 500 souls, which experts believe was mainly involved in small-scale commerce. Indeed, it is almost certainly the largest and earliest ancient synagogue yet discovered in the Western hemisphere. An inscription tells us the name of the man responsible for it, Mindis Faustos.

Two features make absolutely clear a continuous presence over several centuries. First of all, there is a mix of styles. Some of the walls are made of triangular blocks set at an angle, a technique known as *opus reticulatum* which was used in the first century of the Common Era (the century when Titus led his army of conquest into Israel). When the synagogue was later expanded, *opus vittatum* – bricks laid in horizontal rows – was employed instead. This was the building method of the third and fourth centuries. The strange design also reflects the two stages of construction. Certainly the position of the Ark just to the left of the entrance, tucked away in the corner and set back from the essentially rectangular hall, is highly unusual.

Many of the most famous surviving sights of ancient Rome have some connection with the Jews. The Arch of Titus stands at the head of the Via Sacra, looking down on the Colosseum (partly built by Jewish slaves in the years CE/AD 72–80) and the Forum. The Talmud says that Jews should not pass under it, but today wiring and safety regulations anyway make this impossible. Close to the Forum is the grim Mamertine Prison, where some of the Jewish rebels against Roman rule were publicly executed during Titus's triumphal procession.

The Appian Way is the main link between Rome and southern Italy, and hence Africa and the East. It was almost certainly along that route that envoys came from Judas Maccabeus (who is still commemorated each year in the festival of *Chanukah*) seeking the protection of Rome. The alliance eventually led to Roman domination and the victories of Pompey and Titus, who certainly brought back their prisoners along the Appian Way. Yet the road, as a major artery of trade, was also the site of many Jewish settlements. It is here that we can also find some of the Jewish catacombs, whose sarcophagi (many of them in the Museo Nazionale delle Terme) provide evidence for the richer Jews who worked as merchants. The tomb of a Jewish actress called Faustina, for example, is decorated with theatrical masks while Jewish symbols like the *menorah* and *shofar* are scratched into the stone.

As so often in Jewish history, ancient places are associated with events in modern times. It was in Ostia and the towns nearby that groups of Soviet Jews recently spent a few months on Italian soil before moving on to Israel; Rome's small Lubavitch community provided the welfare services. The catacombs on the Appian Way were also the scene of a terrible massacre during the brief German occupation of Rome. When partisans succeeded in assassinating 33 SS officers, a horrendous reprisal killing – with a ratio of ten Italians for every German – took place in the Ardeatine Caves. Nearly a quarter of the 335 victims were Jewish.

The birth of Christianity obviously had a major impact on the Jews – in the first instance because it was just considered to be a cranky variety of Judaism! Yet when the Emperor Constantine made the whole empire Christian in the fourth century, a form of doctrinaire religious anti-Judaism replaced Roman racial and opportunistic attitudes. The crucial point, nonetheless, if one surveys the whole history of the Roman Jews from the time of Titus to the birth of the ghetto in 1555, is how much everything depended on the whims of individuals. A good emperor or Pope (from the Jewish point of view) would be succeeded by a bad one; a reign would start well and end badly, or vice versa, in response to the ever-shifting pressures of religion, economics, politics and personality.

Thus, the Jews fared well under Julius Caesar and Augustus, the founder of the Empire, but persecution was at least one result of the waverings of Tiberius and Claudius. Broadly speaking, hostility to Jews and the Jewish religion as such was not a crucial factor, since the Roman Empire contained an immense variety of cultures, nations and religions and so had to be reasonably tolerant of diverse views. Papal decrees, on the other hand, often dealt far more directly and specifically with Jewish rights and duties.

The most heart-rending example of how Papal personalities and attitudes affected the Jews occurred in our own century, during the late 1930s. For various reasons, Adolf Hitler was reluctant to confront the Catholic Church head on. When there were strong clerical protests about the euthanasia programme in 1940–41, it was abandoned. When Pius XI's 1937 pastoral letter '*Mit Brennender Sorge*' ('With Burning Concern'), criticizing Nazi racial ideology, was read out in churches all over Germany, the Nazi press and radio were furious; Hitler, however, decided against any direct assault on the Pope or the German Catholic hierarchy. Perhaps, as has been argued, a strongly worded Papal condemnation of antisemitism would also have at least delayed the persecution of the Jews; many of the perpetrators and collaborators all over Europe, after all, were practising Catholics (or from a strongly Catholic background) who would surely have been reluctant to ignore unequivocal guidance from the Pope.

Such a document – an encyclical entitled *Humani Generis Unitas* ('The Unity of the Human Race') – was indeed drafted on the instructions of Pope Pius XI, but it was still undelivered when he died in 1939. His successor, Pius XII – a 'conservative' who supported at least the anti-communist aspects of Nazi rule – decided to suppress it. A crucial opportunity of using Papal influence to relieve suffering had been missed. Of more immediate concern to the Roman Jews, the Pope failed to provide any warnings or condemnation of the appalling round-up in October 1943.

This occurred shortly after the Germans took control of Rome, a terrible period which lasted from September 1943 to June 1944 (and for a longer time in the more northern parts of Italy). Some 4,000 Jews still lived on the site of the old ghetto, another 3,000 across the Tiber in Trastevere. A few road blocks were enough to seal off the whole area for a rapid SS raid. A total of 1,259 people were arrested. By the following June, about 1,700 Jews in all (out of 12,000) had been deported. There are some vivid eyewitness accounts of the October round-up, the miraculous escapes and the stories of neighbours willing to adopt Jewish babies on the spur of the moment. Yet the horror of the event cannot disguise one crucial fact: most of the Jews of Rome were still living in the traditional areas of the city – and this no less than 22 years after Mussolini's march on Rome ushered in the Fascist regime!

This no doubt reflected the over-optimism and caution of some communal leaders, but it also says something about what Fascism had been like in practice. Mussolini passed a series of tough racial laws in 1938, but this was largely in response to German pressure and attracted much public opposition; exceptions, or officials willing to bend the rules, were common. Indeed, Mussolini himself expected the rules to be bent in the interests of humanity: Jews were usually treated reasonably well in Croatia and the French Riviera when Italian troops took control and, when compelled to make concessions to the Germans, the Duce characteristically remarked: 'I was forced to give my consent to the extradition, but you can produce all the excuses you want so that not even one Jew will be extradited. Say that we simply have no boats available to transport them by sea. . . .' When the Germans introduced far more systematic persecution, many people risked severe penalties to help the Jews they knew. A joke went the rounds in 1943 about a tourist who asks to see Michelangelo's famous statue of Moses; 'Oh, he's been hiding at a friend's house for some time,' the guide tells him.

Pope Pius XII, as we have seen, lost an opportunity to warn the Jews of Rome in 1943, and also failed to speak out against the Holocaust. If one thinks of him as one visits St Peter's Square, Bernini's famous colonnade – like two great stone arms held out to offer an embrace to the whole of humanity – can seem very stony indeed. Yet the Pope's failure, fortunately, was by no means always reflected in the behaviour of other clerics and Vatican functionaries. At the very least, Jews who threw themselves at the mercy of the local priests were rarely turned in to the authorities. Many were actively helped, hidden away, provided with false papers, food, money and contacts. Convents and monasteries often made ideal safe houses. Even the Poor Clares in Assisi admitted a group of Jews into their cloister – a building where no men had set foot for seven centuries! Despite some notable exceptions (and the fact that war criminals as well were often hidden on Church property after 1945), Italian Catholics performed impressively in living up to their humanitarian ideals. In all, about 85 per cent of Italy's pre-war Jewish population survived, partly because of the general disinclination to take restrictive regulations too seriously. If Mussolini himself encouraged his officials to bend the rules, sympathetic gentiles had little hesitation in doing so. The same applied to the Jews themselves. It is a striking and depressing fact that in many countries Jews told to report for internment often did so; Italian Jews were far more likely to ignore such 'orders' and quickly make private arrangements for securing the forged documents they needed.

Today, of course, the Vatican continues to be a mighty and enigmatic presence in Rome. It contains the Sistine Chapel and what must be the world's greatest collection of artworks on themes drawn from the Hebrew Bible (particularly as interpreted in accordance with the Christian and humanist ideals of the Italian Renaissance). St Peter's houses a column said to come from the Temple in Jerusalem – and traditionally believed to weep once a year in memory of the Temple's destruction! – which inspired Bernini's famous baldequin; this in turn, as I describe later, provided a thrilling architectural motif in one of Venice's loveliest synagogues.

Most of the signs since 1945 are positive. Just as nostalgia for the days of Fascism is only a marginal current in Italian politics, so the Catholic Church has put much of the past behind it. The reforms of the Second Vatican Council, although not without their problems, eliminated most of the Church's traditional antisemitism, such as the reference to the Jews as 'Christ-killers' in the text of the Mass. The Church remains deeply divided, but Pope John Paul II made a historic visit to the main synagogue at Rome and established an annual Day of Judaism to promote inter-faith dialogue in 1990. Day-to-day relations are reasonably good, despite occasional unfortunate remarks, controversies about Waldheim and the convent at Auschwitz, continuing differences over Israel and the role of religion in state education.

In earlier centuries, of course, the great symbol of Jewish oppression by Christians was the ghetto. The Jewish Museum above the Great Temple contains casts of inscriptions from Ostia and the catacombs, many beautiful ritual objects and a marvellous seventeenth-century Chair of Elijah, with an elaborate wooden tracery of a crown, harp, Tablets of the Law and palm leaves against a background of red cloth. There is a brief section on Nazi persecution, but the bulk of the exhibits come from the ghetto period. The Papal Bull of 1555, *Cum nimis absurdum*, which established a ghetto on Venetian lines, is on display, together with later decrees which imposed other restrictions or humiliations on the Jews. Popular hostility – and 'games' such as rolling Jews along the street in barrels lined with nails – echoed the official attitudes. Attendance in church for sermons was made compulsory from 1584.

There are eighteenth- and nineteenth-century prints and sketches which manage to make the ghetto look appealing. John Ruskin (1819–1900), the celebrated English art critic, visited Rome in 1840 and, with youthful enthusiasm, refused to be impressed by the works of Old Masters like Raphael; instead, he produced a most beautiful sketch of 'old clothes hanging out of the old windows in the Jews' quarter' and wrote rhapsodically: 'So completely is this place picturesque, down to its door knockers, and so entirely does the picturesqueness depend, not on any important lines or real beauty, but upon the little bits of contrasted feeling – the old clothes hanging out of a marble architrave, that architrave smashed at one side and built into a piece of Roman frieze, which moulders away the next instant into a patch of broken brickwork – projecting over a mouldering wooden window, supported in its turn on a bit of grey entablature, with a vestige of inscription. . . .'

Although these words capture beautifully the atmosphere of Rome, other descriptions of the ghetto stress the dirt, darkness, dangers of flooding, insanitariness and desperate overcrowding. Most of the old housing, as one might expect, has been swept away, but there is enough remaining on the ground to make exploration worthwhile. Just behind the Great Temple, and close to the Ponte Fabricio, is a church called San Gregorio della Divina Pietà; most unexpectedly, a panel outside depicts the crucified Christ with a quotation from Isaiah in Hebrew and Latin which refers to 'a rebellious people, which walketh in a way which was not good, after their own thoughts; a people which provoketh me to anger'. Since the church was located just next to one of the ghetto gates, this was hardly meant as a friendly gesture.

Another of the ghetto gates was once in place just by the Piazza Mattei, where the palace of the gatekeeper still stands, along with a marvellous Renaissance fountain of bronze tortoises and beautiful Grecian youths. There is a similarly attractive fountain in the Piazza delle Cinque Scuole (named after the five 'schools' or synagogues once housed in a single building in the ghetto), near the site of a third gate. Far more evocative, however, are the roads like the Via della Tribuna di Campitelli which lead down from the Piazza Campitelli to the Great Temple and the Tiber. Tall houses on both sides create a dark, steep,

Typical street scene in the Rome ghetto: the Piazzetta del Pancotto in 1886 (Weidenfeld Archive)

The entrance to the Rome ghetto by the Pescheria Vecchia (Mary Evans Picture Library)

narrow and airless alley which induces a feeling of claustrophobia. To have lived there when they were also filthy, ill-lit and enclosed within walls must have been utterly soul-destroying.

In times past the ghetto gates provided Jews with some protection against hostility. What is depressing is that there is still enough hostility and terrorism to justify constant tight security around the Great Temple and Jewish school. As one reaches the bottom of the Via della Tribuna di Campitelli, a parked car full of very bored policemen and women stands in one's way. Yet in every other respect this exit from the ghetto is extremely exhilarating. One threads one's way past the ruins of a Roman theatre and out into the clear light of day. Straight ahead is a sort of paddock full of palm trees, the first sight of

Rome's marvellous Great Temple. Then one glimpses the segmented aluminium dome which emerges from a square stone base. Nothing could form a greater contrast with the dismal ghetto. The dome is visible, rising out of the trees, from vast distances away, from across the river and from many other districts. Even in a city as dominated by fine churches as Rome, the Great Temple stands out as a proud and moving monument to the Jewish presence on the banks of the Tiber. The general effect, as I have suggested, is a bit like an opera house. Steps lead up to the main doors behind a porch created by four huge columns in 'Assyrian–Babylonian' style. The dome surges up behind the pediment of the façade, where the Tablets of the Law explode out of a golden sun-burst. Below is a series of windows, again created from four massive columns and flanked by two huge palm branches which echo the real palm trees all around.

The interior is also decorated in what might be described as a theatrical style, and the apse containing the Ark is rather like a stage. The most extraordinary decorative motif is in the dome, where overlapping scales in bright reds, blues and greens create an impression of a butterfly's wing. Even the glass in the square lantern at the top is largely yellow, like the rays of the sun, although there is a small transparent disc in the centre. The dome emerges with a riot of colour from a solid grey square drum, and the same idea is repeated many times. The basic structural elements of the synagogue are in dour grey stone, but the detail is exuberant. Austere pillars support the women's gallery, for example, but there are many touches of gold and charming tree-like lamps sprout from the railings above. Orange and yellow are the dominant colours in the stained glass behind.

Steps lead up to the separate raised three-sided section at the back. Huge square ridged columns surmounted by elaborate capitals and sets of tiny pillars form the 'curtain wall'. Ledges all round the apse support gilded *menorot*. The Ark curtain is reached up another set of steps, and it is framed by gilded columns – gold palm branches creep up from the base – and a grand pediment with the Tablets and a golden crown.

The well-known Jewish writer, Chaim Bermant, once gave a nice summary of the Great Temple's appeal. 'Perhaps the most magnificent synagogue in Europe,' he claimed, 'it is a baroque extravaganza, massive, lofty, domed, with the sort of basilica one might expect to find in one of the grander Renaissance churches. Only the array of candelabra in the apse behind the Ark suggests that this may, after

The splendidly operatic Great Temple on the banks of the Tiber, 'perhaps the most magnificent synagogue in Europe' (Ancient Art and Architecture/Ronald Sheridan)

all, be a synagogue.' Despite the Vatican and the Arch of Titus, and all they symbolize, the Great Temple ensures that a visit to Jewish Rome is never depressing.

It is worth briefly considering this in context. Architecturally, and at the risk of gross generalization, the majority of Europe's synagogues are purely functional. There are marvellous hidden jewels, as in Amsterdam, Venice and Toledo, disused or barely used synagogues moving in their very dereliction, as in Prague, and a number in the derivative and rather pompous styles of the nineteenth century. The Great Temple is unusual – and makes such a fine symbol of Jewish survival in the first city of the Diaspora –

because it is highly visible, beautiful and impressive without being at all pretentious or grandiose. Now, this may seem rather surprising. It could only have been built (in 1904) by a Jewish community which felt relaxed, secure and welcome as an accepted part of the Roman scene. Yet even though the ghetto gates had come down in 1848, Jews were largely confined to the area until 1870. By the 1920s, Mussolini's Fascists were in power, and antisemitic legislation followed in 1938. If there was a moment of true tolerance, after millennia of contempt, it was remarkably brief. Why did the Jews of Rome feel so safe at the beginning of this century?

The answer can be found in the values which were forged in the struggle to create a modern Italian nation-state. I have already stressed the ancient foundations of Jewish life in Rome. To all intents and purposes, there have been Jews in Italy as long as 'Italy' has meant anything. What is even more significant is that when, in the nineteenth century, Italy was united as a political entity, Jews were involved in its creation (and hence in the national foundation myths). As in the United States but unlike most other countries in Europe, Jews were not immigrants in an already existing state; they were part of the state from day one.

It was the armies of the French Revolution which first brought liberal ideas to Rome, as to so much of Europe. In February 1798, a Roman Republic was set up under French auspices and Pope Pius VI went into exile. A Liberty Tree was erected in the ghetto and the Jews were granted civil rights in return for a large payment. In September, the city was recaptured by the Neapolitans – and the Jews had to pay up again. Another reversal of fortune occurred in 1800, when General Bonaparte successfully took control of Italy, and the former Papal states became part of his empire. The arrangements his Sanhedrin introduced in France applied to Italy as well, until his fall from power in 1814.

The Congress of Vienna then ushered in an era which tried to put the clock back to pre-Napoleonic (and pre-Revolutionary) times; the Papal regime, attempting to maintain Rome in a state of medieval torpor, was even more benighted and backward than most. Yet, in opposition to this, the seeds had been sown for the movement which was eventually to unite Italy. Its signature tune, so to speak, came to be 'Va, pensiero' from Verdi's *Nabucco* (1842), the famous chorus of captive Hebrew slaves longing for freedom in their own land. (Verdi used a Biblical story partly because censorship regulations made direct expression of political views impossible, but this also provides a good example of how 'liberation movements' have sought and found inspiration in the Hebrew scriptures.) The ghetto, which might be regarded as a modern form of slavery, was a good symbol of all the reformers were fighting against.

The decisive event occurred in 1870, when the walls near the Porta Pia were breached and the Pope lost military control of Rome. Italy was now a single state, and Jewish soldiers had taken part in the decisive battle. The new government, naturally enough, was anticlerical and anti-authoritarian in spirit, and it is hardly surprising that Jews were granted full civil rights at once, on 13 October 1870. Seizing the new opportunities available to them, they soon took up leading positions in politics, business, education, the professions, the arts and even the Army. The first Jewish Prime Minister, Luigi Luzzatti, was elected in 1910. The age of the ghetto ushered in an age of Enlightenment.

Headlong assimilation naturally produced problems of its own. Most Jews were strong supporters of the ruling House of Savoy and a fair number joined the Fascist party in the early days (neither proved reliable allies). Great professional achievement went along with declining religious commitment and increasing intermarriage. Yet in 1938, when the option of conversion allowed Jews to sidestep many of the difficulties they faced, the vast majority were unwilling to abandon their heritage in this cynical way.

Today, there are about 15,000 Jews in Rome, a further 12,000 in Milan and about 33,000 in all Italy. Not all can trace their ancestry back to the time of the Caesars – the Jews expelled from Libya by Colonel Gaddafy were often Italian speakers and came to Italy – but there is something awe-inspiring about the continuity of their presence. They were here before the Roman Empire existed, before the Pope, before Christianity – and they are still here. If 'purity of blood' is a meaningful and desirable ideal, the Jewish community may well be 'purer' than their Italian fellow-citizens, the product of centuries of intermarriage between the original Romans and waves of 'barbarian' invaders.

Yet sheer physical survival is one thing, creative achievement is another. If we look for a Golden Age of Jewish life in Rome, it is probably the period immediately after their emergence from the ghetto, movingly symbolized in the Great Temple. At certain periods in the past, notably in Renaissance times, the climate was tolerant and Jewish scholars came into close contact with their Christian colleagues, but such moments of calm could be suddenly shattered by a hostile Pope.

Fascism and the German occupation obviously destroyed the over-optimistic expectations of assimilation, and there is little hope of recapturing earlier levels of integration. There are now comparatively few Jews in Parliament because many of the politically active fled during the Fascist era. Yet Jews, no longer at the mercy of the arbitrary whims of popes, emperors and dictators, retain a strong position in Italian life; their rights are protected by a modern democratic constitution, antisemitism is a fairly minor factor, and a writer like Primo Levi has been acclaimed as a genius all over the world. While the smaller communities are ageing and dwindling, Rome and Milan have a highly significant Jewish presence whose greatest days may well be still to come.

Rome is the mother-city of one great branch of European Jewry, but the Diaspora proper was succeeded by a second – and almost equally significant – Sephardi diaspora. These two events established the basic patterns for modern Jewish life in Europe. Yet if the Jewish presence in Rome has been continuous, the immense cultural explosion of medieval Spain came to an abrupt end five centuries ago. Towns such as Toledo, to which I turn next, offer unforgettable architectural marvels, but even today they lack a living Jewish presence. There could be no greater contrast with the vivid excitement of Rome.

2

TOLEDO

I SET OUT to find the Jews of Toledo, but I arrived 500 years too late. There are no Jews in town any more – or rather, to be absolutely correct, just one. Yet Toledo contains two of the greatest Jewish monuments of Europe – monuments richly evocative of a golden age, of the era before the great scattering of Sephardim which had such a pivotal role in Jewish history. The blame for their banishment rests firmly with the Catholic Church at its most triumphalist. Jewish Europe has always been inextricably – and often tragically – bound up with the history of the Church. This emerges most clearly in Rome and Toledo. In Rome, the Vatican is a constant presence; in Toledo, whether visitors find it uplifting or oppressive, the whole city has an intensely Christian atmosphere.

To understand the style and significance of the Jewish remains, it is necessary to sketch in the early history of Spain. The country's distinctive contribution to European life derives, of course, from the three separate cultures which shared power in the Middle Ages. After the death of Mohammed in the year 632, the great era of Islamic conquest began. The Moors – Arabs leading an army of Berber soldiers from North Africa – invaded Spain from Gibraltar in 711 and rapidly took control of almost the whole peninsula; the surviving Christian forces were confined to the far North. Toledo, the former capital, fell to the Muslims in 712. The Arab advance was finally stemmed – at Poitiers, hundreds of miles over the present-day French border – but the Moorish period in Spain was to last almost 800 years. For the whole period Jews played a major role in commerce, medicine, scholarship and court life.

Now Toledo, which was controlled by the Moors until 1085, contains no masterpieces of Islamic architecture to rank with the

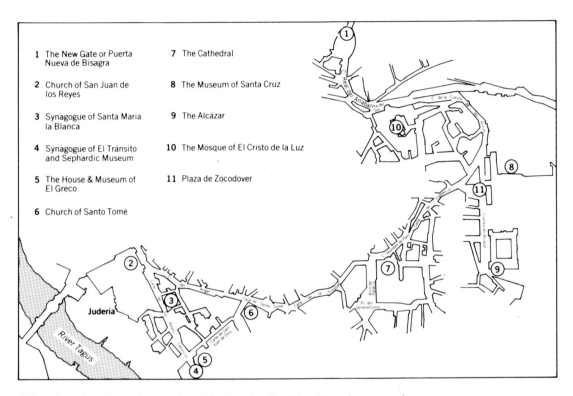

1 The New Gate or Puerta
  Nueva de Bisagra

2 Church of San Juan de
  los Reyes

3 Synagogue of Santa Maria
  la Blanca

4 Synagogue of El Tránsito
  and Sephardic Museum

5 The House & Museum of
  El Greco

6 Church of Santo Tomé

7 The Cathedral

8 The Museum of Santa Cruz

9 The Alcázar

10 The Mosque of El Cristo de la Luz

11 Plaza de Zocodover

Alhambra in Granada or the Alcázar in Seville. Yet the complex
warren of little lanes and the absence of a clear focal point reflect
the town's Arab past. And if Toledo, like Jerusalem, is a walled city
dramatically situated on a rocky outpost and built of limestone, its
walls too were constructed by Muslims. (The surviving sections of
the city wall, the squat and crudely carved gates, however, hardly
bear comparison with the walls the Sultan Suleiman the Magnificent
built around Jerusalem.)

Walking uphill from the main gate – the Puerta Nueva de Visagra
– visitors pass a brick church called Santiago del Arrabal, which
incorporates a tower from a former mosque (and played an inglorious
role, as I shall describe, in anti-Jewish persecution). Further on, and up
a steep hill to the right, is a charming little mosque, to which a church
was tacked on. Built in 922, it is now called the Ermita del Cristo de la
Luz and consists of a square split into nine equal compartments (like
a noughts-and-crosses or tic-tac-toe board) by four central columns.
A slightly different vault crowns each compartment, and horseshoe
arches link the columns with the walls and each other. Both the general
Mudéjar style and the specific horseshoe motifs are very prettily used;

in one of Toledo's famous synagogues, they form part of a far grander ensemble.

The crucial year in Spanish history was 1492. It was then that 'the Catholic Kings' – Ferdinand of Aragon and his wife Isabella of Castile – took Granada and completed the Reconquest of Christian Spain from the Moors, then that Columbus set off on his epochmaking voyages of discovery. The long slow process of Catholic expansion had finally borne fruit. Yet it was a process which had taken hundreds of years. After the fall of Toledo (1085), the Moors were squeezed into smaller and smaller areas of Spain and moved their headquarters from Cordoba to Seville and finally to Granada. The royal court was based in Toledo and then moved to Madrid in the sixteenth century (partly because the Toledan clergy were considered too arrogant!). In other words, each of the first four towns was once a 'capital city', each has its own combination of Moorish, Jewish and Christian treasures. Toledo, which was 'occupied' for the shortest period, may have minimal Moorish remains, yet its Christian and Jewish heritage are superb.

When the Reconquest was completed in 1492, the rulers of rechristianized Spain expelled both the Jews and the remaining Moors. This undoubtedly counts as one of the most terrible moments in Jewish history – perhaps the most traumatic event between the fall of Jerusalem and the Holocaust. Yet there are two very important points to bear in mind: the preceding centuries had been an age of great Jewish achievement in both the Christian and the Muslim sectors of the country. What is even more significant, at least for the purposes of this book, is the scattering of the Sephardi Jews which followed. Almost all the cities I explore, and particularly Amsterdam, London and Venice, were transformed; important new centres grew up in North Africa and Palestine; and since some Jews (or Jewish pseudo-Christians) travelled with Columbus, it was also the beginning of the major settlements in the New World.

The surviving remains of Moorish Toledo are far less extensive and important than the Christian city. There is a story that the horse belonging to the conquering king, Alfonso VI, respectfully fell to its knees in front of the little mosque I have described; a candle from the former Visigothic church was discovered still burning – over three and a half centuries after the mosque had been built there! The first mass of the Reconquest, therefore, was celebrated on the spot.

This naïve legend is charming, but there are many other buildings in Toledo built to the greater glory of the Church Triumphant and its kings. Much of the walls are Moorish, but the huge main gatehouse is stamped with the double-eagle coat of arms of the Holy Roman Emperor Charles V. (One expects to find such symbols tiled on the cathedral roof and all over the imperial capital in Vienna, but it is momentarily surprising in Spain – a good reminder of the extraordinary period when the Habsburgs controlled not only the territory of present-day Austria, Hungary and Czechoslovakia, but also the Low Countries and Spain.)

There is also a sculpture of Charles V trampling underfoot an enemy in chains in the courtyard of the Alcázar. This building, constructed in stages by successive monarchs, loomed over the city like a gloomy block in the days when El Greco painted his famous 'View of Toledo', and is still looming there today. It is now an exceptionally distasteful example of Fascist and Catholic kitsch: the museum commemorates the siege in 1936 when the Loyalist forces refused to surrender to the Republicans even though they had captured and threatened to kill the commander's son. Being a true Spaniard, the general refused to give in and little Luis was shot. The famous telephone conversation between father and son is reproduced on the walls in dozens of different languages.

Toledo's cathedral, on the other hand, is magnificent, and the battles of the Reconquest are pictured with a close attention to detail in carved reliefs on the 54 wooden stalls of the choir. The church of San Juan de los Reyes was once intended to be the burial place of Ferdinand and Isabella, but when they completed the Reconquest of Spain by taking Grenada, they decided to move their mausoleum to the city of their greatest triumph. (The cross which was placed on the Alhambra as a token of final victory is one of the prized relics in Toledo's cathedral.) The outside walls are still decorated with chains which once fettered the freed Christian prisoners of war.

It is a curious feature of European history that the defeat of the Moors in 1492 was followed almost at once by the rise of another Islamic threat to the heart of Europe, in the form of the Ottoman Turks under Suleiman the Magnificent. Budapest, Rhodes and Belgrade were all conquered by Muslim forces in the 1520s, and Vienna narrowly survived a siege. It was not until the crucial naval battle at Lepanto in 1571 (which Shakespeare alludes to in *Othello*) that the tide was decisively turned. The commander of the fleet was Don

John of Austria, an illegitimate son of Charles V. His standard can be seen in the wonderful cruciform museum in the former Hospital de Santa Cruz. As one walks down the main coffered gallery, more and more of the deep-blue forked banner comes into view, until the great golden motif of Christ on the Cross is fully visible.

It is hard not to be impressed by these monuments to Catholic triumphs, but it is equally important to realize the human costs. A scrolled inscription in the cathedral draws these out. The year 1492, it proclaims, deserves to be celebrated for three great achievements: the capture of Granada, the Expulsion of the Jews – and the repair, redecoration and whitewashing of the church! (No one, of course, yet realized the crucial significance of the 'discovery' of America.) The Christian moment of glory may have ushered in a period of exploration and prosperity, but the impact on the Jews was disastrous.

If the northern entrance to Toledo has Moorish echoes and the centre of the city is Christian, the south-west quarter is dominated by the Jewish presence – and by El Greco. It is impossible to ignore El Greco in Toledo. His 'View of Toledo' is now in the Metropolitan Museum in New York, yet for all its idealization, mystery and mystical vision the main features of the view have remained almost unchanged since the early seventeenth century.

One of El Greco's greatest masterpieces, the 'Burial of the Count of Orgaz' (from the late 1580s), is on display in the church of Santo Tomé. The scene is both legendary and fanciful. The count, who died in 1323, is being carried to his grave by St Stephen, the first Christian martyr, and the fourth-century St Augustine, while the black line of grieving courtiers includes El Greco himself, his son and other contemporaries. Only a few sweeping clouds separate them from the Virgin and saints in heaven, and an angel's yellow drapery brushes against the bald head of a mourner. No image could better convey the sense of the Christians, down the centuries, as one big happy family. Yet this fierce sense of unity had only been achieved, in Spain, by forcibly expelling non-Christians from the state.

Down a slope from the church, past El Greco's House, is the Calle Reyes Católicos (or Street of the Catholic Kings). At one end is the church of San Juan de los Reyes and at the other is a big sign saying Zona de Monumentos. In the middle is the Sinai restaurant, owned by Toledo's only Jew, Albert Elmalem Chocron. There are stone lions on columns to either side of the door, an ornate metal grille fences off a balcony with a tiled floor above, and above that is an open patio. The name Sinai appears in huge mock-Hebrew lettering outside, and windows are decorated with advertisements for marzipan in Hebrew and Japanese.

Señor Chocron was born in Morocco, worked in the rag trade in New York and set up a kosher restaurant in Madrid in 1967 – the first on Spanish soil for five centuries. He moved to Toledo in 1972, but the

The unforgettable horseshoe arches in the Santa Maria la Blanca synagogue (Spanish Tourist Board)

requirements of *kashrut* kept prices 50 per cent higher than elsewhere and he was unable to make a go of it. It now serves 'Jewish-style' food (one of the partners spent six months at Bloom's in London to gain experience). There is a small Jewish community established in Madrid with kosher butchers, suppliers of kosher Israeli wine, but there are no kosher restaurants and no longer any Spanish kosher wine. Despite being Toledo's one and only Jew, Señor Chocron has received more than his fair share of abusive phonecalls and there were two attacks on the restaurant in the mid-1970s. More pleasant to relate, the lunchtime-only Sinai has proved very popular not only with visiting groups but with the local priests, who now yield to no one in their enthusiasm for gefilte fish and matzo-ball soup!

The restaurant has been decorated with a silver *menorah*, Star of David tiles, a frieze just below the ceiling with the words of the blessing for the wine. There is also an intriguing Jewish slightly 'oriental'-style lantern from Cordoba, with light of different colours emerging from each side. Behind a grille and among seats in the basement is a very simple *shul*, which is sometimes used by groups. It consists of nothing more than a large free-standing *menorah*, a cupboard full of cups and ritual objects and a Star of David on the wall. Yet this is far and away the least important of Toledo's three synagogues; the other two are both masterpieces.

The earlier synagogue was built at the start of the thirteenth century. It was later converted into a church and given the name of Santa Maria la Blanca, after Saint Vincent Ferrar led a mob from Santiago del Arrabal to throw out the Jews. It was later used as a home for reformed prostitutes, an army storehouse and a dance hall. From the outside the synagogue has the charming but unimposing aspect of a country church. Behind an immense old wooden door is a courtyard scattered with conifers and palms. The building is simple and four-square, the façade pink, and a little overhanging roof with visible supports creates a rustic porch before the main entrance. The larchwood door is also venerable, decorated with typical inlaid star and zigzag motifs.

Attractive as this is, the interior is a real surprise, particularly if one has the place to oneself and only the sounds of birds and cicadas interrupt the peace. Four rows of white walls pierced by horseshoe arches create five 'aisles' with separate pitched and beamed larchwood ceilings. The general effect recalls both Toledo's little mosque and one of the supreme Moorish masterpieces, the Great Mosque of Cordoba. The columns are octagonal and decorated with pine-cone capitals, and just above and between the arches a sort of triangular frieze descends, seemingly made of porcelain although actually plaster. Rosettes in the centre recall the small circular windows running along both sides of the synagogue. Above each column is a scallop shell in relief, and above them a row of columned blind windows with five-lobed arches at the top. The walls of the central 'aisle' are also decorated with a fretted band of vibrant zigzags which interlace into eight-sided stars.

The floor is covered with red herring-bone tiles set off with occasional bands of colour and recurring star motifs. The central 'aisle' leads to a square niche where the altar stood. A golden dome emerges from an octagonal canopy; conch shells adorn each corner and between them are *putti* holding up a coat of arms. The two inner 'aisles' also end in separate niches, which are roofed over with golden conches. Again, interlocking gold bands create eight-sided stars around rosettes. A single Star of David hidden in a frieze makes it certain that the building was once a synagogue, although without a separate section for women.

Even more remarkable, perhaps, is the Transito synagogue, also located on the Calle de los Reyes Católicos. This too was later transformed into a church, and the entrance on Calle Samuel Levi is surmounted with an open bell tower and a cross. There is a single main hall without aisles, although part of the women's gallery survives on the right, the wooden beams decorated with floral designs and Hebrew lettering. Another gallery on the back, West wall was probably used for a choir. A frieze made of plaster and then an arcade of windows and blind arches surround the hall above the galleries. On the East wall, however, there are just two adjacent windows which are clearly intended to resemble the Tablets of the Law.

The floor is again made up of red tiles in herring-bone patterns, calligraphic devices and interlocking punched-out eight-sided stars embellish the cedar of Lebanon ceiling, and five pairs of wooden beams provide support. On the wall under the women's gallery is a niche containing an elaborate Christian tomb below a coat of arms and a canopy with rosettes in relief. At the East end of the main walls run two brightly coloured tiled benches.

The East wall itself, however, is the most extraordinary. It forms an immense plasterwork frieze with three lobed windows framed by delicate little columns opening on to a niche behind. Elaborate arabesques in green, red and white play all over the side panels.

Detail of the extraordinarily intricate and elaborate decoration in the Transito synagogue, once the private synagogue of Samuel Levi Abufalia (Spanish Tourist Board)

White bands like knotted snakes with Hebrew inscriptions surround the shield-shaped coats of arms of Castile and Leon. For this was the private synagogue belonging to Samuel Levi Abufalia, a court Jew and adviser of Pedro I. (An earlier member of the family was a well-known versifier, famous for his outspoken poetry on erotic themes.) He was given permission to build it in 1357 and fell from favour in 1361, accused of fraud.

Next door to the synagogue is the El Greco House, a turn-of-the-century pastiche of a sixteenth-century mansion built around a lovely tiled inner courtyard. There are some marvellous pictures on display, and a fabulous view over the Calle de los Reyes Católicos to the Tagus gorge just beyond. This was once the site of Abufalia's palace, and one gets a very good sense of his wealth by looking at the size of the grounds and his synagogue next door. Yet for all his prominence he never felt totally secure: a secret passage is meant to lead to a spot outside the city walls on the banks of the river. But Abufalia was unable to escape; he was executed by the king he had served in Seville.

★

Together with the synagogue of Cordoba, these are the great Jewish monuments of pre-Reconquest Spain. The subsequent story is far from cheerful: Expulsion, the Inquisition – and then nothing. A once-great civilization was at an end. Officially at least, there were no Jewish communities in the country until very recently. Franco's dictatorship gave a lot of power to the Catholic church – one can still feel the chill in the Alcázar – although the Americans did pressurize him into accepting a few Jews in the immediate post-war period. The Expulsion decree of 1492 was finally repealed in 1968 and a few synagogues have been built since then. Small communities, mainly in Madrid, Barcelona and Malaga, make up a total of twelve to fifteen thousand.

It is obviously a matter for rejoicing that Spanish Jewish life is slowly being reborn in this way, but it would be a mistake to read the earlier history, as it were, backwards. The 'Golden Age' ended in tragedy, but it lasted close to 800 years. And if, as is often argued,

Entrance to the El Greco House, next to the Transito synagogue, on the site of Abufalia's palace (Spanish Tourist Board)

Jews were treated better in Islamic than in Christian countries until the Enlightenment, the synagogues of Toledo are a moving reminder of what they did manage to achieve in Christian Spain.

Detailed accounts of the 'Golden Age' can be found in books like Yitzhak Baer's *History of the Jews in Christian Spain*, but it is worth mentioning some of the literary remains. The difficulties the Jews faced and their heroic response are vividly revealed in the accounts of the 'disputations' which were staged in Barcelona (1263) and Tortosa (1413). These were rigged trials which allowed Catholic former Jews to use distorted quotations from the Talmud to accuse the Jews of all manner of offences, in front of an utterly biased courtroom. The eloquent defences mounted by Nachmanides calmly answered the charges; they remain classic statements of the Jewish case against all bigoted forms of Christianity.

Conflicts with the Christian powers were one of the major themes of Jewish life in Spain, as throughout European history. Yet we also find many other moods and topics in the work of the famous Hebrew poets of the time. Bereavement, erotic passion, graveyard humour, martial fervour, soul-searching, nostalgia for better times, delight in wine and sensual pleasure, self-glorification – all find expression in exquisitely crafted verse. Much of it has been beautifully translated in David Goldstein's *Jewish Poets of Spain*. The greatest of these poets is usually taken to be Judah ha-Levi (c. 1075–1141), who spent time in many towns of Moorish and Christian Spain. After a period in Toledo, however, he seems to have fled back to Cordoba and come to believe that the only hope for himself and his fellow Jews was the return to Zion:

> It will be nothing for me to leave all the goodness of Spain.
> So rich will it be to see the dust of the ruined sanctuary.
>
> I am a jackal mourning your affliction, and when I dream
> Of the return of your captives I am a lyre accompanying
>   your songs.

He describes with contempt the pleasure-loving Jews of Seville, exhorts himself to set out for Israel, is encouraged by friends to remain and finally starts his journey. Several of the poems use the image of the storm at sea; although ha-Levi misses the daughter and grandson he has left behind, his firm faith in his purpose keeps him going until night ('like a negress clothed in gold tapestry') calms the waves again:

The water and sky will be ornaments
Pure and shining upon the night.
The sea's colour will be as heaven's,
Both – two seas bound together,
And between them my heart, a third sea,
As the waves of my praise swell once again.

Such poetry is particularly moving not only because it expresses one of the perennial themes of Jewish life but because the Sephardim of Spain were all compelled to embark on long and often dangerous voyages after 1492. Some followed ha-Levi on the road to Palestine and soon turned Safed into one of the main centres of Cabbalistic learning. Others went to Egypt, North Africa or Constantinople, the capital of the Ottoman Empire.

Of the cities explored in this book, Venice was the one most directly affected by the Expulsion. In the year 1516, the world's first ghetto was established there on the site of the former *getto* or foundry. Very shortly afterwards, Jews who had resided in Spain came to join the German and Levantine communities to form the 'Third Nation'. Despite restrictions, the commercial prominence of the Most Serene Republic offered immense opportunities and a reasonably tolerant environment. Jews were thus able to take part in the cultural explosion at the time of the Renaissance. Another important Italian port was Livorno or Leghorn, which played a key role in the coral trade and later in the diamond trade between India and the major diamond centres of Europe, London, Antwerp and Amsterdam.

Even more numerous were the Jews who fled from Spain to Portugal. As an escape from danger this proved a very short-lived solution, since King Manuel I issued his own expulsion order only four years later. Yet many decided to behave outwardly as 'New Christians' while awaiting the chance to live openly as Jews. Their trading contacts with 'real' Jews remained highly significant. At a time when the Iberian peninsula was at the centre of commerce with the New World and linked dynastically with the Low Countries, opportunities for those with international connections were virtually unlimited.

The search for economic advancement and comparatively liberal (usually Protestant) regimes took the Sephardim of Spain to Hamburg and Amsterdam. It was from the latter town, in 1655, that a delegation set out to London to convince Oliver Cromwell that the Jews should be readmitted to England. Another important community was founded in the area around Bordeaux and subsequently formed the 'aristocratic' branch of French Jewry until wider opportunities opened up at the time of the Revolution. Even more exciting were the opportunities in the New World. Columbus took some *marranos* (Jewish pseudo-Christians) with him to America, and he himself may have come from a Jewish background, although more tangible evidence – including the oldest synagogue still standing in the Western hemisphere, on the island of Curaçao – survives from the later Dutch colonies. When the Dutch were briefly in control of Brazil in the seventeenth century, their liberal policies encouraged large-scale immigration of Sephardim from Holland. In 1654, 23 of them fled to New Amsterdam. This, of course, became New York, and one of the most significant Jewish centres there has ever been. If the tragic events of 1492 had done nothing, indirectly and over many centuries, but help create Jewish New York, the effects would be incalculable. But the long-term impact of the Sephardi diaspora within Europe was almost as momentous.

A page from the *Barcelona Haggadah* (mid-fourteenth century), one of the greatest Hebrew illuminated manuscripts, revealing the variety of unusual instruments played by the Jewish musicians of medieval Spain (Courtesy of the British Library/Facsimile Editions)

The other key point is the centrality of Amsterdam. If there is a much imitated 'mother-synagogue' for the recent Western Sephardim, it is neither of Toledo's masterpieces but Amsterdam's Esnoga. In more general terms, of course, Moorish or pseudo-Moorish became an accepted style for up-market architectural pastiche, just like mock-Egyptian, neo-Gothic and Greek Revival. (The charming and easily imitated motif of the horseshoe arch, for example, can be found widely in millionaires' mansions on the Riviera, churches and buildings of many other kinds.) Because of the Jewish link with Moorish Spain, it was sometimes considered a particularly appropriate style for synagogues, and there are fine examples in Paris and Prague.

Yet this is a more or less playful form of parody. Toledo's great synagogues have no true successors. Along with the poetry, the marvellous illuminated manuscripts, the disputation records, they offer tantalizing glimpses of a lost epoch of civilization. With Amsterdam, we are jolted back into the modern world.

3

AMSTERDAM

TRAFFIC ROARS AROUND the charmless intersection on Visserplein, a tract of drearily typical modern no-man's-land. Yet all around one can step back instantly into history, into the small section of Amsterdam – the area around Meijerplein, the Plantage and the marvellous Jewish Historical Museum – which makes up one of the greatest Jewish monuments in the world. The Museum, housed in four former synagogues, is a magnificent homage

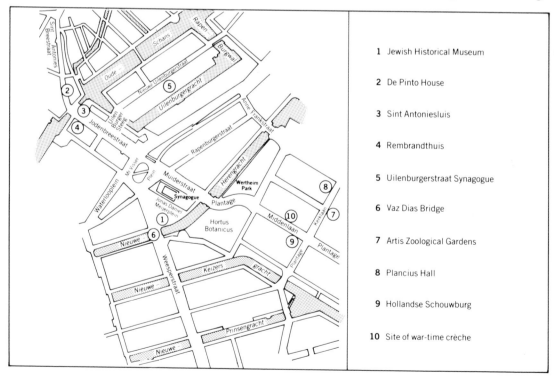

1 Jewish Historical Museum

2 De Pinto House

3 Sint Antoniesluis

4 Rembrandthuis

5 Uilenburgerstraat Synagogue

6 Vaz Dias Bridge

7 Artis Zoological Gardens

8 Plancius Hall

9 Hollandse Schouwburg

10 Site of war-time crèche

to the Jewish tradition and specifically to Dutch Jewish life which has been carefully designed to appeal to Jews and gentiles alike. Indeed, it would be hard to conceive of a more imaginative use of a complex of defunct synagogues.

But that, of course, is the point. The synagogues can no longer be used as synagogues, precisely because such a high proportion of the city's Jews were killed by the Nazis. It is inspiring to reflect on Jewish life in Amsterdam in the age of Rembrandt, the excitement and colour of the Plantage district up until the 1930s, and then one thinks of Anne Frank – and the glorious past just makes the war years and the present seem more depressing. The haughty grandeur of the canal-side houses begins to seem oppressive, and one starts to wonder which of the reserved elderly Dutch were indifferent (or worse) to the fate of the Jews during the War. . . .

Yet this is not totally fair. The old Jewish quarter round the Museum may be largely devoid of Jews, but a very interesting series of photographs inside depicts the variety of Jewish life in the city today: a wedding reception at the Hilton, a left-wing but non-religious Jewish billiards club, a society of homosexual Jews during *Pesach*, the Dizengoff discothèque (named after the famous street in Tel Aviv), the *Minumah* feast, celebrated by Moroccan Jews, where Muslims arrive

The three main synagogues of Amsterdam in the early eighteenth century, the Portuguese-Israelite or 'Esnoga' on the left, the New and Great to the right (Jewish Historical Museum)

just after Passover with supplies of food. All this rightly suggests that Jewish life is still flourishing, on a fairly small scale, in Amsterdam. It is particularly obvious in the south-eastern section of the city. Since the streets here are named after the different rivers of Holland, the area is known as Rivierenbuurt (or River-District).

On the corner of Vrijheidslaan and Vechtstraat, behind a tiny sign and inconspicuous door, can be found Zuurhandel De Leeuw, the sole surviving traditional pickle shop. Today, alas, health regulations demand the use of plastic instead of wooden vats, but everything else is as it was. There is even a model of the pickle cart in which the owner's family used to ply their trade through the streets of Amsterdam. The owner himself was celebrating two recent triumphs. Visitors from New York had just come to ask him if they could buy up his formula to set up a shop back home, perhaps the supreme accolade in the pickle business. In addition, he had just discovered a link between the pickle and Dutch high culture: in a letter by Vincent Van Gogh, the painter describes how he had found inspiration in the vegetables' unusual combinations of colours in the local pickling factory . . .

There are apparently no kosher restaurants and only one kosher sandwich bar now in Amsterdam – the strictly observant who want to eat out have been known to drive all the way to Antwerp – yet around the corner from De Leeuw in Rijnstraat is Betty's Restaurant. This offers delicious kosher-style 'traditional Jewish cooking' in the Dutch mode – lentil soup, sauerkraut and cornbeef, meat dishes cooked in beer – but although they never serve pork or milk-and-meat combinations, it is not strictly kosher or supervised by the rabbinate. The clientele is very mixed. At the end of the war, the owner explained to me, there were only 8,000 Jews left in Holland and the traditions of Jewish catering, as of the Jewish cabaret, were virtually a lost art. It has taken three generations for them to be slowly rebuilt.

Two even more exhilarating signs of Jewish survival can be found not far away. The first is the Liberal synagogue on Jacob Soetendorpstraat, which was dedicated in 1966. The building itself is fortified with security devices and is fairly charmless, but there is a huge stained-glass *menorah* let into the façade which looks out on to the Europaboulevard. Even more impressive is the tablet of the Ten Commandments supported on two columns high above the main entrance, like a banner held aloft proclaiming the continuing Jewish presence.

Nearby, opposite the RAI conference centre on Europaplein, is the Bonbon Jeannette kosher chocolate shop. Although the shop itself is new, there has been a *pâtisserie* on the site since the 1930s and the interior is in Art Deco style. Up-market home-made chocolates are arrayed in tempting displays on all sides and the clientele is obviously very varied, so at first I assumed that the only Jewish aspect was the recipes. The owner, Jeannette Cosman, soon put me right. I asked about Jewish life in Amsterdam, she attempted a few perfunctory answers, then firmly said, 'Let's talk about chocolate!' and brought out some of the specialities.

These included the complete Hebrew alphabet in chocolate, Torah scrolls, *menorot* and *sukkot* for the different festivals, bride and groom wedding dolls, which are sent out all over Holland and even to England. The precise proportions of the ingredients are obviously secret, although nuts, marzipan, puffed rice and sesame seeds – but not extra sugar, additives, syrups or fondants – are mixed in with the chocolate and unpeeled fruit. The results are so good one can hardly argue with the publicity hand-out: 'Once you have tasted her chocolates, you do not ever want to punish your taste buds with another chocolate . . . Her chocolates are entirely different from all mass-produced chocolates because they lack that overwhelming sugar-sweetness, do not leave a fatfilm in your mouth nor the impression of just having finished a five-course dinner. Her chocolates actually smell of chocolate, a taste not many people know.'

Compared to this marvellous shop, the Joachimsthal bookshop next door (with a strong stress on Jewish-interest material), the Sal Meyer butcher and sandwich shop round the corner on Scheldestraat (both under supervision of the rabbinate or ORT) are far less individual, yet they do show that patches of the old Jewish communal life survive in today's Amsterdam. Several of these establishments also attract a significant gentile clientele, perhaps partly out of nostalgia for a notable aspect of pre-war Amsterdam life. (At the turn of the century, about a tenth of the city's population was Jewish.)

In the same area, however, is a monument which embodies many of the complexities of Jewish life in Amsterdam. This is the Lekstraat synagogue, dedicated in 1937, but now functioning as the Resistance Museum. In other words, it is another major Amsterdam synagogue which has had to be imaginatively adapted to new uses because the post-war Jewish population was so tragically depleted. (The annex, however, is still used for religious purposes.) Both the building itself and the exhibits are very moving.

In very general terms, the main synagogues of Amsterdam are built to a single pattern. 'Four-square' is perhaps the first word which comes to mind. They are usually austere, fairly inconspicuous from the outside, more or less square, with four massive stone columns inside and a large main barrel vault flanked by two smaller ones over the women's gallery. The Lekstraat synagogue is like a Bauhaus variation on this theme, white and austere and with very plain wooden grilles on the galleries, yet the galleries themselves seem to float unsupported in mid-air like waves and are pierced by delicate little columns. And the huge copper lamps are dramatic, like inverted torches flecked with bulbs. Railings, marble steps and the marble facing on the back wall, with an empty niche for the Ark, remain in place.

The ground floor deals with Dutch resistance, the galleries with the leading German resisters. There is a good deal about resistance from the churches and creative artists, universities, dockers and doctors. The ephemera are evocative and the photographs exhilarating: partisans taking to the hills, convoys setting out for England in little yachts, crashed trains and underground transmitters, people hiding in cellars, the birth of the Dutch princess Margriet in Ottawa in 1943, 'Welcome ally!' messages ('Remember: we are D for Dutch!' – to join with the A-B-C soldiers of America, Britain and Canada).

All of this represents an understandable attempt to celebrate the positive side of the Dutch reaction to the German Occupation. Yet there is no attempt to disguise the reality of Jewish persecution and resistance. There are photographs of a round-up on the Meijerplein, shop windows with signs saying 'No Jews!', the ghetto created by lifting the drawbridges over the canals and erecting barbed wire, as well as copies of the censored *Het Joodsche Weekblad* newspaper, yellow stars, cards from the Westerbork camp and so on.

Mr F. Douwes, who is not Jewish, grew up in the area before the war and remembers playing football on the site of the Museum where he now works. At the time, about a third of the population was Jewish, mainly reasonably prosperous traders (those who were even richer lived further to the north-east, around Beethovenstraat, where there is still a remarkable 'expressionist' synagogue in Jacob Obrechtstraat which looks rather like a power station with a water-tower supplying the *mikveh*). Yet the atmosphere was one of easy-going tolerance, despite the occasional squabbles over girls. Jewish street musicians would play the fiddle, guitar or mouth organ at every corner, Jewish chess enthusiasts would take on all comers . . . When Fascists in 1941 attacked the popular Koco icecream parlour in Van Woustraat, where chess tournaments were often held, they were sprayed with ammonia and driven back. . . . Yet Mr Douwes also told me of the heart-rending scene in 1942 when Jewish boys of sixteen and seventeen were forced to report to an assembly point. As the curfew came at eight o'clock, they set out with their little packages, and all the streets around echoed with their last farewells to their families: 'Dag vader, dag moeder!'

This was also the area where Anne Frank and her family lived before they moved to Prinsengracht. Their home was on Merwedeplein and every day she would pass Mr Douwes's old house in Roer Straat on the way to the Montessori school in Neirs Straat. Photographs show her holding a rabbit in the Amstelrust park, which is now the site of the RAI Centre.

The Anne Frank House itself remains almost unbearably poignant. Particularly affecting are the marks showing the heights of the Frank children, and the pictures in Anne's bedroom – film stars like Norma Shearer and Deanna Durbin, the young Princesses Elizabeth and Margaret of England, a Leonardo cartoon . . . It could be any teenage girl's bedroom, abandoned only this morning, and its very ordinariness makes the fate of the Frank family seem both more immediate and more incomprehensible. Towering over the House is a huge steeple surmounted by a cross and what looks like a yellow pin-cushion or a strange slavonic crown. Much of the year, visitors have to battle through crowds, but early on a winter morning, when the streets are deserted and a mysterious calm reigns over the canals, only the bells break the silence – the bells, described in the diary, which Anne found so consoling, but her mother so irritating.

It was from the Westerbork camp in the north-east of Holland that Anne Frank and over 100,000 other Dutch Jews (and perhaps 250 gypsies) were transported to the concentration camps in Eastern Europe. The site itself is now an observatory, although the railway tracks have been sheared off and twisted into a grotesque and sinister shape to form a striking commemorative monument. Nearby is a Memorial Centre ingeniously designed to look like a barracks, with an exhibition based on the one in the Dutch section of the museum at Auschwitz. One can also watch the haunting unfinished film, with songs from the Tuesday cabarets, which the commandant compelled the Jews of the camp to make for the purposes of German propaganda.

The other great memorial is the Hollandse Schouwburg theatre on Middenlaan Plantage, the main street in the Plantage district of Amsterdam. From the outside, it looks like an ordinary theatre, with a grey façade surmounted by a sub-classical and slightly saucy pediment presumably depicting a naked goddess between representatives of the arts. And indeed it *was* an ordinary theatre, until it was taken over in 1942 as an assembly point from which Jews were deported. When plans were made after the War to re-open it as a theatre or for storing processed meat, there was an outraged reaction. Eventually it was converted into a memorial.

Much of the back wall did not survive the War, so a simple black octagonal obelisk on a basalt Star of David stands in the open air at the end of two plain covered galleries. By the entrance there is a sort of mourning chamber, with an eternal flame, quotation from the Psalms, cactus from Israel and three very stylized tombstones representing a father, mother and child. Opposite, where there is now a modern building with exuberant multi-coloured window frames, was the crèche for the young children of those detained in the Hollandse Schouwburg. Astonishingly enough, the director and his courageous resistance colleagues managed to remove the relevant files and smuggle out a fair number of Jewish children.

There is still a sprinkling of Jews in the elegant Plantage district as well as many signs of their former presence, yet everything is utterly changed. The Plancius theatre, built for a Jewish choral society, still bears prominently a Star of David just below its name, yet the Dutch police took it over as a garage. The zoo opposite, one of the earliest in the world, still looks wonderful, but the Jews who used it for strolls on the Sabbath have all gone. Yet this was once 'the suburb of the Jewish Quarter', an area where, in the 1920s, over half the population was Jewish.

Something of an antidote to these tragic sites is provided by the Corrie Ten Boom House in Haarlem, which is only fifteen minutes away from Amsterdam by train. The Ten Booms were a family of fervent Christians – an elderly father and two spinster daughters – who set up a sort of humanitarian underground network during the War. They organized escape routes and safe houses for many Jews and students keen to avoid forced labour and even hid away a wanted resistance worker and five Jews. (One was a cantor whose noisy practising added to the risk of discovery.) The house, situated behind a charming old clock shop on Barteljorisstraat, has now been restored to its original pre-war state. Not everyone will find the strong flavour of Christian piety very congenial, but the Ten Booms' courage remains exemplary.

The greatest act of mass defiance during the German Occupation of Holland is commemorated in a large bronze statue of a Dockworker. He stands in the Jonas Daniël Meijerplein, a small scrubby triangle of grass in the centre of Amsterdam. Stocky, four-square and with one foot thrust forward, his posture is of noble simplicity; even the seagulls which keep landing on his head cannot detract from his dignity. In response to the incident at the Koco ice-cream parlour in February 1941, the Nazis abandoned all attempts to appear conciliatory and rounded up 425 Jews. The Communist-led dockworkers immediately stopped work in protest. Public transport came to a halt. Force soon succeeded in breaking the strike, but

The statue of the Dockworker, nobly defiant, stands in the Meijerplein in front of the museum housed in the Great and New synagogues (Joroen Nooter/Jewish Historical Museum)

the event is still remembered each year in a gathering at the foot of the statue.

As elsewhere in Amsterdam, nothing in the area around the Dockworker is quite what it seems. Canals were dug out of dry land, then filled in again to become streets. The *plein* (or open spaces) they link up may once have been islands, self-contained communities where newly arrived immigrants crowded in. Today they are used to host street markets or break up the grid of canals and roads with a patch of green.

To the Dockworker's left is a huge map of El Salvador painted in protest on a housing estate, and what looks like a billboard. The typeface is so fancy that, from a distance, the lettering could almost be Hebrew or hieroglyphics. Cyclists making for the billboard come to a sudden stop and form a silent queue. It is all somewhat baffling, and then one realizes – the 'billboard' is in fact a bridge, raised to allow a boat to pass along the Kaizers Gracht canal.

This is called the Vaz Dias bridge, in honour of a prominent Jewish journalist. The lift bridge to the West, fairy-lit at night and featured in many postcards, is named after Walter Süsskind, a German Jew who saved many children from deportation. Meijerplein itself commemorates the first Jew to be called to the Bar (soon after the armies of the French Revolution in 1796 had established a new constitution which granted full rights of citizenship). Indeed, most of the nearby landmarks are named after well-known Jews (or important resisters) – the result of a touching post-war decision to single out their contribution to the life of the city. And here is also the geographical heart of old Jewish Amsterdam. The brick buildings which form a harmonious ensemble round Meijerplein are the Moses and Aaron church and five synagogues; four of them are now part of the magnificent Jewish Historical Museum.

Perhaps the best approach, however, is from the other side. The Sint Antoniesbreestraat shopping street leads from the central section of Amsterdam, around the railway station, down to the Visserplein. On the left is the De Pinto house, now a library, where a rich Jewish banker from a Portuguese background lived from 1651. This was Isaac de Pinto, whose initials appear in once-gilded wrought iron on the grating outside the windows. The rest of the façade is equally imposing in Italian Renaissance style, with six symmetrical columns, while inside visitors can still admire the gilded beams, elaborate mantelpiece, and restored ceiling paintings. Few other buildings give such a strong sense of the wealth and prestige of some of Amsterdam's Jews during the city's Golden Age. It is hardly surprising that the family were considered almost like the local Rothschilds and 'As rich as de Pinto' became a common expression among the poorer Jews.

To reach the heart of the Jewish quarter one crosses the Sint Antoniesluis bridge, where there was so much street trading in the eighteenth century that some of the old-clothes dealers adopted the family name of Sluis (or 'bridge'); it is here that Sint Antoniebreestraat becomes Jodenbreestraat. When Rembrandt lived there from 1639 to 1660, it was one of the main Jewish streets in Amsterdam. (At the beginning of this century, it was still almost entirely Jewish and the scene of a very popular market.) A virtually complete set of his 280 etchings can be seen in the Rembrandt museum. One shows Menassah ben Israel, who played a central role in the readmission of Jews into England in 1656, and another depicts Ephraim Bueno. It may well be Bueno's daughter who appears in one of Rembrandt's greatest works, the so-called 'Jewish Bride' (in the Rijksmuseum), clearly painted from life even though it *may* be meant to represent Jacob and Rachel or Isaac and Rebecca.

Yet Rembrandt is far more than a Christian painter of genius who used the events of the Hebrew Bible and occasionally Jewish individuals as his subject matter. He produced vast quantities of chalk or pen sketches on the streets around his residence, some inevitably of Jews, and used many of the facial types in his large-scale paintings. (There is also a well-known and mildly satirical sketch which almost certainly depicts the local Jews in the synagogue.) In other words, he used real-life Jews as models for patriarchs, Pharisees and the lecherous elders in the story of Susanna. Most surprising of all, he was one of the few painters in the Christian tradition to take seriously the fact that Jesus was a Jew, and to base his representations of him on the fervent contemporary Talmudic students.

Opposite the Rembrandthuis is Uilenburgstraat, where one can find the so-called Fifth Synagogue, built to the basic design I have outlined, though with wooden columns and galleries. One can still see the Star of David over the gable, one of the main lamps suspended from the ceiling, another like a crumpled spider in a storeroom below, yet the building which was used for its original purpose from 1766 until 1943 has now been converted into artists' *ateliers* and a school of restoration; the courtyard, full of fragments of old buildings, could easily be part of an archaeological dig.

At the end of Jodenbreestraat is the charmless traffic intersection of Meester L.E. Visserplein. Just to the right is Waterlooplein, once an island but now a street market full of stalls offering trumpets or *frites*, tatty old clothes or statues of American Indians, and much else besides. A statue of Jesus looks down disapprovingly from the pediment of the curious Moses and Aaron Church, which has a façade like a Greek temple tacked on to a faceless brown brick box. On the back are niches containing sculptures of Moses and Aaron.

On the far side of the Visserplein is an alley where two large superimposed yellow triangles form the sign for the Jewish Historical Museum. This consists of four disused synagogues: the Great (1671) and New (1752) Synagogues, facing the Dockworker on the Meijerplein; and two much smaller prayer houses behind, the Obbene Shul (1685) and the Dritt or Third Shul (1700–78). Both are now used for offices and the Museum's coffee shop and bookstall. Another alley named A.S. Onderwijzerhof after a Chief Rabbi of Amsterdam gives a back view of the complex; outside is a strange abstract sculpture in black metal resembling nothing so much as a feeding giraffe with an extra leg.

The front entrances to the two main synagogues on the Meijerplein give a good idea of the increasing self-confidence of Amsterdam Jews. Both are basically brown brick boxes with two rows of windows, but the Great Synagogue is far more discreet, with a low arched doorway no bigger than a private house's; even the David's harp and Solomon's seal (symbols of the High German Jewish Community) are fairly inconspicuous in the wrought iron gate.

The New Synagogue clearly echoes the Great, yet is a far more imposing presence. For a start, everything is on a larger scale, a sandstone balustrade, complete with an elaborate swirling decorative motif above the door, surrounds the roof, and above that a weathervane and an octagonal fanlight like a canopy or bonnet add the finishing touch. Even the entrance is picked out by a white stone porch with columns and a pediment.

This porch is imitated in very stylized form by the main entrance to the Joods Historisch Museum, which opens on to a narrow and inviting corridor between the two synagogues. Above, the new windows are just plain sheets of glass criss-crossed with black metal frames – all the modern architecture is elegantly low-key and obviously contemporary so the original synagogue complex makes the maximum impact on visitors; since most of the Museum's magnificent collection of objects date from the seventeenth and eighteenth centuries, the restoration has tried to recreate the synagogues roughly as they would have looked in the 1820s.

Inside, the New Synagogue is built to the pattern already described: square, austere, with white walls and light blue barrel-vaulted ceiling over the two side galleries; the central glass domed fanlight is by far the most unexpected and striking feature. It was originally opened with great ceremony in 1752 ('An orchestra was placed beside the *bimah* and there the musicians performed. One of the performers was uncircumcized, he played the double bass . . .'); it now houses the section of the museum concerned with (Dutch) Jewish identity.

A painting by Martin Monnickendam showing the Great synagogue in 1935, at the time of the service marking the 350th anniversary of the foundation of the Amsterdam Ashkenazi community. (Jewish Historical Museum)

The austere, almost clinical, setting makes an excellent exhibition space, yet it also conveys a message of its own. Here is a rational modern museum which beautifully sums up the universal aspects of Judaism and puts far more stress on relations with the gentile world than folksiness or separatism. The original Ark was destroyed during the War; but on the back wall, where it used to stand, is a large oil painting symbolizing hope for the triumph of justice. There is a good brief account of the Nazi period, when over 100,000 of Holland's 140,000 Jews were deported and killed, and the five themes examined in detail are: religion; Israel and Zionism; persecution and survival; personal history; and interaction with the dominant culture. The last section, for example, reveals how even Torah finials (not to mention complete synagogues) were influenced by the design of Baroque churches; and how Zionism, despite the conference held in the Hague in 1905, never attracted the adherence of more than three per cent of Dutch Jews.

The exhibition on the Jewish religion is housed in the Great Synagogue. An adjacent room, long used as a coal cellar, conveniently turned out during restoration to contain the tiled bath from the former *mikveh*. Again, the main hall is white, almost square, with four great white stone columns surging up to the triple blue barrel vault. The balustrades and grilles on the balconies are still painted in the original combination of greens and blues. The benches visible in old photographs have gone, the *bimah* has given way to a display case, the delicately decorated stained glass has disappeared from the windows in the back wall, but the huge silver Chanukah candelabrum (1753) still stands by the steps which lead up to the restored Ark — a great marble gateway framed by columns, with the curtain now replaced by an abstract painted design in deep blue.

The permanent display provides a good introduction to the events which mark the seasonal and life cycles of observant Jews. Particular stress is given to the increasing involvement of women in progressive Jewish practices, and to the distinctions between Sephardi and Ashkenazi ritual. Even people aware of the essential facts about Judaism are bound to be affected by the extraordinary beauty of the objects which have been collected together from many of the different Jewish communities of Holland: Torah mantles, silver finials like strange pagodas, illuminated prayer books, Ark curtains and a magnificent calendar box for counting the Omer.

The final section of the gallery uses a seemingly small topic – the *tzedakah* or community tax – to show how the Dutch Jewish community has developed from the days of separate poor relief to voluntary contributions to Israel. One gloomy detail is that it took until 1972 to establish the right of Jews and other Dutch war victims to receive state benefits. Interesting exhibits include early diamond-sawing machines (there was only one non-Jewish member on the executive committee of the General Diamond Workers' Union in 1919), collection boxes, orphan-dolls dressed up in their Sunday best, and photographs of beggars, pickle pedlars and old Jewish Amsterdam before and after the War.

To visit the Jewish Historical Museum is a stimulating and haunting experience. Equally stimulating was a discussion I had with one of the curators in the Research Department, Joël Cahen. Mr Cahen is a very restless man and was suffering from jetlag, but he soon launched into a stream of enigmatic, provocative, sometimes unprintable remarks. There were now, he guessed, about 30,000 Jews in Holland (a 1976 census put the figure at 27,000), 8,000 of them affiliated to synagogues. Only the Reform movement was growing, but there was an increasing search for Jewish identity among the community at large. Very strong feelings about Israel were almost universal, although this included a number of Dutch Jews who had gone to live in Israel and had come back in disgust.

Unlike in Antwerp, Amsterdam's diamond business is no longer very lively or dominated by Jews. Indeed, Cahen assured me, it is now essentially a phony tourist attraction. Textiles, however, remain strongly Jewish, and there were significant numbers in law, business, teaching, retail and local and national politics.

All this is perhaps to be expected. The joker in the pack is the presence in Amsterdam of about 5,000 Israelis, mainly from Moroccan backgrounds, who tended to be on the margins of the Jewish community (and sometimes on the margins of legitimate business): 'The native Dutch Jews look down on them, and *they* don't think they need a community.' There were also major differences of temperament and background: 'The Dutch Jews are very Dutch – they're stingy, inhospitable, although compared to the rest of the Dutch, they're very hospitable.'

Young Moroccan Jews, on the other hand, fresh from service in the Israeli Army, sometimes came close to a form of 'Jewish self-hatred' in their contempt for the 'passivity' of Dutch Jews during the German Occupation; in any event, the Holocaust was totally outside their frame of reference. With so much tension between communities and so few Jews around, it was hardly surprising that there was a lot of marrying out. 'There are beautiful girls everywhere in Amsterdam,' said the divorced Mr Cahen as he stared morosely out of the window, 'but it's difficult to find a Jewish partner here; it's almost impossible to find a Dutch Jewish partner.'

Mr Cahen's more scholarly research has also produced some interesting discoveries. We have already seen that Rembrandt's friend, Menassah ben Israel, was instrumental in achieving the re-admission of Jews into England in 1656. It has also long been suggested that the Suasso banking dynasty in Amsterdam largely financed 'the Glorious Revolution' of 1688, the last successful invasion of British soil, when William III and his wife Mary gained control of the country from his father-in-law (the Catholic James II) and brought the comparative religious tolerance of Holland to England. There is even an improbable legend that William was given a chest full of guilders – repayable only if his invasion succeeded. In any event, the Tercentenary celebrations gave Mr Cahen and his colleagues an opportunity to examine the role of the Suassos. The ledgers they discovered in the Bank of Exchange leave little room for doubt that the great Jewish banking family provided the money – a loan of 1.5 million guilders – which enabled the bloodless revolution, one of the key turning points in British history, to take place.

The oldest and most impressive functioning synagogue in Amsterdam, the Portuguese-Israelite or Esnoga, also has an intriguing link with England: it served as a model for the marvellous synagogue in London's Bevis Marks. It is located just opposite the Jewish Historical Museum and, when it was built in 1675, was the largest synagogue in Europe. It faces south-east – towards Jerusalem – and dominates the surrounding scene, although fairly discreetly. Annex buildings encrusting it on two sides were put up on the orders of the town council precisely to hide the fact that it is a synagogue, while the roof is concealed by a balustrade of alternating railings and urns. From the outside, the Esnoga is just a cube of reddish brick with windows, impressive merely because of its size. As you enter, the courtyard outside the synagogue and the flat pillars against the wall deliberately recall the Temple of Solomon. A *sukkah* booth, where meals are served during Succot, stands there all year round. A quotation from

the Psalms – 'And I – in Thy great love – shall enter Thy house' – appears above the main entrance to the synagogue; in Hebrew, this contains both the date of construction and a punning reference to the name Aboab, after the man who was responsible for the decision to build, rabbi Isaac Aboab de Fonseca.

You then move into the sombre and spacious synagogue, built mainly of stone although with dark Italian wood for the triple barrel vault. Rows of huge stone columns create the three separate aisles,

The Great synagogue, again shown here in 1935, now forms the heart of the Jewish Historical Museum (Jewish Historical Museum)

while twelve smaller columns (symbolizing the twelve tribes of Israel) support separate women's galleries in the side aisles. There is no electric lighting, so much of the walls consists of windows square and arched, hanging lamps emerge from sunflower-like decorations in the ceiling, and there are candles on each pew. The Ark, which contains 50 Torah scrolls, vaguely recalls the stepped gables of the canal-side houses. Seats decorated with Gobelin tapestries woven in 1741 are used during Simhat Torah.

For the major festivals like Yom Kippour, 800 to 1,000 people come to the Esnoga. But since it is without electricity and a long way on foot from the centres of present-day Jewish settlement in southern Amsterdam, the attached winter synagogue is used from Simhat Torah to Pesach. This is a tiny room decorated in green with a minuscule women's gallery at the back and what looks like a dining-room cupboard for the Torah scrolls. It is very pretty, but so small that it gives a vivid impression of how a once great community was decimated by the Nazis.

Yet there is also a rather wonderful reminder of the continuity of the community. On the walls are a series of cream panels listing the members of the congregation who died in the years from 5488 (or 1728) onwards. Included are many of the great names in 'Spanish and Portuguese' Jewish history: de Pinto, Periera, Rodrigues, da Costa, Floris . . . Anyone who has read, for example, about the role of the Sephardim from around Bordeaux in the struggles for Emancipation at the time of French Revolution will recognize these names. Here is a great tradition, one thinks, these are the families famous for their philanthropy and learning over many centuries, and it all came to an end in the 1940s. This melancholy reflection is soon proved to be quite mistaken. A cupboard just round the corner stores the top hats which have long been customary in the synagogue; most of the same names still appear on the labels.

In a city where current Jewish life is on a small scale and the old Jewish quarter is essentially a museum, the Esnoga makes a marvellous symbol of precarious survival. Yet it is also, as I have suggested, a model which was imitated by the Western Sephardim in London's Bevis Marks – and far away on the other side of the world. The Touro synagogue on Rhode Island (1763) is the oldest in the United States. The oldest still standing in the whole Western hemisphere (with a rabbi's house – later a Chinese laundry! – next door) was built in 1732

on the Caribbean island of Curaçao. An unusual feature is the sand
strewn over the floor – probably to commemorate the Exodus.

It is a curious fact that none of the European cities with a real
historic Jewish quarter and more than one important pre-nineteenth-
century synagogue – Amsterdam, Prague, Venice and Toledo – has
a strong community today. In all of them, the beauty and evocative
power of the sites cannot overcome the strong sense of loss. Yet Prague
is now coming back to life. The Jewish monuments of Toledo may be
museum-pieces, but since the whole city is essentially a museum the
effect is far less harrowing. The same might be said of Venice, the
world's greatest museum-city. In terms of emotional impact, then,
Amsterdam has something of the sharp poignancy of Vienna. For
in both cities there was a major Jewish component to the exciting
turn-of-the-century mélange – and it has now all but disappeared.

In other ways, however, there are stronger links with my next port
of call, Venice. Quite apart from the historical connections, they both
have genuine former Jewish quarters which leave a similar impression.
A venerable synagogue in each case is still functioning, but only just, as
limited numbers pour in for *shabbat*. Much that is wonderful has been
preserved for tourists, but what was once Jewish territory has blended

Courtyard and entrance
of the Esnoga synagogue
today. Built four years
after the Great, it is now
the only functioning
early synagogue in
Amsterdam (Amsterdam
Tourist Office)

back into the city. Today's Amsterdam, despite the superb décor of the canals, is perhaps best known for its brash modernity. Everybody has heard about the hustling, the drugs, the red-light district, the protest movements and sexual freedom. Yet the obvious stridency has not completely swallowed up the Jewish past. What has gone, if one knows where to look, remains almost equally palpable.

4

VENICE

I T IS ALMOST impossible to be alone in Venice. One can, it is true, set out in the evening and stride purposefully away from the main streets, overflowing with restaurants, down a side alley, then over a little bridge to discover a moment's eerie solitude by the moorings of some deserted palace. But as soon as one starts threading one's way back through the maze again, the bridges glimpsed from afar become unattainable and one suddenly arrives at the opera house, an unexpected *vaporetto* stop or a stray canal-side café. Everything is elusive, but the fiesta is well and truly inescapable.

The ghetto is a good example of this elusiveness. It is not particularly difficult to find, but trying to walk around it is a dizzying experience. After eliminating the cul-de-sacs and the little alleys which suddenly make a U-turn and go back to where one started, one can eventually deduce the right route; at a gentlemanly pace, the complete circuit took me about 25 minutes. There are only tiny glimpses of the ghetto itself from a distant bridge, or the rounded exterior walls which suddenly bulge outwards to accommodate the *bimah* or Ark of a synagogue within. The dominant initial impression is of a hidden and fiercely private world, within which the Jews were both protected and oppressed.

Venice has been saved; rumours about its imminent disappearance into the Adriatic have been scotched. Yet the heart of the city is in the past. The future is secure, but it is a future of mass tourism. The Jewish monuments are totally in keeping with this. The buildings survive, visitors abound, two of the synagogues are still in use (although at different times of year), but the marvellous décor is a memorial to a lost moment of Jewish history. As in Prague, one visits a sort of ghost ghetto, torn between nostalgia and wonder that it has survived at all. One cannot help constantly looking back to a time when there were more residents than tourists.

It is easy to feel the same thing, of course, in the Piazza San Marco. People say that the vast open square which Napoleon described as 'the finest drawing room in Europe' only comes to life when it is full of tourists, but the point is fairly academic: there cannot have been a day for decades when the crowds were absent. As I sheltered from the sun and midsummer masses on a porch, half the world seemed to be there. On my right, a Venezuelan New Yorker was showing her grand-daughters around Europe. On my left, some Italian boys were explaining to a Japanese girl, in something approximating to English, why Italians – so charming, so tender, so attentive – make the best boyfriends. Can it really be, I wondered, that there are still girls so naïve that they have not heard it all a thousand times before? Has Venice *ever* been a real city, or has it always just been a place for carnivals, moon-lit boat trips to the opera and holiday flirtations?

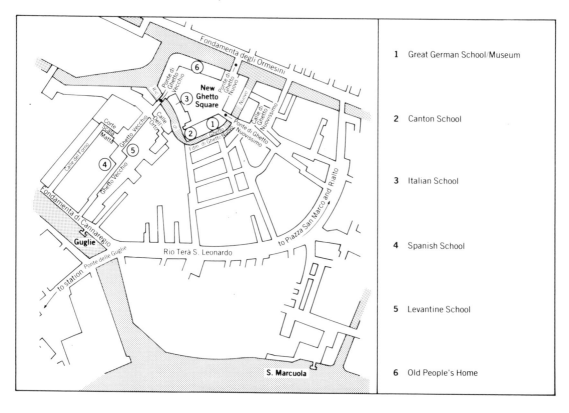

1 Great German School/Museum

2 Canton School

3 Italian School

4 Spanish School

5 Levantine School

6 Old People's Home

Purim players from a book published in 1601 – perhaps the nearest Jewish equivalent of a Venetian carnival? (Weidenfeld Archive)

The answer has to be that Venice has been a magnet for foreign visitors for an astonishingly long time. It was already a sort of home from home for some of the great writers of the Romantic era. And even in the middle of the eighteenth century, the English traveller Lady Mary Wortley Montagu gave a sharp description of her rich young Englishmen compatriots, 'the greatest blockheads in nature', dressing up for the coffee houses, embarking on 'the important conquest of some waiting gentlewoman of an opera queen' and generally treating Venice like a playground.

The trouble with this, of course, is that the more foreign visitors have taken over the city, the more Venetians have moved away. It is obviously one of the wonders of the world, but it is also astonishingly small; the population of the city proper, as opposed to Mestre and the nearby parts of the mainland, is only about 80,000. This marks a sharp decline even since the Second World War; and most of the remaining inhabitants are elderly. The housing is very picturesque, but plumbing tends to be primitive. It must indeed be a strange place to live. As a Jewish resident put it to me: 'Most of the industry's geared to tourism, so it's like living in Disney Land. If you want to eat mussels on a gondola, it's easy to arrange. If you want to buy a loaf of bread, it's far more difficult . . .'

There are many theories about when Venice started its slow decline, at least as a major commercial centre, but one of the crucial turning points was in 1797. It was in that year that Napoleon

Bonaparte, then a general in the French Revolutionary armies, took over the city for the first time. Members of the former Great Council were to be seen dancing around a Liberty Tree erected in the Piazza San Marco. The Most Serene Republic was finished and the gates of the ghetto (the world's first ghetto) were torn down. In towns such as Padua the walls were torn down as well. This makes a marvellous symbol of the moment when the Jews were relieved of their traditional disabilities and entered the modern world, but it also means there is nothing left to see today. In Venice, by contrast, most of the buildings still survive, although few of them are occupied by Jews.

Napoleon is rather an ambivalent figure in Jewish history, but in this first encounter with the Jews he is normally seen as a liberator; he was certainly acclaimed as such in an anonymous Hebrew chronicle of the time. Some people, admittedly, still feel a degree of nostalgia for the intensely separate communal and religious life of the ghetto, but few who have read a detailed description could genuinely want to live locked away in such appallingly cramped, insanitary conditions. A law of 1777 stated firmly: 'The Jews of Venice may never enjoy any Rights of citizenship'; the invading French army, twenty years later, swept all that aside.

The celebrations were both splendid and extraordinary. The provisional government decreed that the ghetto gates must be removed, 'so there is no visual sign of a separation between the Jews and the other Citizens of this City'. Dockyard workers dragged them down, to cries of 'Viva!' and 'Freedom!', and they were hacked to pieces and burnt in New Ghetto Square. A tree was uprooted from a nearby garden and planted as a Liberty Tree; a 'virtuous citizeness' handed over her National Cap to put on top of it. Even the priests were enthusiastic spectators of the speeches and 'patriotic hymns'; the rabbis, it is said, actually joined in the 'democratic dances'. 'Thanks be given to the immortal Bonaparte,' a speaker proclaimed, 'who has broken the bonds of Italian servitude'. Although the first French occupation of Venice lasted only a few months, it had also broken an age-old tradition of Jewish servitude.

The retreating French gave way to a period of Austrian occupation and then to a decade (1805–14) when the Kingdom of Italy was part of the French Empire. With every change of status, it is probably unnecessary to state, the Jews were required to make a large financial contribution to the occupying power. When it came under Austrian control again, the city was in a state of decaying grandeur celebrated by many of the leading figures of the Romantic period. Lord Byron (1788–1826) described Venice as his 'fairy city of the heart' and summed up a typical attitude of the time when he wrote of her as:

> Perchance even dearer in her day of woe,
> Than when she was a boast, a marvel, and a show.

In those days, of course, it was still possible to find solitude in Venice. One of the favoured spots, for those in search of romantic melancholy, was the Lido island, across the lagoon. It is there, for example, that Shelley went riding with Byron. He described it in a poem called 'Julian and Maddalo':

> a bare strand
> Of hillocks, heaped from the ever-shifting sand,
> Matted with thistles and amphibious weeds,
> Such as from earth's embrace the salt ooze breeds,
> Is this; an uninhabited sea-side,
> Where the lone fisher, when his nets are dried,
> Abandons; and no other object breaks
> The waste, but one dwarf tree and some few stakes
> Broken and unrepaired. . .

Needless to say, it is not quite like that any more. The *vaporetto* lets off passengers at a stop called Lido S. Nicolò, where there are rows of parked cars and charmless bungalows, a few fishermen with small boats and a couple of docked ships. What is still there, however, is the walled enclosure containing the old Jewish cemetery. Since land was rented for this purpose in 1386 and the ghetto was only established in 1516, it counts as the earliest major Jewish monument of Venice. (Controversy still surrounds the Giudecca, another of the islands in the lagoon. The name suggests it was an early centre of Jewish settlement, but some people believe that it was originally called the island *del giudicato* – 'of the judges' – because of the conspirators who were exiled there.)

Even in Shelley's day, the cemetery was in disrepair since the French had torn out many of the tombs to make way for fortifications. In 1834, there cannot even have been a wall, since it was the scene of a stormy lovers' quarrel (neither the first nor the last) between the French novelist Georges Sand and the poet Alfred de Musset; in a fit of rage Sand stormed off through the cemetery, leaping from one tomb to the next.

Today, the gate is usually locked, but one can look through the bars at a most atmospheric scene: tall knobbly white graves of local Istrian stone, often marked with Hebrew lettering and shield-like motifs of *shofar*, crown, turret, raised hands or palm branch, emerge from the undergrowth beside the unkempt paths. Sarcophagi are decorated with masks and friezes of flowers and foliage. A mass grave of plague victims is marked by the simplest of stones bearing the legend '1631 Hebrei'. Most of the leading Venetian Jews until the eighteenth century lived in the ghetto and are buried in this cemetery: rabbis like Leone da Modena and Simone Luzzatto, the poet Sara Capio Sullam and her father, and Jews whose search for commercial opportunities and a comparatively liberal regime had brought them to Venice from Iberia, Central Europe or the Levant.

Liberated – and, in a sense, destroyed – by Napoleon, the Venice ghetto was predominantly Jewish until the First World War. Today only the family of the rabbi and a few others still live there, although the current inhabitants are very tolerant and so used to Jews and their customs that they offer New Year's greetings on Rosh Hashanah. The main entrance is located between Gigi's Trattoria and a chemist on the Fondamenta de Cannaregio, a left turn off the main 'road' leading down from the railway station to the Piazza San Marco and the centre of town.

Outside, seafood stalls offer shellfish from the Adriatic while boats awash with flowers, sailors asleep in the bows, churn up the waters in the canal. A dark little tunnel leads into a narrow alley of tall houses, past the bricked-up windows where the guards, paid by the Jews, once sat and past the still visible holes where the gates were attached. A blast of Billy Holiday greeted me as I entered; I walked past a bar, a furniture gilder and a kosher grocery into the Campiello delle Scuole, a small square with the original well and two of the ghetto's five synagogues.

This is the Old Ghetto, dating from 1541, and the synagogues here are still in use, the Spanish School in Summer, the heated Levantine School in Winter. (When I was there, loud pop music started booming out in the small square just as prayers were beginning on Friday and Saturday, but this was presumably a coincidence rather than a deliberate gesture of disrespect.) The Spanish School was founded by Jews expelled from the Iberian peninsula in the 1490s who reached Venice, usually via Amsterdam, Leghorn or Ferrara, in the 1550s. The Levantines were free merchants, citizens of the Ottoman Empire, to whom the Republic made concessions for economic reasons.

Although they look elegant enough and blend in well together, and with the 'skyscrapers' next door to them, the Levantine in pale lemon-yellow, the Spanish in cream, the exteriors are not spectacular. In both cases, the separate section for the Ark or *bimah* can be seen from outside, like a huge lantern half-emerged from the wall (this architectural motif, known as the *liagò*, is also used on non-Jewish buildings as a way of letting in extra light). The interiors of the synagogues, however, are magnificent. Perhaps the most extraordinary sight of all is the *bimah* in the Levantine School (*c.* 1538), a huge ornately carved double staircase in dark walnut which leads up to a grand platform and two twisted columns supporting a great canopy. The balustrades on the staircase end surprisingly at the bottom in two gigantic wooden fruit bowls. The columns with elaborate flowers, fruit and foliage wrapped around them are intended to echo the Temple of Solomon; more directly, they use motifs derived from Bernini's celebrated baldequin in St Peter's in Rome. The prayer leader is illuminated by the natural light which pours down into a domed niche behind him. Since the other dominant colour in the synagogue is the deep red of the curtains, the overall impression is strikingly dramatic.

Nothing else in the Levantine School rivals the overpowering *bimah*, although the convoluted carvings on the ceiling link up with the top of the canopy. The benches, rather like those in a school classroom, are also made of walnut. The Ark, set back in a separate area behind a low brass gate and railings of red marble, is an elaborate classical construction in various shades of grey marble. Flaps with a tight wooden grille open inwards from the women's gallery on one of the long sides of the synagogue. Until comparatively recently they were kept closed during prayers.

The women's gallery in the Spanish School, by contrast, is oval in shape, with a wooden balustrade below the separate grille windows rather reminiscent of the paupers' gallery in a theatre. The Ark is again cordoned off by wooden double gates and a low balustrade which echoes the one in the gallery. Four striped black columns support a triangular tympanum, out of which surge the Tablets of the Law surrounded by golden sun rays, a white arch and the crown; the whole ensemble is set against a deep blue-green arch which almost reaches up to the women's gallery. The *bimah*, at the opposite end of

the synagogue, is a canopy on four columns which emerges from the wall like a four-poster bed. The 'roof' carries an elaborate wooden structure of scrolls and amphoras which is linked by the gallery to the rosettes on the ceiling. While the yellow walls and red curtains dominate the lower levels, the eye is carried up towards the solid and violently contrasted deep brown structures above. The overall effect is flamboyantly theatrical.

The main street of the ghetto swerves through the Campiello delle Scuole and then continues in a virtually straight line, past a shop selling Jewish souvenirs, another selling dresses and a travel agent, over a bridge and into New Ghetto Square. This large open space contains three synagogues, an old people's home, and a Jewish museum; but the salient impression is that a former Jewish domain has become just an ordinary, poor section of Venice. Boys kick footballs in and out of the columns which form the porch – like a miniature Roman temple – of the Italian School; pots of flowers create tiny gardens on the terrace above. Parents lean from the windows of the Great German School to call to the kids amid a pile of bikes below. The five- and six-storey buildings, among the first 'skyscrapers' in Europe, were erected to get as many people as possible into a confined space. Some are of bare brick, but most are painted in pale orange or red, greys and creams; green shutters and a few blinds cover all the windows. Girls sit on the ornate well heads which date from the sixteenth century. Frisbies are thrown, cats stalk sparrows, bins overflow with rubbish, and a young man lies in his girlfriend's lap on a bench just in front of a series of Holocaust reliefs. Most of the people just sit and gossip, although one sometimes sees a postman passing, a plump priest hitching up his cassock or the occasional chic beauty, sporting yet another inventive variant of *décolleté*.

Along with a Chabad House, there are three businesses in the square. Glamour girls pout from photographs in a shop which seems to sell ornate silver frames. David's Shop is a gift shop, where one can buy Snoopy tiles or tiny glass Pink Panthers with cute Jewish messages, Murano glass and Burano lace, tiny carnival masks, brass candlesticks and *mezuzot* which used to be made in the ghetto. Altogether more interesting is the final shop, owned by

The Levantine School, looking towards the celebrated *bimah* (G. Arici/Museum Management Service)

Gianfranco Penzo, which offers craft works combining 'traditional Venetian decoration with a Jewish theme'. Signor Penzo obtains glass plates and cups, made to his own design, from the master glaziers of Murano, paints them with images or motifs derived from Jewish sources and bakes them in his kiln. He copies, for example, the charming scenes of Jewish life in the nineteenth-century prints by Moritz or puts individual names and dates on plates intended as one-off wedding or barmitzvah presents. The larger plates take 46 days to make and so are not cheap (although they count as duty-free religious objects), but even people who cannot afford his kiddush cups stop to watch a true craftsman at work.

Today there are only about 400 Jews, and 100 young Jews, in Venice proper (600 in the area which includes the Lido and Mestre), since many have moved away in search of career opportunities or the richer communal life of Rome or Milan. A mere 30 or so men regularly attend synagogue in winter, even fewer locals during the summer holiday season. Observance is not very strict and intermarriage is common; the total Jewish population of Italy may not have declined since the nineteenth century, but the historic Venetian community consists of old-established families and is probably on its last legs.

Even people who know nothing of the ghetto, however, invariably link Jews with Venice. And that is because one of the most famous characters in literature is a Venetian Jew. *The Merchant of Venice* is, of course, an antisemitic play. Shakespeare may show us the casual antisemitism of the Venetian Christians, he may let us see how their feverish, vacuous charm depends on Shylock's money, he may even in a sense allow Shylock to put his case, but strong elements of the pernicious stereotype remain. Shylock is both a money lender and an over-possessive father, out of place in a romantic comedy. Antonio is suffering from self-indulgent melancholy, Portia from a sort of girlish petulance, while Bassanio is looking for a rich heiress to settle his debts; Shylock enters talking of money. By the end he has become an inhuman monster, impervious to pity:

> You may as well do anything most hard
> As seek to soften that – than which what's harder? –
> His Jewish heart.

The play celebrates the reckless glamour of the great age of Venetian commerce, when ships risked destruction on 'merchant-marring rocks' to bring back riches from every corner of the earth, as in Shylock's description of Antonio: 'He hath an argosy bound to Tripolis, another to the Indies; I understand, moreover, upon the Rialto, he hath a third at Mexico, a fourth for England, and other ventures he hath squandered abroad.' Yet it is utterly disdainful of money-lending, which is seen as an attempt to breed from 'barren metal' and associated with the Jews.

In this, of course, Shakespeare was not just expressing his own prejudices but reflecting a major Christian tradition. One can still see in New Ghetto Square a house labelled Banco Rosso under the low colonnade. This was one of the three former pawnbrokers or 'paupers' banks' (named after the colour of the receipts they handed out). Since Christians were not officially allowed to practise 'usury' or money-lending, it became a Jewish monopoly as early as the fourteenth century and the Jewish banks obviously played a vital role in seeing to the needs of the poor and making tax contributions to the Republic. Inevitably, this did little to enhance their popularity. However much people need credit, they seldom love their creditors and Christian preachers who railed against Jewish usurers usually got a good reception. The Church did recognize, however, that some form of poor relief was essential, so they set up so-called *monti di pietà* to provide interest-free loans. In theory, these were charitable institutions, but they often ended up charging low rates of interest and thus competing, not very successfully, with the pawnshops.

The history of the Jews in Venice (as elsewhere) thus tended to follow a cycle. When the Church strictly maintained the principle that usury was illicit, the Jews suffered for it. Yet when the Christian attempts to relieve hardship by other means proved unavailing, Jewish usury – and hence the Jews themselves – enjoyed a reluctant tolerance. By performing a necessary although despised function in society, Jews were able to live in comparative safety.

These issues are implicit in *The Merchant of Venice*, which was written in the 1590s when there was no official Jewish presence in England. (There is, however, a possible reference in the play to Dr Roderigo Lopez, a Portuguese 'New Christian' who was executed in 1594 for an alleged attempt to poison Queen Elizabeth: Gratiano accuses Shylock of being 'wolvish, bloody, starved, and ravenous' because he has acquired the soul of an animal – 'thy currish spirit/Governed a wolf . . . hanged for human slaughter'; since the Latin word for 'wolf' is *lupus*, there may be an oblique allusion to Dr Lopez.)

In 1638, however, the Venetian chief rabbi Simone Luzzatto published a series of *Discourses* which set out the opposite case: despite a few Jewish criminals, the community as a whole was not vicious; they made a major contribution to the economic well-being of the Republic. Their main role, he suggests, was as traders. Citizens of an affluent city become more and more reluctant to run the risks of seafaring, so commerce largely depends on newcomers. Jews are particularly suitable because they have no land of their own to return to in old age and so tend to invest their wealth locally. Hardship and large families encourage the Jews to work inventively and hard. Indeed, the Jews in a state are like the feet – their status may be inferior, but they support all the rest.

Luzzatto himself was a maverick – he believed that the Talmud permitted travelling by gondola on the Sabbath! – but his argument is interesting for two reasons. First of all, there are some striking parallels between his *Discourses* and the claims of Menassah ben Israel in the appeal he submitted to Cromwell in 1655. This, as is well known, played a crucial role in securing the Readmission of the Jews to England, so the indirect influence of Luzzatto was immense. In the eighteenth century, help went in the other direction when the Sephardim of Amsterdam and London provided financial help to those of Venice.

The other point is that the underlying issue – the Jewish role in early capitalism – remains a very controversial one. Professor Milton Friedman, alluding to *The Merchant of Venice*, once described how 'anti-semitism produced a stereotype of the Jew as primarily interested in money, as a merchant or money-lender who put commercial interests ahead of human values, who was money-grasping, cunning, selfish and greedy, who would "*jew*" you down and insist on his pound of flesh'. Yet instead of 'accepting the description but rejecting the values that regarded these traits as blameworthy', Friedman suggests, many Jews have denied all reality to the stereotype (one of the explanations of Jewish prominence in left-wing causes). The *Universal Jewish Encyclopaedia*, for example, says that the German scholar Werner Sombart (author of *The Jews and Modern Capitalism* in 1911, later a Nazi sympathizer) 'accused the Jews of having created capitalism' – as if this was, by definition, an insult.

It is easy to reflect on such topics in Venice, a city which is like a perfectly preserved jewel from a golden age of commerce. Its empire is long defunct, yet several of the ports of Cyprus, the Greek islands and mainland are still like miniature fragments of Venice, gems scattered by the Serenissima in her prime. Jews often acted as links in this network of international trade and a tiny ghetto, tragically depleted by Nazi deportations, still survives in Corfu. Not that the Jews were invariably on the Venetian side. One of the most colourful characters in Jewish history, Joseph Nasi, adviser to the Ottoman sultan Selim the Sot, was involved in various schemes to wrest the islands of the Aegean out of Venetian hands. At the height of his influence, he was given the title of Duke of Naxos (an island he never visited), although his plans to become King of a Jewish colony in Cyprus did not materialize even after the successful Turkish invasion in 1570.

In Venice itself, the main outlines of early settlement are clear. From the fourteenth century, the city was keen to encourage money-lenders, and many were Jewish from the beginning. Despite restrictions, hostile legislation and even an expulsion decree in 1397, which did not apply to doctors and was generally carried out in rather haphazard fashion, these people formed the nucleus of a major community. By the end of the fifteenth century, they were also allowed to sell second-hand clothes – which, in practice, were often new clothes with a tiny fault deliberately introduced!

The Great German School, looking through the unusual *bimah* towards the Ark (G. Arici/Museum Management Service)

★

Not long afterwards, in 1516, the earliest part of the ghetto was built – on the site, confusingly, of New Ghetto Square. This was itself a reflection of Christian ambivalence: although it was recognized that the Jews were needed, it was also felt necessary to control and confine them. Yet within appallingly cramped conditions, three hidden synagogues soon sprang up.

The earliest is the Great German School of 1529. (German Jews lived briefly in the city from 1382 to 1397 and were then expelled to Mestre; their descendants are still around today, but the city's single Sephardi rabbi means that they have not used the Ashkenazi ritual in this century.) The basic shape is slightly irregular, but the dark brown benches on the long sides lead up to fake marble panels (real marble was not permitted in synagogues) and then an astonishing oval women's gallery. This is made of gilded wood and in three ascending layers: balustrade, intricate close-meshed grille and open sections divided up by slender columns. A lamp is suspended from the octagonal lantern in the ceiling. The overall effect is like an eighteenth-century jewel box (the gallery was not an original feature), with the gilding echoed in both the Ark and the *bimah*.

The Ark is at the top of four steps; the doors are red, decorated with golden Trees of Life in relief, and framed by Corinthian columns and a pediment above which almost brushes against the golden studs below the women's gallery. The seats for the elders on either side are like miniature versions of the same design. At the other end of the room is the strange *bimah*, like an unattached and enclosed booth or balcony, with thin columns above a low balustrade supporting a canopy. The delicacy and dominant gold tone add a finishing touch to the décor of this lovely synagogue.

Next door to it, in the corner of the square, is the Canton School (1532). The most noticeable feature is the tiny cupola which pops up out of the roof like some curious Oriental fantasy. The word 'Canton', however, has nothing to do with China, but derives either from the name of a donor or from its sense of 'corner' in Venetian dialect. Inside, there is the familiar contrast between dark wood and gilding. Flaps open inwards just below the ceiling from the women's gallery, as in the later synagogues of the Ghetto Vecchio; each is decorated with a motif of interlocking loops. Below, windows looking out over the canal alternate with wooden panels, above which are crown-shaped reliefs depicting Jerusalem, the Red

Sea, the River Jordan and other Biblical scenes. The Ark is similar in shape to the one in the Great German School, although it is gilded all over and decorated with elaborate, beautifully carved floral and semi-abstract patterns.

The most striking structure is the *bimah*. Wooden steps lead up to a separate more or less semicircular niche almost the width of the synagogue. Two pairs of spiralling columns made of intertwining branches – recalling the Temple of Solomon – create a framing arch. The simple three-sided pulpit is again gilded, a completely independent unit which seems to have been lowered on to the steps from above. It certainly stands out against the dark wood behind and seems perched, about to topple, on a single tapering foot. As in the Levantine School, the natural light illuminating the reader from the octagonal cupola behind him adds to the dramatic effect.

The Italian School, finally, is on a more intimate scale. (The use of a specifically Italian religious ritual was largely confined to southern Italy up to around Padua; this small and poor offshoot in Venice survived until the early nineteenth century.) The Ark is set back behind a low wall and double gate and is made of wood. Above it, the cornice which goes all round the room gives way to an arch. Exactly the same thing happens above the *bimah*, a podium which projects forward from a niche reached by a double staircase. Four wooden Corinthian columns support the arch, thereby framing both the *bimah* and the stairs. In contrast to this grand structure and the dark wooden desks and panels along the walls are the stucco panels above.

As in the other synagogues, the original sixteenth-century details have been overlaid by several stages of restoration, and are difficult to reconstruct exactly. What is certain is that the Italian School is the synagogue which blends most easily into the square, with its charming little porch, flower-filled balconies and flats, and five larger arched windows; the eighteenth-century cupola makes a lovely finishing touch.

Something of a historical afterthought in Jewish Venice is the Ghetto Nuovissimo, a T-shaped addition which is reached over the small bridge at the end of the *sotòportego*, or passageway, which opens on to New Ghetto Square. In the charming little Jewish Museum, between the Great German and Canton Schools, is a fine collection of Italian Judaica: beautiful marriage contracts, Torah finials like huge pine-cones, Oriental spice-boxes with trees emerging, Torah shields the shape of flattened crowns, silver cradle amulets. Indeed, there is a strong stress on silver, worked with supreme delicacy into paper-thin roses and flowers.

Yet there is also a sense that Venice is one huge museum, the whole ghetto a miniature museum within it. Although, like Amsterdam and London, it represents one of the early points of call in the post-1492 Sephardi diaspora, the difference in atmosphere is overwhelming. The real turning point for Jewish life in London was the mass eastward movement after the pogroms of 1881. Of that specific moment, on which so much depends, the East End is the great memorial. Venice, by contrast, remains a blessed city largely because one can almost forget the nineteenth and twentieth centuries.

The ghetto has its particular flavour of separateness and enclosure, yet it is also very visibly Venetian. There are always film crews in Venice diligently searching for the elusive atmosphere of carnival, decadent glamour and mystery. From the night scene in Visconti's *Senso* (1954) to *The Comfort of Strangers* (1990), many have used the ghetto as a charming backdrop. And it is a charming backdrop, of course, but it is also far more than that. Its history and hidden riches make it perhaps the most evocative site in Jewish Europe.

The back 'entrance' to the ghetto, leading to the Ghetto Nuovissimo (G. Arici/Museum Management Service)

5

LONDON

Familiar images of wartime London show crowds sheltering in the tube stations during the Blitz, the short period when the city faced the brunt of Hitler's war machine. Particularly poignant are the famous series of drawings by Henry Moore. A comparatively small proportion of the population spent nights underground; there were a few terrible accidents and anxieties about health risks; but the sense of security and camaraderie was genuine.

Yet what was there to do in an air raid shelter as the bombs rained down outside? Entertainment of various kinds was soon improvised – and a curtain was hastily rigged up for performances by a husband-and-wife Yiddish theatre troupe. Gentiles who knew not a word of the language were treated to operettas like *Yossele and Feigele*, which tells the story of a lovelorn Hasid and his innocent sweetheart. Exceptional circumstances had brought a romantic melodrama with songs out of the 'ghetto' in front of a far wider audience. When the 'All Clear!' sounded and the actors left the shelter, they were cheered on their way by one and all. There could hardly be a greater contrast with what was beginning to happen to the Jews in virtually every country in continental Europe.

It also makes a marvellous symbol of Jewish life in London. Yiddish theatre, like much of the Jewish culture of Eastern Europe, was brought by the immigrants of the 1880s. It flourished briefly in the East End and then, as Jews integrated into the wider community, slowly began to die. When the Second World War ended and young Jews moved away from the area, a living form of theatre became a conscious act of nostalgia, a loving recreation of a dead tradition.

★

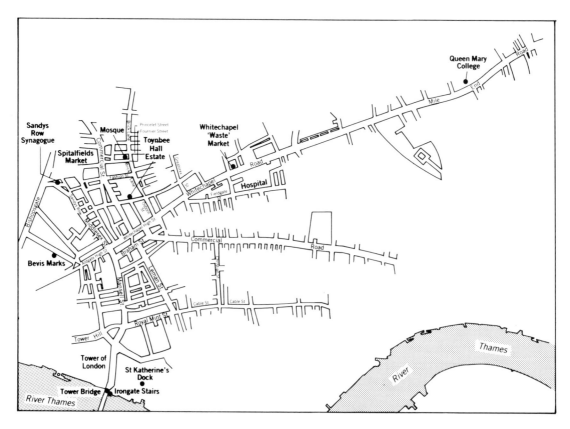

The Jewish East End is in many ways a lost world. I once attended a play called *From Stepney Green to Golders Green*, a title which neatly summarizes the route taken by many Jewish families from the original area of settlement into the affluent suburbs of north-west London. It consisted of typical scenes from the past. Jeers and cries of 'You killed Jesus!' greeted Jewish children in their playgrounds at Easter, while mothers pushed pretzels and bagels to them through the railings. An uncle taught his newly arrived nephew the only English words he needed to be a hat salesman – 'Very nice! Very cheap!' – while the baby slept on in an orange box in the rat-infested house. The widest pavement in London, along the Whitechapel Road (now the scene of an Asian street market), was once known as 'Monkies Parade'; teenage flirtations blossomed into romances over pickled cucumber and chips, and sometimes ended in marriage. Larry the Lamplighter served as *shabbas goy* for several streets. And it was a standing joke to heat up coins over a fire, so they would burn a hole in the beggar's hat. . . .

All these incidents had been recalled by people who had grown up in the East End and were now Old Age Pensioners. When I saw the play in a Jewish old people's home, most of the audience was glum, sickly and semi-senile. Yet they suddenly came back to life as scenes from their childhood unfolded on stage. There are still echoes of such times for those who know where to look on the streets of the East End.

London's Jewish sites have a unique, often poignant fascination, yet the area still often looks and feels like a set for a film about Jack the Ripper. The street lighting may have improved a good deal since 1888 (partly in response to the outcry about the appalling crimes), but there is dereliction on all sides. Bomb damage during the Blitz only adds to the feeling of neglect.

Many of the great working-class sections of European cities, transformed by waves of Jewish immigration in the aftermath of pogroms in 1881 and 1903, have been given more or less successful facelifts. The Gorbals in Glasgow may still be fairly grim, but acres of cramped and insanitary tenement housing have been swept aside. All around the East End, too, there have been major improvements: the City of London is slowly expanding, parts of Spitalfields have become fashionable and the Docklands have been turned into a surreal combination of Dickensian housing and sleek, ultra-modern (but often empty) luxury residences and offices. Yet in the central section of the East End, around Whitechapel, it is not difficult to imagine the Victorian slum. Today's Jewish population may be ageing and numerically small, but nowhere else does one get such a strong sense of the particular moment when Jewish life was transformed by mass migration across Europe – and, of course, across the Atlantic, to American equivalents of the East End such as the Lower East Side.

A slightly larger area includes all the major historic Jewish centres of London. If one starts in the very centre, near Bank, one can find a street called Old Jewry. This is located within the City, as bounded by the original mediaeval walls, and represents a settlement which dates from before the Expulsion in 1290. Moving east, one also moves forward through the centuries. One of the gates in the walls was called Aldgate, where the City starts to blend into the East End. It was here that the Jews first took up residence after they were officially readmitted in the 1650s. Jewry Street and Bevis Marks, the oldest synagogue in England, provide the most obvious surviving evidence. Outside St Botolph's church, long a centre for improving

'The Jewish Family' by Mark Gertler (1913) depicts in nobly stylized form a typical immigrant family from Eastern Europe (Tate Gallery)

Christian-Jewish relations, is a simple sculpture of a crouched human figure below a stylized canopy; this is *Sanctuary*, by a Holocaust survivor called Naomi Blake.

Further on is the huge Whitechapel intersection known as Gardiner's Corner, the heart of the late nineteenth-century '*shtetl*'. Until the Second World War, it was the undisputed centre of Jewish institutions in England. This is no longer true, but one of the main exodus routes has led yet further east, along the grim monotony of the Mile End Road – roughly parallel to the Thames – to Ilford and Redbridge. Since most of the immigrants originally arrived by water, some people have seen in this a superstitious desire to maintain a link with the point of arrival (as well as family left behind) in case of renewed hostility. Equally important, however, has been the movement towards areas of northern London such as Finchley and Golders Green. This has long been known colloquially as 'the North-West Passage'.

It is impossible to explore Jewish London without constantly coming across the sites of the Ripper murders (guided tours give morbid visitors a chance to see them for themselves). The first victim was killed at the end of a sinister little alley just behind the Whitechapel Road, the main artery through the district. Another body was left in Mitre Square, near Aldgate. There was even a Jack the Ripper pub in Spitalfields, although feminist protest meant that its name was changed to the Three Bells. Jack the Ripper's ghastly exploits have, inevitably, led to much prurient conjecture, although the market for books on the subject has unearthed some vivid social history. No one who has read any of them can suppress a shudder or forget that these are haunted streets, where the drink-sodden prostitute victims once plied their trade in dark alleys and courtyards. And a celebrated clue (or non-clue) has a direct link with the Jewish history of the area.

On the night of 30 September 1888, two murders took place. The first was in Berner Street, Whitechapel; a fragment of the victim's bloodstained apron was found in Goulston Street, near the famous 'Petticoat Lane' street market. The second, as I have mentioned, was in Mitre Square. It was also in Goulston Street that an illiterate and enigmatic piece of graffiti was discovered on a patch of brickwork. This read: 'The Juwes are The men That Will not be Blamed for nothing.'

Or something similar. There are several versions of the exact wording, and we shall never know which is correct. For while the Acting City Police Commissioner called Major Smith ordered that the chalk scrawls be photographed, the Metropolitan Police Commissioner, Sir Charles Warren, decided to erase them. This may have had something to do with rivalry between the different police forces, but the most natural view is that Sir Charles believed the graffiti to be an irrelevant piece of antisemitic griping which could only increase the level of inter-racial tension. Yet the alleged 'police cover-up' has been used ever since as the cornerstone of many overheated conspiracy theories.

Thus, the word 'Juwes', we are told, has nothing to do with the Jews but refers to three Masonic figures called Jubela, Jubelo and Jubelum. Those who are not paranoid about the Freemasons can take their pick from a dizzying range of different speculations about Jack the Ripper's identity, involving a Russian doctor, an eccentric homosexual Cambridge academic, clairvoyants, deranged midwives, the poet Swinburne, an insurance salesman called Smith, the painter Walter Sickert, major Establishment figures and even, inevitably, the Royal Family.

At the time of the murders, the reaction was far simpler. They had taken place in an area with a large Jewish population and could not, it was said, have been committed by an ordinary Englishman, so antisemitic attacks became commonplace. One policeman put forward the view that 'in stating that he was a Polish Jew I am merely stating a definitely established fact', although others made impressive efforts to calm the situation. Much was made of the fact that some of the murders took place on Jewish holidays, and the spectres were soon raised of a bloodthirsty ritual slaughterer roaming the streets with his knife, or a religious fanatic inspired by the denunciations of prostitutes in the Talmud. Only in the 1930s (and again, briefly, after the War), with the deliberate provocation of Oswald Mosley's strutting British Union of Fascists, would hostility towards the Jews erupt with comparable ferocity.

This could certainly be very ugly. The playwright Harold Pinter has described some instances from his youth in the 1940s: 'I went to a Jewish club, by an old railway arch, and there were quite a lot of people often waiting with broken milk bottles in a particular alley we used to walk through.' It would be absurd to skate over such examples of British antisemitism, yet it is equally important to stress a crucial difference between London and the capital cities of continental Europe. Jewish refugees who arrived in the late 1930s were often treated with peculiar insensitivity, for example when they were interned as enemy aliens. British policy in Palestine was influenced by both antisemitism and romantic pro-Arabism. Yet, with the minor exception of the occupied Channel Islands, Jews were not deported to concentration camps from British soil.

No one can tell, of course, what would have happened if the rest of Britain had been occupied by the Nazis; yet a huge psychological difference remains. Jews all over Europe, even if they personally were protected by non-Jewish fellow-citizens, have to live with the plain historical fact that many of their compatriots took part in genocide. British Jews do not; while some are very sensitive even to mild instances of antisemitism, it is also not unusual to find 1930s' refugees who strongly believe in a 'British tradition of tolerance'. If such a tradition exists, one might find an example in the famous demonstration against fascism which took place on 6 October 1936, the Battle of Cable Street.

The first history of the Jews in England, D'Blossiers Tovey's *Anglia Judaica* (1738) was nominally inspired by Christian hostility. Yet although the author quotes many antisemitic legends and accusations, he clearly regards them with a sceptical eye and gives some pretty broad hints that they were spread for mercenary motives: 'the Jews always seem to commit such dastardly crimes when the reigning king is in need of money!' The Expulsion of the Jews in 1290 achieved nothing. Whatever the faults of Jewish money-lenders and traders, their Christian counterparts, unburdened of competition, had proved just as grasping. He is unable, Tovey concludes, 'to find any evidence of any good whatsoever arising from the Jews' banishment'.

The only new Jewish institution in 1738 was the Sephardi burial ground at 329 Mile End Road, the third oldest in England, which had been bought five years before. Apart from that, the Jewish East End then consisted of two great monuments – the Sephardi synagogue at Bevis Marks (1701) and the Ashkenazi Great Synagogue (1690) close by. The total Jewish population of England Tovey estimated at 6,000. The Readmission was made official in the year 1664 shortly after King Charles II recovered the throne and put an end to Oliver Cromwell's short-lived Republic (1648–60). Yet it is Cromwell who is usually given the credit for it (Freud called his first son Oliver in gratitude), since Charles merely gave formal legal acceptance to the *de facto* Jewish presence in the city. What were Cromwell's motives? It is safe to assume that there is no truth in Tovey's story that the Jews were willing to pay £500,000 to be let back in – provided that they were also given St Paul's Cathedral as a synagogue and the Bodleian Library in Oxford as a business centre!

In reality, the main factors seem to have been a combination of religious idealism, Messianic convictions, hard-headed commercial calculation and the personal intervention of Menassah ben Israel (the friend of Rembrandt and rabbi of the Great Synagogue in Amsterdam, whom I mention in the chapter on that city). Furthermore, since there was a wave of Cossack persecution against the Jews in the late 1640s, the search for a refuge had acquired a new urgency.

On the whole, the Puritans who formed the basis of Cromwell's republic were devoted readers of the Bible and admirers of Jewish achievements, some believing in tolerance and others keen to get

the chance to try and convert some genuine Jews! Jews and Christians alike pondered the significance of prophecies in Daniel and
Deuteronomy that the promised Redemption would not come about
until the Jews were scattered to the four corners of the earth. As more
or less reliable evidence reached Europe of a Jewish presence in China,
the Americas and Tartary, everything seemed to be going according to
plan. The great exception was England, whose very name in French –
Angleterre – seemed to indicate that it counted as one of the earth's
'angles' or corners.

Such speculations had their influence on Menassah, Cromwell
and his associates. Yet considerations of trade were equally significant.
The great Sephardi diaspora which followed the Expulsion from Spain
in 1492 had brought a number of 'New Christians' to London and
had played a key role in Amsterdam's increasing prosperity. By
officially readmitting the Jews Cromwell hoped to lure to London
instead men who would build up British trade with Spain and
the West Indies and could draw on contacts all over the world to
obtain intelligence. Menassah ben Israel's book *The Hope of Israel*
(1650) skilfully combined the religious and commercial arguments
for readmission, and a pamphlet entitled *Vindiciae Judaeorum* (1656)
answered the objectors.

The decisive breakthrough, however, occurred not in the kind
of sonorous declaration favoured by the French Revolutionaries but
more or less by chance. When war broke out between England and
Spain, Spanish merchants in London were deprived of their property.
A 'New Christian' called Don Antonio Robles appealed, claiming that
he was in reality both Portuguese and Jewish. Cromwell encouraged
his Council to uphold this claim – thus granting official acceptance of
the Jewish presence in London and implicit protection from the most
powerful man in the land.

The Jews may have been readmitted by the back door, but the
community slowly built up from there. A plaque marks the site of the
first synagogue, which was located inside a building on Creechurch
Lane from 1657 to 1701. It soon became a major social centre, with
fascinated British visitors who knew little about Judaism coming to
watch the religious practices of the exotic newcomers. Another plaque
marks the site of the former Great Synagogue (destroyed by bombing
in 1941) in Duke's Place. The original Ashkenazi *shul* stood there from
1690, and exactly a century later it was replaced by a neoclassical
synagogue which became firmly linked with the Chief Rabbi and

accepted as the major religious centre of Anglo-Jewry. Duke's Place soon changed its name to Bevis Marks and there, in a courtyard behind a locked gate, is the splendid synagogue of the same name.

The architect is said to have been a Quaker who refused payment for work on a religious building, and the general flavour is rather like that of a Dissenters' meeting house. There are extremely plain arched windows on all sides, and twelve solid plaster columns support the women's gallery. These are cream in colour, but the railings above are darker, and the wood panelling, seating, oak benches from Creechurch Lane, central pulpit, Ark railing and wardens' box pew, complete with wooden canopy, are all very dark indeed. The basic structure has a kind of austerely imposing dignity. But the detail is far more dramatic. Lighting was originally supplied by brass Dutch candlesticks, candelabra and impressive low-hanging lamps, which emerge from gilded rosettes in the white ceiling. These use the motif of oak leaves and ostrich feathers, the former as an act of homage to Charles II, who hid in an oak tree during his escape from

The Ark in London's oldest surviving synagogue at Bevis Marks (Valerie Chazan)

England. (To light up the whole room or extinguish all the candles, in the days before electricity, took half an hour.) The Ark is a triple cupboard using gilded Spanish leather and influenced by the altars in Sir Christopher Wren's famous series of nearby City churches. The doors are dark brown, with gold garlands above, green wooden columns on each side and a background frame of cream plaster.

As with many synagogues, the setting is discreet, so the very impressive interior comes as a lovely surprise. The surrounding courtyard once housed many communal buildings such as a girls' school where they were taught sewing and basic numeracy in both Spanish and English. There is also a war memorial which gives a good idea of the range of different countries in Europe, the Balkans, the Near East and even further afield which have supplied London with Sephardim. One estimate is that about 20,000 out of Britain's 400,000 Jews are Sephardi.

Like many other Sephardi synagogues, including ones on the other side of the world – on Rhode Island and on Curaçao in the Dutch West Indies – an important stylistic influence on Bevis Marks was the surviving 'Esnoga' synagogue in Amsterdam. The 'Dutchness' of the ceremonies caused problems as late as 1879, when part of the community defected – because the cantor insisted on wearing a silk top hat instead of the traditional tricorn hat which had reached England solely because of its popularity in seventeenth-century Amsterdam! More generally, its location away from centres of present-day Jewish settlement meant that sister Sephardi congregations have arisen in areas like Maida Vale, Wembley and Holland Park.

The second, and far larger, wave of Jewish immigration into the East End came in the 1880s and following decades, until the First World War brought it to an end. It was already well established as the classic immigrant area of London, home in turn to exiled Huguenots (French Protestants), to the Irish and later, after the Jewish period, to Bengalis. Since London was then still a major port, the Jews generally arrived by boat from Hamburg and touched dry land on the Irongate Stairs just below Tower Bridge. It is not easy to imagine the bedraggled refugees today, since the former wharf now forms part of the de luxe marina in St Katherine's Dock, but one can recreate some of the first rungs on the ladder towards assimilation into British life. Many started off in the Jews' Temporary Shelter on Leman Street, founded in 1885.

This street (and the parallel Mansell Street, where the Shelter moved around 1930) is very close to the docks, and the Superintendant would go down to meet new arrivals. Accommodation was spartan but clean and welcoming; when Stefan Zweig wrote a fund-raising pamphlet called *House of a Thousand Destinies* in the mid-1930s, he expressed eloquently its importance: affluent Londoners may never have heard of it, but, 'In Poland, in the Ukraine, in Latvia, in Bulgaria, from one end of Europe to the other, all the poor Jews know of the Shelter in London.' It could fitly be described, he concludes, as an 'unknown and incomparable monument of Jewish and human dignity'.

This is certainly true, although generous motives were always combined with anxiety about the effects of mass Jewish immigration. As early as 1882 the Board of Guardians of the Jewish Poor announced in the East European press that they could not supply poor relief to new arrivals in London, and the JTS pamphlet I have mentioned stressed that many of the residents were short-term transmigrants waiting for the next ship to take them to the *goldeneh medina* in the United States. While they were on British soil, the Shelter would not only feed and house them but make sure they did not compete with British labour or place a burden on British taxpayers or charities. During its days in Mansell Street, some people criticized the Shelter and its single-sex dormitories for becoming too much like a workhouse, yet it is impossible to deny the vital role it played, over many decades, in relieving human misery.

It is a sign of the decline of the old East End that the JTS, although still functioning, has moved to Willesden in North London. Sale of the larger accommodation in the East End means that it is now essentially self-supporting. The atmosphere is that of a plain but pleasant kosher boarding house, with signs reading 'No smoking on *shabbat*'. There are 30 beds but no long-term residents, so the Shelter usually takes in the temporary homeless (abandoned wives and so on), patients and their families in London for operations, elderly people whose families are on holiday and the rare waves of Jewish immigrants who still make for British soil. About 200 Iranian Jews stayed there, for example, at different times over an eighteen-month period following the fall of the Shah. Since it is still well-known for being able to take in people at a moment's notice, conmen who have been doing the rounds of the London jewellers but claim to have lost their money also occasionally turn up.

Some of the other Jewish charitable institutions survive in the East End. The Soup Kitchen for the Jewish Poor, dating from 1902, is still functioning on Brune Street – the name is openly blazoned across the cornice – in a building in a 'charity' style which could easily belong to the Salvation Army or another of the similar organizations long spawned by the East End. The luncheon club in the Morris Kasler Hall on Greatorex Street still brings together for fish and chips many of the surviving Jewish residents of the area. Customers are greeted by an immense manager who adds his own faintly melancholy air, and the whole place exudes a strong sense of what the East End was once like.

Other places which used to help the newly arrived Jews have more or less disappeared. At the head of Middlesex Street, close to the vast Broadgate development on Liverpool Street, is a former

A satirical scene from 1872 – the golden age of street trading! – in Middlesex Street or 'Petticoat Lane' (Anne Cowen/*Graphic*)

warehouse set at an odd angle to the road; an upper window was once used as a grain chute for supplying the poor. Opposite, in Frying Pan Alley, is the original site of the Jews' Free School. At one point this was said to have been the largest school in the world, but it too has moved away to North London, leaving only an undistinguished little plaza with offices, flags and an underground car park.

The incoming Jews brought with them ways of life very unlike those of Britain's established Jewish community. They were poor, largely Yiddish-speaking, often committed to radical (and later Zionist) causes, and worshipped in small-scale, enthusiastic *chevrot* which had none of the decorum characteristic of older synagogues in more affluent districts. Established British Jews, on the other hand, had fought throughout the nineteenth century to acquire the full rights of citizenship, and in the process they had become extremely anglicized.

It is probably not surprising that it was a Rothschild, Baron Lionel, who became the first Jewish Member of Parliament, in 1847, although he then had to wait for over a decade before a law was passed

The opposite extreme of Jewish life in London: the grand mansion built by Baron Rothschild in Piccadilly, 1862 (Anne Cowen/*Illustrated London News*)

allowing an unconverted Jew to swear the Oath of Allegiance on the Old Testament. In most other respects, the Rothschilds and a few of the other leading families acquired the titles and life styles of the British aristocracy; in the Vale of Aylesbury, once nicknamed 'Rothschildshire', a series of their palatial country houses full of art works still stand. Waddeston Manor, for example, is open to the public. There was also a Rothschild building of a rather different kind in the East End. A lonely arch survives in Wentworth Street to commemorate the 'Four Per Cent Industrial Dwellings' (or Charlotte de Rothschild's Dwellings) which were built in the 1880s and stood here until the 1980s. Commercial investors were promised an annual return of four per cent, but the current Baron Rothschild made a gift of cash and land which amounted to £17,000. This, curiously enough, was the birthplace of Abraham Saperstein in 1908, the man who subsequently founded the Harlem Globe Trotters.

The new immigrants also soon embarked on the process of becoming fully British, slowly abandoning their East European heritage. A living Yiddish theatre, for example, flourished for a time and then succumbed to the pressure to assimilate. Short-lived radical groups flared up and then disappeared. Yet hidden away in the East End traces of some of these lost traditions can still be found.

Since the East End was a famously poor quarter in the capital of a great empire, it always attracted a good deal of attention. Pioneering sociologists as well as bold writers and artists brought back descriptions of their glimpses into the abyss. Reformers, missionaries and philanthropists made strenuous efforts to combat poverty, ignorance, heathen ideas and the demon drink. Today, there are still many touching reminders of these self-help and charitable institutions set up in Victorian (or earlier) times.

It is also stimulating to explore areas where vestiges of the different waves of immigrants are all jammed in among each other in a tiny space. The synagogue still in use in Sandys Row was built specifically for immigrants from Holland in the nineteenth century. Nearby Artillery Lane was originally a cramped mediaeval passage. The overflowing prosperity of the City of London has introduced a few wine shops and restaurants, but there are also several local Asian grocers. At the end of the road, on the corner of Crispin Street, is a modern 'night refuge' for the homeless. Opposite is a wide sweeping green shopfront from 1757, often considered one of the finest Georgian shop exteriors in London; the Huguenots may have long since blended in totally with the surrounding British society, yet their distinctive sense of design is one of the constant delights of Spitalfields.

It is not only the juxtapositions which reveal the history of the area; certain individual buildings have changed their function as one wave of immigrants has succeeded another. Most obviously, some of the former kosher butchers tried to capture the new clientele by selling halal meat. A more striking example is on the corner of Brick Lane (scene of a Sunday street market) and Fournier Street. As the latter name suggests, the elegant houses were once used by the French silk weavers, so they had a large brick chapel on the corner. One can still see the sundial, the date (1743) and the inscription below: *Sumus umbra* ('We are but shadows'). It was subsequently taken over by the grotesquely unsuccessful London Society for the Promotion of Christianity Amongst the Jews. In 1892, it became the Great Synagogue, Spitalfields; now, inevitably, it is a mosque.

Down Brick Lane in either direction one can see similar signs of the different layers of history. The changing racial composition of the area means that most of the children at the Christ Church primary school are now Muslims. Yet on each of the drainpipes, in a curiously touching ecumenical gesture, a Star of David is visible. The most obvious Jewish businesses are Elfes monumental masons, suppliers of funerary stoneware, and the Sova Trading Company, one of the few Jewish survivors in the East End segment of the 'rag trade', where a few rabbinic figures huddle over ledgers amid mountainous piles of clothing scraps. The majority of such businesses are now owned by Asians, but roads like Fashion Street were once dominated by Jewish traders.

Nearby Princelet Street (formerly Princes Street) was also a Huguenot stronghold and now has a strong Asian presence. An up-market sari shop forms part of a 30s' building which may once have been a sweatshop. It was on this site that the first purpose-built Yiddish theatre was constructed in 1886. The leading actor, Jacob Adler, was a distant relative of Chief Rabbi Dr Adler. Tragedy, alas, soon struck. A terrible fire in January 1887, possibly started by a rival troupe, put an end to the club when it had hardly started. 'A fire in Princes Street' became a proverbial phrase locally for a disaster. Adler decided to seek his fortune in New York; the Chief Rabbi, glad to see the back of him, put up most of the money for the company's fare.

The establishment, keen to anglicize the newcomers, tended to look askance at the raucous and popular tradition of Yiddish theatre.

Even the *Jewish Chronicle* referred to Yiddish as a 'Judisch-Deutsch dialect, a language we should be the last to encourage any efforts to preserve'. When the United Synagogue took over Adler House, Adler Street, in 1947 for the Beth Din, this was widely regarded as a conscious attempt to end theatrical performances – including Saturday matinées! – on the site.

Yet Princes Street was far from the only venue. Even the buildings have now largely disappeared, but there were at least seven main theatres and music halls over the years, many of them either on or very close to the main thoroughfares of the Whitechapel and Commercial Roads. The repertoire was equally broad. Classics like *The Dybbuk* and *The Golem* obviously featured prominently, along with comedies, love stories and plays on Biblical or historical themes. Works often regarded as antisemitic like *The Merchant of Venice* and Eugene Scribe's *La Juive* were adapted, and *King Lear* was given a happy ending! Cromwell's meetings with Menassah ben Israel, a contemporary blood libel trial in Hungary, even the extraordinary story of Flight-Sergeant Cohen (who took over a Mediterranean island in 1943 and thus acquired the nickname of *The King of Lampedusa*), all found their way on to the stage. The movie star Paul Muni, later to play the role of Emile Zola in a film about the Dreyfus case, emerged from this tradition.

A theatre which burned down over a century ago, however, is not the only powerful reminder of Jewish life to be found on Princelet Street. No. 19 is a characteristically elegant Huguenot weavers' house built around 1720, which had fallen into Jewish hands by the nineteenth century: at one point, it was owned by a pickle and sauce manufacturer called Lewis Abrahams. Later tenants constructed a workshop in the garden. When an association of Polish Jews known as the Loyal United Friends Friendly Society was looking for a suitable site for a synagogue in the late 1860s, it seemed ideal.

This synagogue functioned from 1870 to 1970 and can still be visited. It is the third oldest in London, but it has a significance far beyond that. The later nineteenth century in the East End saw the mushrooming of little *chevrot* – places of worship which were also used for meeting friends and self-help societies – usually established by fellow-immigrants from specific towns in Eastern Europe. Very few survive. Princelet Street is highly unusual in that the synagogue was not just a corner of a private house but purpose-built. Restoration is in progress, but the current state is wonderfully evocative. Lighting was provided by three hanging lamps and from a large but squat lantern fanlight, with almost the whole ceiling consisting of pale purple, blue and green stained glass. The walls are cream, but six thin brown spiralling metal pillars support the women's gallery. A gate at the far end leads up two steps to a curved recess with the Ark. Like the oblong raised and railed pulpit in the centre, this is made of brown wood. Especially touching are the little gilded memorials painted on to the women's gallery. The children of Fanny Rinkoff, for example, gave £7 so that her name could be remembered there. She died as recently as 1953.

Movement away from the East End left the synagogue without a congregation, and the building, complete with archives, furniture, vestments and prayer books, was long left abandoned. This sad fact has now been put to good use by the decision to hold exhibitions, usually on a Jewish theme, within. The long-term plan is to turn it into the Jewish section of a broadly based museum of local immigration, with upstairs rooms displaying Huguenot and Bengali material.

There is yet one more, and far more controversial, Jewish link with Princelet Street. A few doors from the synagogue, in the offices of the Runnymead Trust, I spoke to David Rosenberg, one of eight people on the editorial board of *Jewish Socialist* magazine. Jews, he suggested, ought to be on the left and fighting alongside other minorities, yet many communal leaders were trying to pull them to the right and away from their traditional and natural allies. He and his colleagues had been closely involved in combating antisemitism and the rise of the National Front and in encouraging dialogue between Palestinians and liberal Israelis. Most of them were neither religiously observant nor uncritical Zionists (what he described as 'the two official forms of Jewishness'), but they saw themselves as culturally and ethnically Jewish and located their socialist convictions partly in the terrible history of Jewish persecution.

Jewish socialists, of course, differ from other socialists in their perspectives on certain issues. A good deal of their time, I was told, was spent attacking the kind of 'uncritical pan-Arab nationalism' which is sometimes found on the left. Most Jews would support such efforts, yet in almost every other respect it is safe to say that *Jewish Socialist* represents a very minor current within Anglo-Jewry. (It has even been the object of smear campaigns, according to David Rosenberg.) Nonetheless, the editorial board is largely made up of descendants of immigrants from Russia and Poland who arrived in the 1890s or early this century. The majority brought with them Bundist or other radical ideas. Today, many people have no time for such beliefs, yet it is hard to deny that they represent one of the genuine traditions of the Jewish East End.

Almost all the distinctive features of the East End can be discovered on the Whitechapel Road (later the Mile End Road), the main artery through the area. The obvious place to start is Bloom's – 'the most famous kosher restaurant in Great Britain' – which offers pickles and sandwiches to take away as well as 'continental'-style sit-down meals with waiters to match. Just next door at no. 88, Albert's shirt shop has a remarkable heraldic decoration over the door. This features a Star of David, together with Lions of Judah brandishing swords and supporting shields, each adorned with a *menorah*. We have now reached the cultural heart of Whitechapel. Here the splendid art gallery abuts the library, long used by intellectually ambitious Jews as the first step in their escape from the ghetto. A plaque commemorates the tragic soldier-poet of the First World War, Isaac Rosenberg (1890–1918). Behind the art gallery are other reminders of the East End's fiery political past, Freedom Books (specializing in anarchism) and the Aldgate Press. Not far away is Toynbee Hall, originally founded as an idealistic attempt to bring education from the academic heartlands of Oxbridge to the poor of the East End.

Further up the Whitechapel Road, you can hardly miss the huge modern red-brick mosque, incongruous in its Saudi-financed grandeur. The façade includes the Albaraka International Bank and Bad Influence shirt shop, and the tape-recorded calls to prayer boom out, seemingly unregarded, to the pubs, garages and Salvation Army hostels around. In reality, worshippers often enter through the back gate, and it is there that one gets an extraordinary surprise. Jammed up against the mosque and the entrance to a linked building belonging to the Islamic Funeral Services – one finds the tiny little Fieldgate Street synagogue. Twice bombed during the War, it was twice rebuilt with donations, and makes a marvellous symbol of the tenacious Jewish presence in the area.

Beyond the mosque is 'Monkies Parade' and the London Hospital, where the 'Elephant Man', John Merrick, spent much of his life. Opposite is a stone monument to King Edward VII erected by the local Jews in 1911 'in grateful and loyal memory'. A little further on is a building which housed until 1980 another missionary

Behind the mosque on
Whitechapel Road – a
sign of changing times!
(Valerie Chazan)

society known as the Hebrew Christian Testimony to Israel. Genuine
conversions – they sometimes offered financial inducements – were
almost non-existent, and the mission was replaced by a shop selling
cookers, which has given way to a drama school.

By now, we have reached a small area which seems to be devoted
to essentially Christian charitable institutions. It was here that William
Booth preached the sermon which founded the Salvation Army. Two
statues of him (one currently brandishing a Kentucky Fried Chicken
carton) dominate a little piece of scrubland by the side of the road.
Behind are the glorious Trinity House almshouses, built as residences
for 28 retired ships' captains in 1695. Close by, Frederick Charrington,
heir to one of the main breweries in the area, set up his National
Temperance Hall to campaign against the evils of drink!

As in Glasgow, there were plans to build a People's Palace in
the East End in the 1880s. Charrington came to one of the meetings
– to insist that no alcohol should be sold on site! In the event,
entertainment, exhibitions and education were all provided, and

many a Jewish match developed between young people who met at the dances. It is still to be seen on the Mile End Road, with reliefs on the façade to represent the different arts. The technical school for workers became Queen Mary's College (London University), an offshoot which now uses the former People's Palace as well. Professor William Fishman, who teaches there, is perhaps the world's leading authority on the social history and Jewish politics of the area. Fishman typifies one of the two main escape routes generally used to get out of the East End – education and the world of entertainment. Since most people are not cut out to be either boxers or music hall performers, education perhaps counts as the easier option. Yet it was never very easy. The future professor was virtually a juvenile delinquent at the age of eleven: 'I was badly behaved when younger but keen on learning. It was either prison or university!'

There is one final great Jewish sight on the same road. Plans were made to build a gigantic department store, in suitably imposing style: a great row of classical columns along the first floor and an Egyptian obelisk stuck on the top! It never really worked out and the absurd monument, currently occupied by Blockbuster Video and a DIY shop, is not improved by the grime. But the best thing about it is that one of the shops on the site, Spiegelhalter jewellers (now Carmel Foods), would not be bought out. It breaks into the middle of the grand façade like an irrelevant cream block, defying all the attempts of the architects to give a bit of extra class to the area. For small businesses everywhere who refuse to be bullied by the big boys, it makes a wonderful symbol of defiance.

For all the vital remains of the Jewish East End, one thing is clear: there has been a massive exodus from the area since the Second World War, and even before it. The absorbing London Museum of Jewish Life (formerly the Museum of the Jewish East End) is located in East End Road – but it turns out to be an East End Road in Finchley, North London! One famous episode, however, has resonances far beyond its own time.

The three areas of major Jewish settlement were Whitechapel; Spitalfields and St-George's-in-the-East. We have already explored the first two. If Spitalfields is dominated by Hawksmoor's magnificent Christ Church, St George's stands in the shadow of the church of the same name. This Hawksmoor masterpiece is more or less abandoned, but its castle-like tower looms like a fortress over Cable Street and the surrounding area. Opposite is the beautiful vaulted warehouse of Tobacco Dock, which was recently transformed into a shopping centre and entertainment plaza. Beyond you enter a quite different world, a tranquil complex of antiseptic waterside housing for the affluent.

But Cable Street remains solidly working-class. It can easily be reached from Gardner's Corner – up the Commercial Road, and then right into Christian Street. That was the route taken by protestors on 6 October 1936, when Sir Oswald Mosley and his black-shirted British Union of Fascists – with, it is usually agreed, tacit police support – planned a march through the area shouting provocative slogans. Where Cable Street meets Royal Mint Street, a pitched battle took place and Mosley and his cronies were forced to retreat. A plaque still marks the spot; Arnold Wesker's play, *Chicken Soup with Barley*, gives a stirring account of the day.

A great swirling mural also commemorates the event in a dizzying picture of flying pliers, leaflets, bottles and fists. Mounted police confront the marchers with a banner reading 'Bar the Road to British Fascism!' The real chimneys of the building are incorporated into the mural, and from every window spectators hurl encouragement, abuse or domestic objects they have to hand. The great chant of the day – 'They shall not pass!' – was confirmed by events. Mosley naturally tried to make the best of it: 'The government surrenders to Red violence and Jewish corruption. We never surrender.' He was soon proved utterly mistaken: the Fascist movement in Britain, never a very real threat, rapidly crumbled.

The Battle of Cable Street is sometimes treated as an almost sacred event, although it hardly put an end to official antisemitism or attacks on Jews. Yet combined Jewish and gentile mass actions to confront the Fascist threat were by no means common in the 1930s. I have mentioned in this book some of the great moments in which their fellow-citizens expressed their solidarity with Jewish suffering – the dockers' strike in Amsterdam, the huge procession in Paris to protest about the desecration of the cemetery in Carpentras, the rescue in Copenhagen – but they remain very few and far between. Cable Street is certainly worthy to be put alongside them.

Jewish London is obviously flourishing in all sorts of ways, although its focus – cultural, political and geographical – has moved far from the East End. (The closest surviving sector is the ultra-Orthodox quarter in Manor House and Stamford Hill.) The marvellous series of events, exhibitions and talks to celebrate the Jewish East End, held in the summer of 1987, might be said to mark the end of an era. Few people will regret the end of the sweatshops, grinding poverty and powerlessness, yet perhaps something has also been lost, amid the immense gains.

London remains easily the second Jewish city in Western Europe. If one judges by the standards of an ideal world, it is not hard to find a significant level of antisemitism in England; compared with most of continental Europe over the last 50 years, the picture is spectacularly brighter. And yet a paradox remains: the contribution of British Jews (particularly native-born Jews) to cultural and intellectual life is, by the highest standards, unimpressive. Where are the British equivalents of Freud, Mahler, Einstein, Proust, Schoenberg, Lévi-Strauss, Primo Levi? None of the great names in British science, and not even the chess players, Professor George Steiner once lamented, are Jewish. Harold Pinter, a rare world-class literary figure from the Jewish East End, was victimized in his youth. The whole issue of the relationship between oppression, even persecution, and creativity is ferociously complicated and very delicate; but perhaps the environment in which the bulk of British Jewry grows up is too comfortable to foster certain kinds of achievement? As Harry Lime suggests in *The Third Man*, the Swiss have enjoyed 500 years of peace and prosperity – and only managed to invent the cuckoo clock!

The Third Man is probably the most famous film set in Vienna, the great contrast to London in this respect, a far smaller capital where many of the major currents of modern art and thought were forged around 1900 in an explosion of largely Jewish talent. Despite the city's famed *Gemütlichkeit*, the climate for Jews was distinctly cool. Yet if creativity thrives on opposition, Vienna unquestionably offered 'opportunities' which were not available in London. The price of comparative tolerance may indeed be a dearth of geniuses; but most people will consider the price worth paying.

6

VIENNA

VIENNA IS BUILT to a very simple design, and its backbone is the magnificent stage set – slightly overpowering by day, wonderfully evocative at night – of the Ringstrasse. The broad boulevard replaced the huge city fortifications in the later nineteenth century, largely for reasons of crowd control, and contains an eclectic collection of grand buildings: a barracks (now a police headquarters) like a Florentine palace at one end; the neo-gothic *Rathaus*, or Town Hall; the Greek-temple Parliament dominated by a huge statue of Athena, goddess of Wisdom (with her back to the building!); the monumental gateway leading to the Hofburg imperial palace; the Renaissance-style University; and Baroque Burgtheater.

The former Great Temple on Tempelgasse, a typically overpowering piece of nineteenth-century Viennese architecture (Austrian National Library)

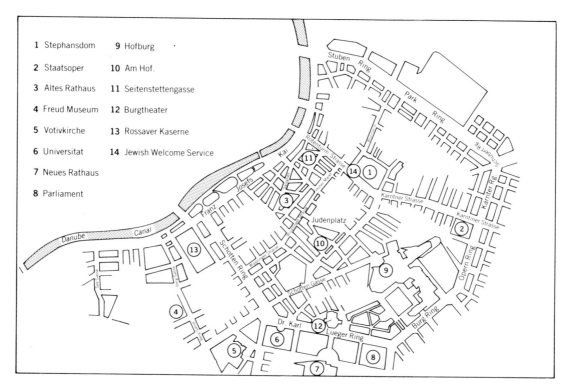

1 Stephansdom   9 Hofburg

2 Staatsoper   10 Am Hof.

3 Altes Rathaus   11 Seitenstettengasse

4 Freud Museum   12 Burgtheater

5 Votivkirche   13 Rossaver Kaserne

6 Universitat   14 Jewish Welcome Service

7 Neues Rathaus

8 Parliament

The first piece of this marvellous ensemble to be completed, rather surprisingly, was the *Staatsoper*, or State Opera House. Yet it is also rather appropriate. The Viennese are obviously enthusiastic connoisseurs of opera; and there is also something distinctly operatic about Vienna. The splendour, the grandeur, the elaborate protocol and rituals of politeness are real enough and have a certain appeal, but one often has a sense of something far less pleasant lurking underneath, like the Phantom said to haunt the Paris Opéra.

A strange symbol of the murky Austrian past can be found just behind the opera house, on the Albertinaplatz, in a memorial to the city's Jews. There is a perfectly decent monument by the canal in Moritzplatz, on the site of the former Hotel Metropol (once Gestapo HQ), and there is an informative museum dealing with the Austrian resistance in the *Altes Rathaus* (or Old Town Hall) on Wipplingerstrasse, but Alfred Hrdlinka's sculptural group (1988) is far more arty and ambitious. It is also obscure and rather offensive. It consists of a huge tablet; an uncompleted pair of marble legs and buttocks emerging from a block on a concrete base; a concrete base supporting nothing; and a concrete base supporting some emaciated and tormented marble figures. In the centre is the only straightforwardly affecting element, a seemingly abstract block of metal which turns out to be portraying an elderly Jew forced to kneel on the ground to clean the street.

Such scenes were, of course, common in 1938, and it is moving to be reminded of them. A commemorative monument half a century later is basically a fine gesture, yet I was left with a strong feeling of unease. This is partly because the group is unfinished and unlikely ever to be finished, though whether through the sculptor's inability, indolence or conscious choice *à la* Michelangelo is unclear. But it is also because of the context. Just behind is the celebrated Albertina collection of graphic art, which is surrounded by a huge wall (the height of the original city walls); on the terrace above is a typically grand equestrian sculpture of a successful general called Archduke Albrecht. Now Vienna is crammed with crushing monumental sculpture, but here, just next to a memorial to Jewish humiliation, the Austrian triumphalism leaves a distinctly bad taste.

While it is impossible to disguise the tragic nature of the recent Jewish history of Vienna, we should bear in mind one great earlier achievement. In 1782, before the French Revolution, Emperor Joseph II issued an 'Edict of Tolerance' which granted Jews far greater freedom of residence and movement as well as new educational and occupational opportunities. Since the aim was essentially to end Jewish isolation and make Jews useful to the state, these liberal measures were accompanied by restrictions on the use of Yiddish and Hebrew and the power of the rabbis; Jews were also required to serve in the army and adopt German names. Poorer Jews considered the package a very mixed blessing, but there is no doubt that it offered important new opportunities for the more affluent and educated.

This spirit of (comparative) tolerance is celebrated in the Judenplatz with a statue of the dramatist Gotthold Ephraim Lessing. Lessing (1729–81) was a crucial figure in the German Enlightenment and wrote several philosemitic plays such as *Nathan the Wise* and *The Jews*. In the latter, a Baron is saved from robbers by an anonymous Traveller who turns out – a startling *coup de théâtre*! – to be a Jew. The stone Lessing is dressed in a great coat, glancing down at a book, and stands with one foot thrust forward, proud, immensely tall and impressive.

Even the Judenplatz contains a less pleasant memory, a plaque on No. 2 (just next to the house where Mozart lived shortly after

Joseph's Edict) commemorating an attack on the local Jews in 1421. For this was one of the old Jewish quarters of the city; Stars of David from a former synagogue are still visible in the first-floor windows at No. 8, which now by coincidence houses the Misrachi prayer room. The small roads linking the Judenplatz to Am Hof, where Harry Lime disappears in *The Third Man*, are also fascinating: Schulhof was once the garden of the Jewish district, an ancient *mikveh* was discovered in Kleeblattgasse. Am Hof (or 'At the Court') was also crucial, since court Jews in charge of the Mint once operated from what is now the site of the Österreichische Länderbank.

Far more than most cities, Vienna has a clear central focus. The Inner City is a fairly small area bounded by the horseshoe-shaped Ring and the Danube Canal. In the middle is the Stephansplatz and the magnificent St Stephen's Cathedral, and from this hub roads fan out towards the opera house, the former imperial palace of the Habsburgs, the university and the Frans-Josef-Kai (quay) on the canal. *Fiakers* stand around the cathedral waiting for tourists, but much of the area is closed to cars.

It is not difficult to find signs of the once-strong Jewish presence. In the window of a bank, greatly to my surprise, I discovered a small exhibition of the verse collections and Shakespeare translations of Erich Fried, who left Austria just before the War, became one of the best-known German poets of his generation and lived out the rest of his life in London with his English wife and English-speaking children. Fried was a haunting as well as controversial figure and a most eccentric man who would scour rubbish dumps for odds and ends and kept an urn containing the ashes of his mother in his study, concealed by an American Indian head-dress.

Fried was only one of many Viennese Jews who produced a major body of work in exile. In Autumn 1987, the city authorities had the ingenious and touching (if rather belated) idea of paying homage to twelve Jewish victims of National Socialism by displaying samples of their verse on posters all over Vienna. Some perished in the camps, some committed suicide, some lived out their lives (or still live) in Germany, New York or London, and only two of them decided to return to Vienna. There are other reminders of the incredible importance of Jews in pre-War Vienna as booksellers, publishers, journalists, editors and creative writers. On the Graben Hotel at 3 Dorotheegasse, a plaque commemorates a stay by Kafka and Max

Brod. Another plaque can be found on the former bookshop of Moritz Perles at 4 Seilergasse. Little remains of all their intense literacy; today's dull Austrian press has few admirers.

Such indications of the lost past inevitably form much of the Jewish interest in Vienna, yet there is also a Jewish Welcome Service catering to anyone who wants to find a suitable synagogue or learn more about the city's Jewish culture and heritage. This has been run for eleven years by the community and the State of Vienna and has an office on Stephansplatz. It shares a back room with Israel Tourist Information, behind a *bureau de change* and an office providing sightseeing tours. One enters through a broken wall, as if in Jerusalem, and neon 'sunlight' comes flooding down from a vaulted ceiling, while stylized metal palm trees around a gravel pond stretch up to the 'sky'; to avoid flooding, the pond has unfortunately had to be kept dry. This, of course, is intended as a striking and very life-affirming evocation of the elements and the spirit of Israel.

In this context, we should remember that Theodor Herzl, the founder of political Zionism, was very much a Viennese figure, a journalist for many years on the *Neue Freie Presse* who was deeply affected by the rise of antisemitism in Austria as well as by the Dreyfus Affair in France. He was buried in the almost unused Jewish cemetery in Ruthnergasse, although his remains were later reinterred in Israel.

To penetrate deeper into the spirit of Vienna, and the immense Jewish contribution to its culture, we must return to the opera house. No work better captures the bitter-sweet charms of old Vienna than *Der Rosenkavalier*, composed by Richard Strauss to a supremely entertaining libretto by Hugo von Hofmannsthal. Their earlier operas *Elektra* and *Salome* had been far more radical, but in 1911, not long before the First World War finished off for good the venerable Austro-Hungarian Empire, one of the greatest partnerships in operatic history set out to create the definitive Viennese opera. Astringent yet sentimental, nostalgic yet intensely modern, it brings together material from all the golden days: the eighteenth-century décor of the age of the Empress Maria Theresa, the waltzes of the nineteenth-century Strausses, and the sharp psychology and sexual sophistication of the Freudian era.

On one level the opera is a celebration of a city, yet its great theme is how men and women, in rather different ways, have to come to terms with the passing of time. The over-extended, grotesquely vain and lecherous Baron Ochs must learn to give up his hopes of marrying a fifteen-year-old bourgeois girl who is due to inherit a fortune. The Marschallin (in her early thirties) must renounce her delicious affair with a seventeen-year-old – and all to ensure the far more fitting triumph of young love. Yet when she is overcome by melancholy thoughts, she tells us in a famous monologue, she sometimes feels compelled to get up at night to stop the clocks. . . .

Intentionally or not, this makes a wonderful symbol of Vienna, very much a city in which the clocks have stopped. To some extent, this has always been the city's reputation: it was at the Congress there in 1815 that diplomats came to dance and to restore the *status quo ante* after Napoleon's defeat. Yet today's stagnation is far more significant. At the Café Central on Herrengasse, a model of the poet Peter Altenberg sits for all time near the door, his hand poised on a cup of coffee and a spoon still resting on his glass of water. The vaulted interior of the Central has been beautifully restored and coffee houses remain a wonderful institution, but no one goes to them any more to plot revolutions, found artistic movements – or even for the best conversation in Europe. (There are, however, plans to recreate the Central's great rival, the Café Greinsteidl, so we can perhaps expect a revival of the 'battles' when separate literary cliques held court in the different coffee houses. . . .)

Post-war Vienna is a shadow of its former self, and one of the main reasons is the tragically depleted Jewish presence. The historian Steven Beller describes the prophetic satire of a writer called Hugo Bettauer, who imagined in 1922 what Vienna would be like without its Jews: no operetta, no worthwhile theatre, no patrons of the arts; no centrally placed coffee houses for intellectuals; no native Austrians capable of running banks; no spas, no prostitutes; and no high fashion in a city largely consisting of peasants. . . . Such a picture, of course, contained a good deal of humorous exaggeration, yet many people *do* feel that cultural life in today's Vienna is dull and unadventurous, and that the whole atmosphere is far more staid and provincial than in the past. Even the Ringstrasse has a curiously hollow impressiveness, particularly now that the grandest residences have been taken over by airline companies and the local branch of Weight Watchers.

When Gustav Mahler (1860–1911) was appointed *Hofoperndirecktor* or Director of the Staatsoper in 1901, he reached one of the supreme

The *Kaffeehausliterat* included most of the great names in Viennese literature, many of them Jewish. The Cafe Central, illustrated here, and its great rival, the Griensteidl, were their favoured haunts (Austrian Tourist Board)

pinnacles of Viennese life (holders of the post today expect to receive more, and more unsparing, press coverage than even the President of the Republic!). Yet it was also Mahler, a Catholic convert, who could write in a moment of despair: 'I am rootless three times over: as a Bohemian among Austrians, as an Austrian among Germans, and as a Jew everywhere in the world. Everywhere I am regarded as an interloper, nowhere am I what people call "desirable".'

Mahler, of course, was part of the extraordinary upsurge of creativity and experimentation produced by what is sometimes known as the 'Vienna 1900' generation. Many of the names are well known: Freud, the 'Second Vienna School' of Schoenberg, Webern and Berg, the 'Austrian School' of economists, architects like Otto Wagner and Adolf Loos, Wittgenstein, Otto Weininger (the classic case of Jewish self-hatred), Karl Kraus, Hermann Broch, Stefan Zweig, Schnitzler, Robert Musil, and many, many more. These people, and their equivalents in painting and design, established many of the intellectual and artistic themes which have dominated twentieth-century culture ever since.

They were also predominantly, although not exclusively, Jewish; the culture of the time thus represents a unique – and uniquely fruitful – synthesis. Now, Richard Strauss, as it happens (unlike the earlier dynasty of waltzing Strausses), was not really a Viennese figure nor from an even partially Jewish background; indeed, his behaviour during the Nazi period was at least opportunistic and perhaps worse. But Hugo von Hofmannsthal *was* more or less Jewish, from a typical assimilated – or rather *assimilating* – background.

To describe Hofmannsthal and some of his most famous contemporaries as 'more or less Jewish' sounds fairly vague, although it is true both in terms of family background and in that their natural habitat was the theatre, the opera house, the coffee house or the consulting room rather than the synagogue. Many, of course, were intensely ambitious to gain glory in the highest reaches of academic and artistic life. Yet there was always one undeniable fact which Jews in Vienna, however assimilated and successful, could not escape: from 1895, and alone in Europe, the city was run by an openly antisemitic mayor, Karl Lueger, whose brand of populist rhetoric would later prove a great inspiration to Adolf Hitler.

It is undeniable that Lueger had a major impact on the infrastructure of Vienna, in terms of trams, street lighting, schools, parks and abattoirs, so it is perhaps appropriate (as well as slightly disturbing) that part of the Ring is named Dr Karl Lueger-Ring in his honour. It has also been suggested that Lueger himself was not a doctrinaire antisemite: before coming to power, he used to spend time in the Café Greinsteidl, along with the Jewish literary figures of the Young Vienna group; when a fervent follower accused him of attacking Jews in public while socializing with them in private, Lueger replied: '*Wer ein Jud' ist, bestimme ich*' (It's I who decide who's a Jew'). This may be one of the classic statements of political opportunism, but it was hardly calculated to reassure the Jews of Vienna. At the very least, Lueger was happy to *use* antisemitism to further his political ends. He was, alas, far from being the last Austrian politician of whom that could be said . . .

One might also put the matter more generally. As Steven Beller points out, certain concepts and forms of behaviour were accepted as quintessentially Viennese under the Empire, and to some extent remain so today. The imperial bureaucracies tended to operate with the sluggish inefficiency which is known as *Schlamperei* or 'slovenliness'; *Protektion* (i.e. having friends in the right places) was essential if one wanted anything done. Flattery, an obsession with titles and appearances and a delight in *Wiener Schmäh* (a talent for telling plausible lies) were all very common. And, of course, there was a general atmosphere of *Gemütlichkeit* (the rather oppressive 'cosiness' one can still find in many Viennese restaurants). All such aspects of the Austrian way of life, it seems clear, helped create 'insiders' and excluded everyone else.

What still remains on the streets of Vienna 1900? The city is full of memorials to Beethoven and Schubert, a hotel and even a liqueur are named after Mozart, and there is no denying the imperial splendour of Habsburg Vienna. Yet since the Jewish contribution to architecture and the visual arts was comparatively minor, there is no need to go there to sample the specifically Jewish achievements of the time. Today it is far from being the world centre of psychoanalysis or free-market economics, and other major cities offer just as many opportunities to sample the music of Schoenberg or Mahler.

The place most evocative of the city's Jewish past, sad to say, is the Central Cemetery (familiar to many people from the final scene of *The Third Man*). In many ways, this is a strikingly *unevocative* place, with none of the flamboyant funerary sculpture common in Latin countries; restraint and decorum are the key notes. The illustrious dead are buried separately, in a section adjoining the main path which leads to the Lueger Memorial Church. Nowhere else in the world can there be graves or memorials to so many famous composers (most of them shamelessly neglected by the Viennese during their lifetimes). Here is one of the places that Jews, in death, have achieved equality with their gentile equivalents. Schoenberg's grave – an ugly white cube set on edge on a simple base – may not be in the inner sanctum along with Beethoven and Brahms, but it is nearby. There are few wreaths placed on it, yet it is still heartening to see Schoenberg's compelling greatness frankly acknowledged by his native city.

Another route to social acceptance, of course, was conversion to Catholicism, and the superior status this granted applied even after death: the writer Karl Kraus, for example, is buried in the well-maintained main section of the cemetery. Visitors looking at the names on the tombs also get a strong sense of how multiracial Vienna was as the centre of the Empire, and particularly the number of ambitious immigrants from the industrial heartlands of Bohemia and Moravia. Several of the best-known Jewish figures like Freud and Mahler were also born in what is now Czech territory.

The old Jewish section close to Gate I makes a poignant contrast, a monument to disappointed hopes. It was consecrated in 1879 and received about 100,000 people in the years up until 1928; writers like Arthur Schnitzler and Frederic Torberg were buried here in later years. There is also a very Austrian obsession with rank and titles, so one can see the graves of every sort of minor imperial bureaucrat as well as a 'newspaper-clipping-compiler', chief rabbis, the cantor Salomon Sulzer, for whom Schubert wrote a Psalm setting, Freud's religious instructor Samuel Hammerschlag, and families with close variants of my own surname.

The dominant impression is the intense aspiration to assimilate, with many of the graves of the affluent in typical neo-gothic or neo-classical styles which owe nothing to the Jewish tradition. Since this aspiration was tragically unfulfilled and the diminished present-day community has more pressing demands on its resources, the cemetery remains neglected and overgrown, tombs blown over or disappearing in the undergrowth, a strange deserted spot where

A view over the small Jewish cemetery in Seegasse (Austrian Tourist Board)

feelings of gentle melancholy are soon transformed into anger and sorrow.

There is far less to say about the new Jewish section of the cemetery near Gate IV, which was added in 1917. This was the only 'park' Jews were allowed to use during the Nazi era and it was virtually a battlefield near the end of the War, yet even the domed ceremonial hall which was burnt during *Kristallnacht* has been rebuilt. A series of moving stained-glass windows depict a stylized death camp and Theresienstadt ghetto, although the chimney flames seem to be transformed first into tears and then into a burning *menorah* in a final image of the rebirth of Jewish life.

There is another and infinitely more beautiful Jewish cemetery close to the centre of Vienna. Visitors walk straight from the street through the hall of the modern (no longer Jewish) old people's home at Seegasse 9 and into the courtyard behind. One catches brief glimpses of sickness, senility and disability and suddenly emerges into the perfectly maintained cemetery, which was used from about 1540 until 1783, devastated by the Nazis and restored in the 1980s. The graves display a discreet eighteenth-century elegance, made of marble and sandstone which glow a wonderful red in the evening light, and the well tended grass and ancient trees add to the charm of the scene. Research in the archives discovered a document dating from 1670 – when Emperor Leopold used a fire at his palace as an excuse to expel the Viennese Jews – between the city and a rich Jewish family. In return for a huge fee, the municipality agreed to maintain the cemetery and graves forever. It remains a startling sight.

Nearby is the fascinating Sigmund Freud House. Freud believed that his Jewishness, his exclusion from the 'compact majority' of Austrians, had encouraged his independence of judgement, his oppositional stance and his intellectual courage. It is perhaps appropriate that Berggasse 19, where he lived from 1891 until 1938, is several blocks beyond the Ring, on the outside looking in. Bruno Bettelheim, who grew up in Vienna, saw a further significance in Freud's choice of a house on 'Mountain Street', half way up the hill from a largely Jewish flea market to the far more bourgeois area around the University of Vienna. Certainly, Freud achieved middle-class comfort but never complete intellectual or social acceptance.

A deep foyer is decorated with frosted glass windows at the back depicting a huntress and a goddess, presumably Spring, holding fruit and a basket of goodies. A wide staircase with an elaborate wrought-iron railing, illuminated with a kind of street lamp, leads up to the Museum. The original well can still be glimpsed in the garden, although the stables are now used as garages.

Visitors pass an ornate bronze ashtray in the floral Art Nouveau style, hang up their coats in the hall and proceed, like patients, into the waiting room. When Freud left Vienna, he took most of his furniture to London (where it can be seen in another Freud Museum), but his daughter Anna arranged for the plush orange and deep-red chairs and sofa in the waiting room to be shipped back. Her legacy of 600 books is displayed in an Anna Freud Memorial Room. Freud's consulting room and study are decorated with photographs of them in 1938 by August Aichhorn and Edmund Engelman. Their most striking feature is the incredible clutter of books, blankets and statuettes, some of which are also on display. The bulk of the collection, however, consists of first editions and marvellous photographs: family snapshots, Freud about to take his first plane journey, the exterior of the house marked with a swastika, and the flamboyant Princess Marie Bonaparte of Greece with her dog. The Princess was one of the people who encouraged Freud to leave Vienna from as early as 1936; she also provided some of the money to enable him to do so.

Freud once asked himself why it had taken 'a completely godless Jew' to discover psychoanalysis, and both antisemites and his daughter Anna believed that it was in some sense a 'Jewish science'. The issue remains controversial. What is beyond dispute is that Freud was a militant atheist, that he insisted his fiancée give up the Jewish festivals and rituals she had grown up with, and that he devoted one of his books to attacking the 'illusion' of belief in God (*The Future of an Illusion*). Another, which Jewish friends begged him not to publish, is devoted to the controversial thesis (which has gained few adherents) that Moses was an Egyptian (*Moses and Monotheism*).

It is equally clear, however, that the vast majority, perhaps even 90 per cent, of Freud's early followers came from Jewish backgrounds. Ernest Jones, Freud's close associate and biographer, describes how he helped found a sort of inner sanctum of the psychoanalytic movement in 1912 (a group which recalled 'stories of Charlemagne's paladins from boyhood, and many secret societies from literature'). Of the seven members including Freud, Jones was the only gentile, although he claims in rather startling terms that this caused no problems:

'Coming myself of an oppressed race,' (i.e. the Welsh!) he tells us, 'it was easy for me to identify myself with the Jewish outlook.'

When the Nazis took over Austria in 1938, Jewish analysts naturally tried to escape, but the gentiles were presented with a difficult dilemma. Should they remain in Vienna and try to keep the flame of psychoanalysis burning, even if this meant inevitable compromises of their integrity, or should they get out while they had the chance? Jones tried to encourage a certain Richard Sterba to stay at his post and refused to give him financial assistance. When Sterba left Vienna nonetheless, Jones commented 'Oy, our *Shabbas goy* is gone.'

In the event, only one analyst was killed by the Nazis, two spent the War in Vienna and none came back afterwards. It took almost 30 years for psychoanalysis to be fully re-established in the city of its birth, but there are now about 100 analysts training or practising, as many as in 1938. Freud now appears on the new 50-Schilling notes, visitors and school parties flock each year to the Museum, and there is a full programme of lectures, conferences and symposia. In Freud Year, 1989, there was a larger conference on Philosophy and Psychoanalysis and seven leading contemporary artists produced works which are now on display in the Museum of Modern Art at the Liechtenstein Palace. At last, it seems, the most famous Viennese of them all is receiving the attention he deserves of his native city.

Regardless of any other merits, Freud's case histories and books like *The Psychopathology of Everyday Life* speak volumes about the manners, suppressed feelings, professional rivalries, family lives and sexual hang-ups of his Viennese contemporaries. His fascinating study of *Jokes and their Relation to the Unconscious* is a wonderful anthology of Jewish jokes, even if the explanations sometimes seem humourless or far-fetched. A whole civilization, in other words, lives on in Freud's works. The briefest glance at the statistics is enough to confirm that this great civilization has been utterly destroyed.

If there were nearly 150,000 Jews in Vienna in 1900, 175,000 in 1910 and a peak of just over 200,000 (almost eleven per cent of the population) in 1923, there must be less than 15,000 today. Even this represents a significant recovery, since absolutely tiny numbers survived the War in Austria underground (perhaps 150), in forced labour gangs or 'privileged mixed marriages'. As many as 93 Jewish places of worship were destroyed during *Kristallnacht* (9–10 November 1938). And there is little doubt that popular antisemitism

The crammed and diverse Jewish quarter of Vienna around 1875 (Mary Evans Picture Library)

was stronger in Austria than in Germany in the late 1930s: in his well-known memoir, *Last Waltz in Vienna*, George Clare describes how much safer his family felt after they had managed to leave Vienna and find lodgings in Berlin. The only positive aspect of such blatant persecution was that many Jews realized there was no future for them and got out of Central Europe before the outbreak of war. Nonetheless, about 65,000 Viennese Jews were killed in the camps.

The immediate post-war years were almost as bleak. Dr Zelman of the Jewish Welcome Service described to me his own, typical, story. Born in Poland, he had been sent to Auschwitz, liberated from Mauthausen and had then come to Vienna. This, needless to say, was not out of any particular affection for the Austrian people. Like many camp survivors, he was very sick, and Vienna was the obvious haven in Central Europe, offering hospitals, educational opportunities and a good base from which to emigrate. Better still, the 'American Joint' (Distribution Committee) was there in force to ensure they got a favourable reception.

The Waldheim affair had also left an unpleasant taste. A certain number of Jews had left Austria, many more had wanted to. Dr Zelman was not convinced that Waldheim was a true antisemite, accepted that many other politicians tell lies, and was even willing to overlook his unsavoury past. What he could not forgive was that Waldheim was a liar *about the Holocaust*, and that he was a politician in the Lueger mould, happy to make opportunistic *use* of antisemitism to further his own political ends. The only mildly reassuring aspect was that Vienna was the one part of Austria where Waldheim had not won a majority.

All this sounded more and more depressing. But quite by chance the President of the Jewish Students Union arrived while I was speaking to Dr Zelman. Here, at last, was a grain of hope. If Viennese Jewish life after the War consisted largely of sick, traumatized and often old Jews straight from the camps, the great shot in the arm for the community had been the Soviet Jews who had arrived over the last ten years. Some had tried life in Israel and returned to Vienna. Here, Dr Zelman assured me, were the young and energetic people, often from illiterate families, who could ensure a bright future.

Herr R. (who asked not to be named) painted a similar picture. He is a Viennese Jew, forced to flee in the 1930s, who worked in the theatre in Germany, Switzerland, England and the United States and decided, rather surprisingly, to retire in Vienna. Vienna after the War, he told me, was exactly as depicted in *The Third Man*, full of racketeers, competing Allied authorities and international adventurers scurrying around in the deprived and bombed-out city. In his view, the Waldheim affair was very welcome. It had certainly brought antisemitism to the surface ('although not so strong as to worry about'), but it had cut through decades of suppression and forced Austrians to confront their less than glorious past. Now one could not go to a dinner party without the Jewish question coming up, sometimes at tedious length ('Philosemitism is getting as bad as antisemitism'), but the neo-Nazis were a negligible factor. Jörg Haider and his FPÖ party, which skilfully woos the nationalist vote by innuendo rather than an explicit programme, was far more dangerous, but this was nothing new: roughly the same proportion of the population had supported nationalist politicians since the 1850s. In any event, Viennese food, culture and life-style offered a unique set of attractions, and it was there that Herr R. wanted to end his days.

The fullest picture was provided by Dr Hodig of the Israelitische Kultusmeinde Wien (or Vienna Jewish Community). Without question, antisemitism in Austria was still strong, the press was often hostile and stories about blood libels were still popular in rural areas like the Tyrol. Yet the community had 'good to excellent' relations with many church leaders, who were active in fighting such pernicious superstitions, and Catholic students had expressed solidarity with the Jews at the time of the Waldheim affair. Nonetheless, these few hopeful signs were hardly enough to encourage complacency.

The specifically Jewish scene was far more optimistic. Up until about the 1970s, many Jews had 'lived on their luggage'. The new generation had made a conscious decision that Vienna was their home and they were going to stay. There are now eleven synagogues in Vienna. A new kosher restaurant, cultural centre and two schools (one of them a Lubavitch school for Soviet immigrants) were all recent achievements; a new Sephardi centre was also planned. All had built on good relations with the Mayor and city authorities, despite the minimal Jewish presence in local and national politics.

Numbers were not easy to come by. There were 6,200 registered Jews and perhaps 5,000 others; immigrants from the European sector of the Soviet Union were usually secular and reluctant to get in touch with the authorities, but one could make estimates from the applications to welfare organizations. A new community of religious Sephardi Jews from Soviet Asia had replaced the pre-War Turkish group. A rabbi had been brought in from Israel to allow such people to maintain their own traditions while integrating in other ways. Achieving this successfully, Dr Hodig suggested, 'represents the future of our community'.

Such Soviet Jews have tended to move into the traditional working-class area of the 2nd district or Leopoldstadt. (This is located, with the Prater amusement park, between the Danube canal and the Danube itself. Prayer houses cluster along the north bank of the canal.) They work in markets and small shops, often selling to tourists from Eastern Europe, or as craftsmen and shoemakers. Already they are a key factor in Viennese Jewish life, yet some politicians hope to welcome thousands more over the next few years. The strain on Jewish welfare resources will be immense, but so will the new possibilities.

Dr Hodig's office is located in by far the most important street in today's Jewish Vienna, Seitenstettengasse, which descends towards the canal in an elegant white curve from Judengasse. A large grey building on the corner is the Arche Noah kosher restaurant, and below are three gates which lead to all the major institutions: the Stadttempel (or main synagogue), communal administration, newspaper and museum.

The Stadttempel was built in 1824–26 and is so closely packed in by houses that it was vandalized but not destroyed during *Kristallnacht*. Indeed, prayers were held there until 1944. Now restored to its former state and reached through vaulted halls hung with a series of plush purple and deep-blue Ark curtains, it is a most beguiling building, with an intriguing resemblance to the Staatsoper of the 1860s. In both cases, the form is an almost complete oval and layers of white balconies, picked out with stylized gold botanical motifs, rise up towards a ceiling with a central source of bright light (from a white and gold fanlight in the synagogue) and painted sun rays all around. In the synagogue, however, the ceiling is painted pale blue and covered in stars and the two balconies are supported on white scrolled columns with charming tree-like lamps above. The upper balcony is almost hidden by a sort of *trompe l'oeil* effect and two columns frame the grand Ark, with richly decorated curtains, semicircular fanlight and moulding with rosettes above. Again, the palm branches and scrolls add a touch of gold against the dominant white colour scheme.

Almost equally impressive is the Jewish Museum which has been created from the major Max Berger collection. Along with photographs of the synagogues destroyed by the Nazis and scenes of present-day Viennese Jewish life are many ravishing ritual objects which can be enjoyed for their sheer beauty as well as the insight they afford into Jewish customs. The display may have neither the intellectual impact of the Jewish museum in Amsterdam nor the rather chaotic poignancy of the museum in Prague, yet it remains a superb collection for one man to have assembled.

★

The splendid Stadttempel, the only surviving nineteenth-century Viennese synagogue (Austrian Tourist Board)

There is much to absorb and stimulate in Jewish Vienna today; but is there anyone who keeps alive the spirit of earlier times? One of the things the major figures of 'Vienna 1900' had in common was an intense desire to search out the truth beneath appearances and a refusal to accept comfortable clichés. This is obviously true of Freud, yet Schnitzler also savaged bourgeois hypocrisy, Karl Kraus launched a ferocious one-man campaign against loose thinking and poor writing, and Mahler and Schoenberg pursued their personal vision to the point where they had to subvert the traditions of Western music.

Ever since the War, many ex-Nazis have gone unpunished and the realities of the Third Reich have been played down. The great Austrian myth, which the Allies colluded in, is that the country was merely the first victim of National Socialism; the many collaborators, Nazi sympathizers and denouncers of their Jewish neighbours are often forgotten. If there is one man who has stood up for the truth against such comfortable illusions, it is the world's greatest Nazi hunter, Simon Wiesenthal. His small Documentation Centre is hardly a tourist attraction and does not welcome visitors, yet its existence is crucial. Many memorials demand that we 'Never Forget', but few people really live by the principle. And yet, despite the harrowing nature of the material he deals with, Herr Wiesenthal describes himself as the happiest of men. For whenever two ex-Nazis get together and have an argument, he claims, there is always one of them who ends up saying: 'Now you just be careful – or I'll report you to Wiesenthal'!

Wiesenthal's career leaves one with two very strong feelings – how inspiring that such a man exists, how tragic that he should have to! Jewish Vienna, despite all the reminders of the glorious past and the genuine achievements of the post-war years, leaves one with a sense of despair. In the 1930s and 1940s ordinary Austrians tended to be notably more antisemitic than ordinary Germans and, unlike the Poles, they did nothing to defeat the Nazis by struggling to liberate their land. Exclusiveness and xenophobia are still strong today. The only minor consolation is that Jewish ideas and influences, despite the Nazis' best efforts, were passed on. Adolf Hitler, fortunately for us all, funded research into rocketry rather than the atomic bomb because of his contempt for 'degenerate Jewish science'. His attempts to destroy 'decadent' art, music and psychology – associated with the key figures from Vienna (and the Weimar Republic) – were equally unsuccessful. Much of their work remains a crucial chapter in the common heritage of mankind.

7

COPENHAGEN

F OR THE GERMANS, Denmark was something of a model protec-
torate. The country was invaded by surprise in April 1940
and taken over with hardly a shot fired. The occupation was
largely peaceful. Farmers (in a predominantly agricultural economy)
rejoiced at acquiring a captive market. From a commercial point of
view, conditions could hardly have been better: 'Suddenly they found
they had a customer who didn't ask the price,' a leading figure in
today's Jewish community explained to me, 'they just wanted you

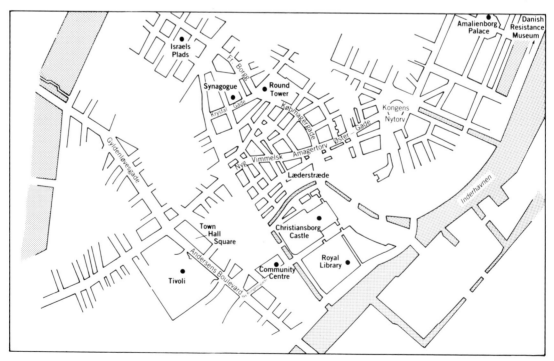

to deliver. So you went to the Danish National Bank and got your money, and you got rich. As long as the Germans succeeded on the various fronts, there weren't really any problems.'

The Danish King and Parliament continued to carry out their functions, despite the obvious compromises involved. Respect for law and order hampered the growth of a resistance movement. Collaboration of the more unpleasant sort was uncommon – the Danish Nazis were considered both a joke and an irrelevance, even by the Germans – but patient compliance, at least in the early days, was widespread. To round up a few thousand Jews should have been the easiest thing in the world. Yet there is no simple relationship between resistance and attitudes to the Jews. The Polish partisans, with a most glorious record in fighting the Germans, were often as antisemitic as their persecutors. The Italians were nominally allies of the Nazis, but many private individuals showed great courage in protecting Jews within Italy; humane officials were equally adept at bending the rules in Croatia and on the French Riviera. The Danes, as is well known, managed to save over 98 per cent of their Jewish fellow-citizens.

What makes the Danish case so unusual and inspiring is not only that most of the Jews were saved, but that the country acted in accordance with the pre-war (and post-war) democratic traditions it tried to maintain in appalling circumstances. The Danes behaved well not so much out of sheer human solidarity, but out of commitment to a set of noble ideals. Jewish life in Copenhagen is now on a fairly small scale, yet one is constantly aware that this was the setting for one of the most remarkable dramas of the twentieth century. Far more than elsewhere in Jewish Europe, it is one extraordinary episode which makes the city a haunting place to visit.

The basic events are set out in the fascinating Museum of the Danish Resistance on the edge of Churchill Park (in the north-east of the city, not far from the famous statue of the Little Mermaid). It is both smaller and simpler than the parallel museum in Amsterdam, but the story it tells is far less ambivalent. From the outside, the building looks like a featureless wooden shed or perhaps an improvised little church on an army base, since there is a home-made armoured car parked in the forecourt and a stained-glass window celebrating 'The Light of Freedom' (1983).

The exhibition is displayed in a single corridor around a court-yard which contains barbed wire from one of the camps on Danish soil and a replica of the monument to the resistance in Elsinore. An organizational chart shows the structure of Gestapo power in Denmark, with propaganda photographs of German soldiers feeding the pigeons or relaxing with their Danish girlfriends. Others show the rantings and ravings of the Danish Nazis or a restaurant converted into 'The German Corner' cultural centre.

Most of the museum, however, concentrates on resistance activities, with a selection of arm bands, weaponry parachuted in by the British, a reconstruction of an illegal workshop, and pictures of bombed-out buildings. The successful attack on Gestapo HQ was a triumph, since it destroyed many papers which incriminated resisters, although there was also a tragic occasion when a school was attacked in error and a series of planes all aimed their bombs at the same burning target. Despite the loss of life, German attempts to use the event to turn the Danes against the Allies soon foundered. As always in such exhibitions, there are also marvellous images of liberation, some featuring the armoured car now displayed outside.

Only a short section of the museum considers the Rescue of the Jews, although this contains many moving photographs of the little ships conveying their human cargo across to Sweden. There are also photographs and dinner tickets from Terezín, to which a few Danish Jews were deported; astonishingly enough, they were later allowed to return home, after intense lobbying by the Danes and the famously controversial Red Cross visit (see the chapter on Prague). In an almost incredible episode, the Swedish Red Cross sent 35 buses for the Danish Jews – although it was far from easy, in April 1944, to find a zigzag route through the bombed-out cities and the Allied armies which were rapidly closing in.

On the way back from the Resistance Museum to the town centre, one passes through the cobbled main courtyard of the Amalienborg Palace. Although there are guards in picturesque uniforms outside, it would hard to imagine a more charming and approachable royal residence. The style of the Danish royal family is similarly informal, and King Christian X's behaviour during the German occupation was of crucial significance. Although almost 70 when the Germans took over, the King soon decided to continue his daily rides through the city; despite the lack of security, he frequently stopped to talk with his subjects. (A mounted statue commemorates these scenes in Bredgade, close to the royal palace.) Now, on one level, this might be regarded

The moment of freedom! A fishing boat carrying its secret cargo of Jews arrives at the Swedish port of Gothenberg (Museum of the Danish Resistance)

as a form of compliance; by continuing business-as-usual, the King was giving a sort of legitimacy to the occupying power. Yet it also counted potentially as a form of defiance: by retaining his prestige and influence, the King could also retain an impact on events. In the event, he used every opportunity to express the humane national consensus about the Jews.

It seems to be a legend (although a plausible one) that Christian offered to wear the yellow star himself in the event of Jewish persecution in Denmark. He did, however, attend a centenary service in Copenhagen's main synagogue in April 1933, a significant gesture of solidarity at a time when the new Nazi regime in next-door Germany was just starting its boycott of Jewish businesses. He sent a New Year's letter to the same synagogue in 1942, expressing sympathy in the aftermath of an arson attack. He intervened when persecution was imminent. He once stated that the Danes had no 'Jewish problem' because they had never (unlike the Germans, presumably!) had feelings of inferiority *vis-à-vis* the Jews.

And he refused to ingratiate himself with the Nazis: when Hitler sent birthday greetings in September 1942, the King's reply by telegram was brisk almost to the point of rudeness: 'MY UTMOST THANKS, CHRISTIAN REX.' The Führer was livid and used the opportunity to replace a 'moderate' German administrative chief in Denmark with someone he considered more reliable. Among other things, he clearly hoped for increased efforts to set the Holocaust in motion on Danish soil. After almost two and a half years of occupation, little had yet been done.

The basic attitudes of the Danes were familiar to the Germans, of course, and reflected in their cautious policies. They even found their way into the horrifying telegram which introduced the Final Solution. On 8 September 1943, Dr Werner Best, the new SS-*Obergruppenführer* in Denmark, sent a wire to Berlin which included the words: 'IT IS MY OPINION THAT MEASURES SHOULD NOW BE TAKEN TOWARD A SOLUTION OF THE PROBLEMS OF THE JEWS AND THE FREEMASONS.' It was not going to be easy. The current state of emergency, Best stressed, provided a perfect opportunity; at a later date, persecution would be likely to unleash a storm of protest. The King and the Rigsdag (or Parliament) would refuse all co-operation with the German authorities; a general strike might well occur. The fairly cosy relationship between Danes and Germans, which assured a steady supply of agricultural produce, could easily break down. Now was the time to act, although the operation would require an additional contingent of police to carry through successfully.

The last point, a request for more men, was highly significant. There is reason to believe that Best was comparatively immune to Nazi dogma; like most German officials who had actually spent time in Denmark, he had soon become very aware of the disadvantages of starting persecution there. But, as so often in the history of the Holocaust, bureaucratic rivalry was a major factor: fights between different ministries in Berlin were reflected in a long-standing conflict between the military and civilian occupation forces in Denmark.

After the war, Best naturally produced a flurry of excuses. His telegram, he claimed, was merely written confirmation of orders which had come from Hitler. Indeed, by forcefully pointing out the difficulties of the plan, he was subtly trying to prevent it happening! His real motives were probably far more banal: he hoped to tilt the balance away from the soldiers back in favour of his own, civilian administration – and the Jews were to be sacrificed to that end.

If Best was keen to consolidate his own power base, he was also keen to maintain good relations with the Danes. A successfully accomplished deportation would be utterly unacceptable to public opinion, yet his masters in Berlin demanded action. There is evidence that the administration deliberately let slip hints of what was going to happen, most notably to G.F. Duckwitz, shipping attaché to the German legation, who immediately warned the Danish Social Democrats, who in turn warned the Jews. The chairman of the very comfortable and assimilated community, C.B. Henriques, at first refused to believe them. Yet as soon as he was convinced, the news was rapidly circulated, particularly when many of the Jews were assembled in the synagogue the next day for Rosh Hashanah. Assistance to the Jews was widespread and spontaneous – and the vast majority of them suddenly disappeared, into hiding and then spirited away across the narrow sound to neutral Sweden. By opening up such links to the neighbouring country, a supply source was made available to the Danish resistance, which rapidly began to build up strength.

The Germans had made a fatal mistake, and condemnation of their actions was not slow in coming. Bishops read out a prepared statement in their churches, claiming that persecution was in conflict with Christian concepts of brotherly love, the Danish ideal of justice and the firmly established link between Jewish prophecies and their alleged Christian fulfilment. Dr Best, therefore, made a grotesque attempt to regain popular support.

The state of emergency, which had been imposed on 29 August, had resulted in the internment of many Danish soldiers. Intense resentment about this was magnified by rumours that they might be sent to fight on the Russian Front. Just after the attempted deportation, an announcement was made that the authorities had managed to put an end to all Jewish attempts to 'poison the atmosphere'; at the same time, the interned soldiers were to be released. The whole nation, including the Army and Navy, was outraged. Not only were they utterly unconvinced by stories of Jewish malevolence and disgusted by the round-ups themselves; they were deeply resentful of attempts to use the issue of the interned soldiers as a distraction. However much they wanted to be released, release on such terms was quite unacceptable. Such a principled response, of course, was extraordinarily rare in occupied Europe.

★

Edvard Lehmann's 'Musicale at the Henriques Residence' (1868), a typical scene of cultured Jewish bourgeois life in nineteenth-century Copenhagen. A descendant of the family members depicted played a key role in the events of 1943 (Royal Library)

Denmark, like most of the Nordic countries, has a strong tradition of links with Israel (many Finnish Christians are such committed Zionists they would make Theodor Herzl seem like a moderate!) and a major organization of Danish Kibbutz Friends. A group of young Zionist pioneers were among the Jews caught in Denmark and then transported to Sweden during the German occupation. There is a Denmark Square in Jerusalem to express gratitude for the Danes' wartime behaviour; and in 1968, 25 years after the rescue took place, the former Green Square in Copenhagen (behind a little vegetable market on Frederiks Borggade) was renamed Israels Plads. A chunk of rock from Eilat, now splashed with whitewash, serves as a rather incongruous memorial.

It is also possible to reconstruct the stages of the rescue in Copenhagen and the little harbours on the shoreline stretching North along the Danish Riviera up to Elsinore, and indeed beyond, where Jews were hidden in churches, boathouses, tileworks and private residences during the day and then picked up on deserted beaches at night. A great T-shaped pedestrian precinct makes exploration of the city easy. On Købmagergade, the base of the T which goes from the site of the former city gate at Nørreport to the bridge leading to the Royal Library and Parliament, is the austere Round Tower. Since it was originally built as an observatory, strips of windows open out in almost every direction, although it is tacked on to the drab grey Trinity Church. The main synagogue is just round the corner; it was here that the Torah scrolls were concealed during the German occupation.

The Jews in flight, however, tended to make for the northern section of the city. Since doctors, like the clergy, were very active in humanitarian resistance work, the hospital at Bispebjerg helped save many lives. There was little risk of betrayal, ambulances were seldom stopped in security checks, and it was easy to admit Jews under false names, secrete them away in different wards or farm them out to other hospitals. Collective responsibility had the great advantage that, even if they were betrayed, it was hardly possible to arrest the whole staff of a large hospital.

The coastal road goes up through Hellerup, where there is a memorial park for the resistance, and into the countryside, past the modernist luxury villas, past the royal hunting park, and into Rungsted. This small town is famous mainly because it was here that Karen Blixen wrote *Out of Africa* and most of her other books; much of her house (a restored sixteenth-century inn) is now open as a museum, but the author's ageing housekeeper still recalls the procession of Jews in hiding who made brief stays before setting out for Sweden.

Most of the crossings started from the little ports between Rungsted and Elsinore, and between Elsinore and Gilleleje (one of the latter, Hornbæk, is still a popular Jewish resort, with several summer synagogues). A small memorial on the shore at Snekkersten commemorates the efforts on the Jews' behalf of an innkeeper called H.C. Thomsen. All the way along the coastal route one is aware of the looming presence of Sweden just across a finger of sea; during the war years, it was like a dream land of freedom lit up at night while Denmark was blacked-out. The short hop from Hamlet's town of Elsinore to Helsingborg is now one of the busiest stretches of water in the world. (Most of the passengers come from Sweden, many attracted by Denmark's more liberal licensing laws. A certain amount of rowdiness is the result, so graffiti in the Danish port towns often say things like: 'Keep Denmark clean; take a Swede back to the ferry!') If one reads accounts of the 1943 rescue, one gets the feeling that the crossing was almost as busy then. Certainly, activity was constant in the days which succeeded the attempted deportation on 1–2 October 1943.

There are, of course, several factors which worked in the favour of the Danish Jews. They were few in number, mainly comfortably off and could easily hide, since they were indistinguishable from their fellow citizens in terms of language, dress and, often, eating habits. In contrast to the situation in other countries, Danes were not cowed into complete submission by a reign of terror or the constant threat of death. Furthermore, the Holocaust came to Denmark comparatively late: a middle-aged Jew said to me dramatically that, although he was grateful to his fellow citizens, he would not be sitting there alive in front of me if it had not been for the Allied victories in Stalingrad and El Alamein. With the tide of the war shifting away from the Axis, the behaviour of Swedes, Danes and even Germans naturally started to change. Sweden had been nominally neutral, but its policy of so-called 'neutrality' usually involved efforts not to offend the Germans. By October 1943, however, they were far more willing to open their doors to persecuted refugees.

All such factors are significant, but they cannot eclipse the most significant fact of all: unlike the inhabitants of many other European countries, the Danes *wanted* to protect their Jewish fellow-citizens and considered it a matter of national honour to do so; external factors assured their remarkable success rate. It is very tempting to consider the history and the monuments of Jewish Copenhagen in the light of the events of 1943.

To start with, the community has always been small, assimilated and reasonably affluent. A good deal of unrest accompanied the decree of 1814, which granted the Jews full rights of citizenship; but since then, the general atmosphere has been fairly tolerant, even if certain invisible barriers continued to operate. In the nineteenth century, therefore, Jews achieved great successes in the wider culture, while intermarriage, more or less sincere conversions and the attractions of bourgeois life lured many away from traditional Jewish observance. As so often in European history, ambitious Jews felt it was not prudent to be *too* Jewish. Between 1834 and 1901, there was even an absolute decline in numbers from 4,000 (0.38 per cent of the population) to 3,500 (0.14 per cent). Provincial communities more or less ceased to exist.

There are some beautiful paintings of cultured Jewish bourgeois life in Copenhagen, including one of a musical evening at the Henriques family residence. M.R. Henriques (1815–1912) was a crucial figure in musical circles. His sister Dorothea married Moritz Melchior, chairman of the Chamber of Commerce, and presided over a salon whose guests included Hans Christian Andersen. The last two Chief Rabbis of Denmark were both Melchiors, Marcus and his son Bent. It was also a Henriques, it will be recalled, who at first refused to believe that the Germans were really planning to deport the Jews in 1943. Some writers have criticized what they see as the excessive caution and political passivity of communal leaders.

The main synagogue is also fascinating in this respect. Inside, it is decorated with austere splendour, but the side facing Krystalgade could hardly be more discreet, a neutral and completely anonymous-looking building in mustard-coloured brick. (The tight security outside provides the main clue that it could be a synagogue.) It is a wonderful symbol of a community which was rich, proud of its traditions yet extremely careful to avoid calling attention to itself. Inside, the dark wooden seating takes up most of the floor space and rows of solid grey octagonal columns support the women's gallery. Against this rather dour background gold lotus-leaf capitals form a vivid contrast. The same motif is repeated in more delicate form on the layer above. On the back wall, two short double staircases lead up to an Ark curtain which breaks dramatically into a crisscrossed gold screen. Each square is decorated again with lotus leaves, and an Egyptian-style cornice creates a sort of crenellation effect at the top. The monumental style obviously shows the influence of Napoleon's Egyptian Expedition, an episode with particularly rich resonances for Jews (see the chapter on Paris).

The earliest Jewish settlements in Denmark are usually dated to 1622, far later than in many European countries, when Christian IV (1588–1648) encouraged rich Sephardi merchants to take up residence in the town of Glückstadt. Since this never succeeded in becoming a serious rival to Hamburg, they were never a significant presence, and a true Danish community only became established with an influx of

Joseph Theodor Hansen's 'Interior of the Copenhagen Synagogue' (1879). This was built in 1833, attacked by arsonists in 1942, yet still standing today (Royal Library)

poorer Ashkenazis much later in the century. Religious freedom was granted in the new fortress town of Fredericia in 1682, where an early Jewish cemetery still survives.

In Copenhagen, a jeweller called Meyer Goldschmidt was allowed to use his house for private prayers from 1684, and the first cemetery was built in 1693. (This can still be seen in Møllegade, to the north-east of the city; a newer cemetery, dating from 1886, is located on Vestre Kirkegårds Allé.) The first public synagogue was not consecrated until 1766. Jews were not allowed to join guilds, but the authorities sometimes provided facilities for Jewish businesses in an attempt to encourage enterprise and break the guild monopolies. This sometimes led to hostility, which occasionally erupted into physical violence. Yet persecuted Jews who claimed to be manufacturers were often admitted into the country for humanitarian reasons: the College of Commerce, for example, wrote in 1757 that, 'We acknowledge that these are unfortunate, ill-fated people; they are hated everywhere and civil rights are denied them in most of Europe.' Attitudes like this, of course, were to come to the surface again in 1943.

Statistics make the progress clear. There were only nineteen Jews in Copenhagen in 1682; by the end of the eighteenth century, there were something like 1,500 (and another 200 or so in provincial towns). These are very small numbers, yet all the while a far larger collection of Jewish *books* (which also needed to be 'rescued' during the war) formed part of one of Europe's great libraries. This is the Royal Library, in central Copenhagen, set in an interior courtyard with a lovely garden; a suitably grim statue of Søren Kierkegaard looks on.

The celebrated Judaica collection was a significant part of it from the time of its inauguration in 1673, and the stock has been increased by purchases, donations and adventurous expeditions ever since. In 1761, for example, a team of six bold scholars set out for *Arabia Felix* (or Yemen); unfortunately, only a single survivor, Carsten Niebuhr, returned five years later, after visiting Jerusalem and Persepolis and crossing the whole of Europe on horseback. Yet he brought with him a superb collection of oriental Hebrew Bibles.

Another substantial addition to the stock came when a trader called Simon Aron Eibeschütz made substantial funds available to the library in 1853. Yet the heart of the current collection was supplied by a bequest from David Simonsen, former Chief Rabbi of Denmark, in 1932. This comprised 40,000 volumes in all, written in Yiddish and Ladino, Judeo-Arabic and Judeo-Persian, along with manuscripts from Yemen – and the first Hebrew text to mention Denmark! During the German occupation, the curator for Judaica managed to hide all the books in cellars or among theology and other sections of the library (ambulances were sometimes used to transport the community's own collection to safety there!). Indeed, even from Sweden he continued his work, acquiring texts from Allied countries; after the war, he was able to obtain much antisemitic material and more serious writing on Jewish themes which was left behind by the parting Germans. Further donations dramatically increased the supply of Yiddish books, Karaite and Falasha literature, and Hebrew incunabula.

Today, this superb collection houses between 80 and 90 thousand volumes, more than 60 incunabula (printed books from before the year 1501) and 400 manuscripts. Facsimiles of the most important *Haggadot* of the world are on display, and (preferably with a few days' notice) the staff are willing to show visitors some of the more fragile treasures. These include early editions of Maimonides's *Guide for the Perplexed* in the original Arabic and the only copy of the Hebrew translation from Barcelona in 1348 where the scribe has written his name in the colophon (only five or six copies of this book exist in the world). There is a superb collection of Hebrew Bibles and prayer books from Spain (one illuminated in 'Arabic carpet' style with exquisite micrographic writing), Bavaria, Naples, Prague and Mantua. Major centres of early printing like Venice and Amsterdam are well represented, including Menassah ben Israel's own Latin and English versions of *Hope of Israel*, the book which played a key role in securing the Readmission of the Jews into England.

By the end of the nineteenth century the small established community of 'Viking Jews' was largely bourgeois, conservative and subject to depletion by more or less opportunistic conversions to Christianity. The long-term future could only be one of dilution and decline. At this point, however, an influx of Jews fleeing persecution in Eastern Europe revitalized the community. Some of these refused to take part at all in the established institutions and formed a small ultra-Orthodox group still represented by the Machsike Hadas synagogue on Ole Suhrsgade. Other small synagogues sprang up in roads like Læderstræde (just off the main pedestrian street known as Strøget). As in London, Paris and Vienna, conflict soon developed between the old-timers and the newcomers both about power within the community and about the appropriate Jewish life-style for the times. Certainly, the establishment, fearing an outbreak of antisemitism, was ambivalent about the sudden arrival of many young, poor, Yiddish-speaking and often traditionalist Jews from Eastern Europe, and this century has seen a slow process of modernization to make the organized community more open, democratic and accountable.

In 1917 Denmark passed laws restricting immigration, which remained fairly tight even during the Nazi period. Nonetheless, another component of today's community are the Central European Jews who sought asylum in the early 1930s and managed to survive the war on Swedish soil. More recently, along with a significant exodus of young Danish Jews to Israel, there have also been a number of Israeli immigrants, particularly just after the wars of 1956 and 1967; some were marriage partners of Danish Jews, others Sephardim who felt Israel offered them few opportunities. Close links – many Danish Jews have children in the Israeli Army – have meant a very strong commitment to Israel. Whereas prominent Jewish figures, notably in the Anglo-Saxon world, have sometimes combined this with unequivocal criticism of particular Israeli policies, the small Danish community tends to feel this could only give ammunition to their external and domestic enemies, notably Arab groups and so-called 'radical' politicians. Tight security at synagogues and other communal buildings is an unfortunate necessity.

The final element is the 2,000 Jews (some of them Jews only in Polish terms and not by any religious commitment or definition) who were more or less expelled from Poland in 1969. Many were veterans of the Second World War and archetypal Jewish socialists, who had survived concentration camps, fought as partisans in Russia or the Polish branch of the Red Army and then gone on to obtain key positions as apparatniks; yet suddenly, after 1967, they were declared Zionists and traitors and deprived of all they had.

Such is today's Jewish community in Denmark. Since the mid-nineteenth century, as elsewhere, large-scale assimilation has been the trend. An official put it very eloquently to me: if the term 'Jew' is given the strict Halachic definition, there are perhaps 10,000 now living in Denmark; as defined by the Nuremberg regulations, there are probably a quarter of a million. Fully paid-up members (who give two per cent of their taxed income, just like adherents of the established church) number about 3,000 adults and their 1,500 children. For many who do not use the Jewish school, attend synagogue or intend to be buried soon, the financial burden often seems too great. A final problem is demographic, since Danish Jews (and indeed Danes in general) are faced with an ageing population; over a third of them have reached the pensionable age of 67.

To some extent, this is a bleak picture, and the community undoubtedly needs more members, commitment and money if it is to remain strong and retain its influence. Yet there are also some very positive factors. It is not plagued by the factions and divisions which can afflict even communities of the same size. There is a single synagogue, a Chief Rabbi and just one other rabbi. Orthodoxy is the norm, but few are bothered by people who prefer Reform or Conservative observances – or those who park their cars at a discreet distance from the synagogue on *shabbat*.

This harmony is well symbolized by the Community Centre on Ny Kongensgade, which houses almost every major Jewish body in Copenhagen. The other great asset is the Chief Rabbi, Bent Melchior, a charismatic personality and one of the leading cultural figures in the country. Most Christian societies retain a residual reluctance to accept moral leadership from Jews, yet Melchior is well-known outside the community, often recognized in the street (rather more often than the Bishop of Copenhagen!) and in constant demand as a public speaker. It is he who maintains links with the established church; when, for example, police planned to storm streets occupied by squatters, Melchior and the Bishop jointly took part in a 'peace watch'.

Comparative flexibility and tolerance also characterize Jewish-Islamic relations. Denmark today has a Muslim population of about 60,000 – Turks, Pakistanis, European converts and even Palestinians – so how does it cope with a problem which creates immense difficulties, for example in Marseilles? A certain amount of conflict and disagreement is inevitable, yet there is also a remarkable example of co-operation: Jews and Muslims share premises and the expensive machinery required by religious law for slaughtering cattle.

We must, of course, hope that Jewish life continues to flourish in Copenhagen. Yet even in the worst-case scenario, if communal commitment goes on declining, this represents a conscious choice. This is utterly different from the situation in much of Europe, where dying communities are a direct result of Nazi persecution.

The cities considered in this book offer diverse rewards. But whereas those featured in earlier chapters contain monuments evocative of great eras in the Jewish past, we turn now to cities where the current scene is far more optimistic, first to Glasgow (which was spared persecution in the 1940s) and then to places which have been transformed or reborn since the War. Sometimes this is the result of external factors, like the end of Communist rule in Eastern Europe (Prague) or French colonial rule in North Africa (Marseilles, Paris), and sometimes the result of a conscious decision to hold on to the traditions of ultra-Orthodoxy (Antwerp). In any event, the present and future of the communities are a cause for hope and celebration. Copenhagen comes into neither category: rather, it is the city's history *during the Nazi era* which is inspiring and exemplary, a story of gentile heroism without parallel in Continental Europe.

This classic image of
the rescue in 1943 comes
from a celebratory film
made shortly after the war
(Museum of the Danish
Resistance)

8

GLASGOW

G LASGOW IS THE liveliest of cities, yet dominating the whole
town – and particularly the cathedral just below – is the
City of the Dead. Optimists now claim that Glasgow is a
pioneering example of a 'post-industrial city'; but the Necropolis is
a strange and moving reminder that it was also, for many decades,
the second city of a great empire. At the top is an immense statue of
John Knox (1505–72), the Scottish religious reformer and scourge

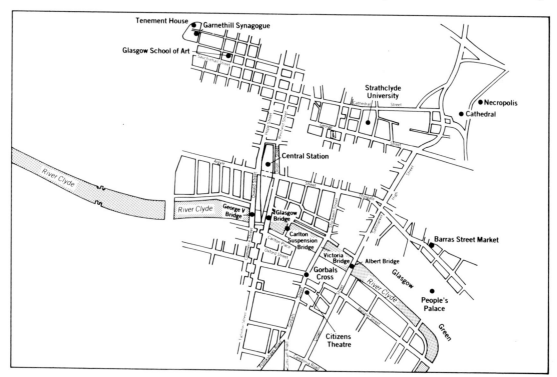

of the Catholics, who sternly surveys a city long torn apart by
tensions between Catholics and Protestants. All around are grandiose
funerary monuments to local dignitaries of the nineteenth century –
bleach manufacturers and professors of theology, mill-owners, actor-
managers, literateurs and even the author of the well-known nursery
rhyme 'Wee Willie Winkie'. Egyptian vaults provided temporary
homes for corpses awaiting burial, two Greek temples are stacked
on top of each other to form a new mélange, and pastiches in just
about every other high-minded style – Moorish, Gothic, Byzantine
and Ottoman – are well represented.

Opened in 1832, the Necropolis soon became a tourist attraction
where visitors went to indulge in uplifting and melancholy thoughts.
'Who,' asked one of the early guide books, 'is not made better
and wiser by occasional intercourse with the tomb?' In theory, the
cemetery was always intended to be non-denominational, but it forms
a continuation of the tightly packed churchyard around the cathedral
and contains more than its share of Celtic crosses. It is quite a surprise

The Jews' Enclosure,
'suburb to the city of
the dead', is now sadly
overgrown (Scottish
Jewish Archive Centre)

to learn, therefore, that the first burial was of a Jewish quill merchant called Joseph Levy.

In 1831, records show there were only 47 Jews in Glasgow, six of them born in the city. Such people were normally buried in Edinburgh, but Levy died of cholera and was interred as quickly as possible. In 1836, the Jews' Enclosure was built, tucked away in a corner just by the fence on Wishart Street, as a 'suburb to the city of the dead'. It was soon full up – 51 Jews were buried there before 1851 – and is now sadly overgrown, yet one can still examine the names on the tombs outside the enclosure of people on the periphery of the community – a man who married out, a woman involved in some minor dispute. Those within, ironically, are now quite inaccessible beneath the undergrowth.

A grand column based on Absalom's pillar in Jerusalem stands sentinel next to a bricked-up ornamental gateway with scrolls supporting an urn; below are inscriptions from Lord Byron's *Hebrew Melodies* and the Bible. There is evidence that all of these were erected at the expense of the Merchants' House, owners of the cemetery, and that even the land was provided cheap – early signs of the acceptance and tolerance Glasgow has always accorded its Jews.

There had only been a short and small-scale Jewish presence in Glasgow *before* the Necropolis was built. A hatter called Isaac Cohen is mentioned in the city records for 1812, a small prayer room was opened in the High Street (near the Necropolis) for *Succot* in 1823, the first circumcision performed in 1824. As the community increased, there was a constant struggle to find larger premises and some fierce disputes on the subject. One concerned a site at 204 George Street, now part of Strathclyde University, which also housed dissecting rooms for medical students and raised the fear that '*Cohanim* and others may meet corpses of all nations.' Another concerned the question of which synagogue had burial rights in the Jews' Enclosure – a religious dispute which had to be settled in the Scottish law courts.

These early prayer rooms and the earliest area of Jewish settlement in Glasgow were around George Square, now the municipal centre of the city where a statue of Sir Walter Scott looks down on the imposing Italianate City Chambers. The first true synagogue was also in George Street and seated 250 people. This was opened in 1858, when there were about 150 Jewish families in the city.

A further significant influx came in the 1870s, when a non-Jewish warehousing firm brought in a group of Jewish tailors who took up residence near the Clyde. This shifted the centre of gravity of Jewish settlement slightly to the south, although the newcomers continued to use the George Street synagogue. Meanwhile, the more affluent Jews were moving into the West End, and it was for them that the first specially built synagogue on Scottish soil was established in 1879. This is the Garnethill synagogue, which is now also the site of the Jewish Archive Centre.

The Garnethill synagogue, specially built in 1879, was far grander and more impressive than the little prayer rooms which sprang up earlier around George Street (George Outram/*Glasgow Herald*)

If the earlier synagogues were little more than converted tenement flats, Garnethill, which stands at the top of a hill close to Charles Rennie Mackintosh's celebrated Glasgow School of Art, is vastly more imposing. 'The style of architecture adopted is "Romanesque" with a "Byzantine" feeling introduced in the details,' wrote the *Jewish Chronicle* at the time of its consecration, although the overall effect is that of a smart English parish church. It is, in any event, a most beautiful building. The Ark is set back into an apse below a skylight, the vaulted ceiling is decorated with a blue and white chequerboard design, while Corinthian columns picked out in gold support a Moorish-style women's gallery with elaborate metalwork railings and huge arches inlaid with purple. A grand octagonal pulpit stands in the centre, while lovely memorial stained-glass windows – plants emerging from pots burst into flower – are let into every wall. A particularly fine example stands at the turn of the grand staircase leading up to the women's gallery. Yet another window is a sole surviving relic of the George Street synagogue.

Upstairs, there was a small exhibition about Avrom Greenbaum, whose Jewish Institute Players were the main focus of local Jewish drama after 1936; the brides' room, now decorated with wallpaper featuring orange butterflies; and, finally, the Archive Centre. This was founded when the Crosshill Synagogue was closed in 1986 and is located in a small room, again with beautiful stained glass in pastel tints. There are fascinating things on display and in the files: the key to the Gertrude Jacobson orphanage, a Jewish Colonial Trust Bond of 1900, a full-scale oil painting of an officer in the Jewish Lads' Brigade and photographs of the local rabbis and other dignitaries of the community. The centre also holds regular meetings, usually with speeches by Scottish Jews who have made good: Sir Horace Phillips, the only Jewish British ambassador, the late Sir Monty Finnison, former Chairman of British Steel, and well-known writers and academics such as David Daiches or Chaim Bermant.

The centenary of the Garnethill Synagogue was celebrated in a grand commemorative dinner in 1979, a well-merited act of homage to the greatest Jewish monument of Scotland. The advertisements and messages of congratulation in the souvenir brochure – from carpet merchants and car washes, furriers, 'forktruck specialists' and many financial institutions – graphically convey the variety of Glasgow Jewish life.

Medicine has long been a particularly popular profession. One

Dr Cosgrove preaching
at Garnethill (George
Outram/*Glasgow Herald*)

of the leading lights of the Archive Centre is a general practitioner, Dr Kenneth Collins, who has also researched and written about Jewish life in Scotland over many years. He lives, like most of Glasgow's Jews, in one of the leafier suburbs to the south of the city, has a practice consisting largely of Asians and has edited a little book entitled *Aspects of Scottish Jewry*. One of the key points about Garnethill, he stressed, is that it was built mainly by recent immigrants from Eastern Europe. To be more precise, they were largely Litvaks, or Lithuanian Jews, who had easy access to the Baltic ports in hard times. Two years after the synagogue was completed, the Russian pogroms of 1881 sent many more thousands of Jews fleeing westwards. Such people, whose descendants now form the bulk of Glasgow Jewry, came from a very similar background.

Some went to London and eventually reached Glasgow, usually in the 1890s. (Researchers can trace the long migrations from the birthplaces of successive children in the larger families – Warsaw, Hamburg, London, Manchester and finally Glasgow, for example.) Others took a more direct route, by boat from Rotterdam or Hamburg to Leith and then by train to Glasgow. On the whole, those who decided to stay on in Glasgow blended in fairly well with people who were much like themselves; there was no long-established, totally assimilated and slightly stuffy Jewish 'establishment', as in London, to look askance at the newcomers.

What were the main characteristics of the Litvaks who came to Glasgow and formed the backbone of today's community? They tended to be fairly worldly, enterprising and well attuned to the Calvinist work ethic of the Scots; Glasgow offered far more opportunities for their energies and talents than the staider city of Edinburgh. (Peddlers, who travelled into Northern England as well as all over Scotland, were common and popular figures in the early years. Some provided a rudimentary but very useful system of credit to their customers. For a brief period, they even spoke their own dialect, an unlikely mixture of Scots and Yiddish!)

In religious outlook, the Litvaks were little influenced by either Hasidism or the Reform movement and remained within the mainstream of Orthodox Judaism. Radical politics was not a particularly strong feature. Even the efforts of the Reverend E.P. Phillips (the first minister of Garnethill who held the post for over 50 years) on behalf of Oscar Slater were given lukewarm support. Slater was a German Jew and a petty crook who was convicted of murder on utterly inadequate evidence. Sir Arthur Conan-Doyle took time off from writing about Sherlock Holmes to join with Phillips in a crusade for Slater's release, yet Phillips's congregation showed little interest in the case.

It would be quite absurd, however, to think of Glasgow Jewry as apolitical, since the newcomers at the end of the nineteenth century brought with them from Lithuania an intense and very early commitment to Zionism. The mother of President Herzog was Glasgow-born, pioneers have left the city to live in Palestine since well before the First World War, and about 1,000 Glasgow Jews did *aliya* between 1948 and the Six Day War. Most of them were children of people born in Scotland and retain a strong Scottish as well as Jewish identity. This led to a good deal of soul-searching when Scotland played football against Israel in the World Cup, but the annual Burns' Night dinner in Tel Aviv is said to be one of the liveliest events in the Israeli social calendar!

After the major influx of Jews in the 1880s and '90s came the German Jews in the 1930s. Dr Collins has written a PhD and a book on Jewish medical students in Scotland (and even articles about Jamaican Jewish medics), a seemingly obscure subject which is actually crucial. There are two reasons for this. The first is that in the 1930s medicine was far and away the most popular subject for study among the Jewish youth, partly because the old-established Scottish law firms, for example, were often unwelcoming to Jews. (Since the War, as one might expect, dentistry, law, accountancy and electronics have all become major employers.) The other is that one very simple measure enabled many German Jews to come to Scotland in the 1930s. This was a decree in 1932 which allowed those with a German medical degree to requalify in Scotland after only one year – a much shorter time than in England. Another contingent of medical students – about 1,000 in the period from the 1920s to early '40s – came from the United States, where a *numerus clausus* or quota system was operating in the major medical schools of the Eastern Seaboard.

A touching story about a particular individual reveals the ingenious ways in which the Scots managed to help Jewish refugees in the 1930s. It concerns a Jewish professor in Heidelberg who saw the writing on the wall in the early Nazi period and got his son safely out of Central Europe. The boy arrived at Edinburgh university with no money and explained the situation. The governing body said they would consider his request sympathetically and asked him to come back later. When he returned, they told him they would accept him and waive all fees – sponsoring the studies of a professor's son would be their contribution to the Heidelberg centenary celebrations which were being held that year. Needless to say, this was a beautifully discreet slap in the face for the German authorities as well as a fine humanitarian gesture.

The new German immigrants never made up a proportion of more than about six or seven per cent of the community, but their arrival led to a certain amount of tension. Dr Rayner Kölmel, a contributor to Dr Collins' book, quotes some heart-rending testimonies of child refugees. Some were lodged in a house next to Garnethill. Viscount Traprain, nephew of Lord Balfour (the author of the Balfour Declaration), allowed a school to be established on his estate which trained 160 Jewish children for emigration to Palestine. Others were fostered by Jewish families.

One described her first meeting with her new 'mother': 'There was nobody to meet me at the Central Station. What could I do? I couldn't even speak the language . . . It was a Saturday.' The girl, of course, had no choice but to search for the address she had been given: 'So I arrive, right in the middle of a Saturday, and she was so rude to me! They were Orthodox Jews, she says, "I wrote to tell them not to come on a Saturday."' More generally, the Litvaks resented the left-wing activism, irreligion and commitment to German culture of some of the German Jews, while the Germans often looked down on people they regarded as *Ostjuden* devoted only to money-making. Most of these tensions, however, were smoothed over in time by the demands of war work and the assimilation of the new arrivals. Some of the German Jews have subsequently moved on, mainly to London, Israel and the United States; but several hundred are still resident in Glasgow.

The newcomers in the 1880s and '90s, and again in the 1930s, moved into one of the most notorious slums in Europe: the Gorbals. Half the Jews in the city lived in this one district in 1936. Although the city has been extensively redeveloped since the War, Glasgow's long-standing bad reputation still derives largely from this one area. Yet if one explores the Gorbals by crossing the Carlton Suspension Bridge, first impressions are exhilarating. Carlton Place, built in the early nineteenth century, stretches along the South bank of the Clyde like

a splendid neo-classical façade. Its only 'gateway' is South Portland
Street, which is lined with buildings belonging to some of the
Gorbals's main charitable institutions: the Guild of Aid, the Medical
Mission Society, Salvation Army Centre and finally, on the corner
of Oxford Street, the second of the public libraries which feature
prominently in some of the Jewish memoirs of Gorbals days. The
street was also the site of the Great Central Synagogue, built in 1901
but now completely destroyed. Another major synagogue, the Beth
Medrash Hagodal, was founded in Oxford Street in the same year.

The Gorbals is fairly grim even today, and it is impossible to
regret the destruction of the old tightly packed and insanitary housing.
What is sad, however, is that so little of the Jewish Gorbals remains.
There are, of course, some noteworthy buildings and monuments
which were already there when the Jews arrived, and others which
were constructed during the Jewish period. Interesting examples
include the booking hall of the now defunct Bridge Street Station
(1890), the grand entrance opposite to the Savings Bank (1888), the

The Gorbals Cross
intersection around 1917,
at the heart of Glasgow's
Jewish quarter
(Strathclyde Regional
Archives)

Coliseum music hall on Eglington Street, which mounted everything
from pantomime and Glasgow's first 'talkie' to Wagner's *Ring*, and
the Caledonia Road Church in 'Greek Revival' style (1856–57).

Yet it is the changes which are far more significant. The Clyde,
of course, is utterly transformed: only a tea clipper called the *Carrick*
now floats as a tourist attraction on a river which used to be one of
the great ship-building centres of the world. Nearby, Gorbals Cross at
the head of Gorbals Street is a crossroads which was once hemmed in
on all sides by tenement housing. There are many descriptions of the
lively scenes on weekends when Jews, Irish, Italians and Lithuanians
would all stand around discussing politics and setting off on family
outings. Today, the tenements have gone, creating a sort of wasteland
around the 'innovative public housing' which has not worn at all well;
the clock tower has gone; and even the Gents' public lavatory in the
centre of the Cross has gone. The once imposing façade of the famous
Citizens' Theatre has been reconstructed in brash 1970s style, next to
lawyers' offices which face the huge new Sheriff Court. The most
impressive building nearby is the Central Mosque and Islamic Centre.
The New Central Synagogue, on the other hand, was first converted
into a plastics factory and then destroyed altogether. Truly, times have
changed!

There is, then, virtually nothing left of the old Gorbals, and
one is reduced to relying mainly on local historians, memories and
memoirs. Yet because Glasgow is a city with a very strong tradition of
left-wing politics, there is more to see than there might be elsewhere.
A Tenement House, for example, has been preserved for posterity
by the National Trust with all its furnishings intact; although it is
located in the West End near Garnethill, it gives a good idea of what
the more salubrious parts of the Gorbals were like. There is also the
remarkable People's Palace, a museum of labour history in a sort
of grand greenhouse. An old pharmacy, newsagents and the box
office of the Palace Theatre in the Gorbals are all recreated with
the original objects, and displays feature many interesting artefacts
like the catechisms and tune books which were used at socialist
Sunday schools. Close by is the Barras Street market which had a
large proportion of Jewish traders in days gone by.

One of the most colourful descriptions of the Gorbals in the 1930s
appears in Chaim Bermant's *Coming Home*. Glasgow was quite unlike
Barovke, the village he had come from, but the Yiddish posters,
bakers with Jewish bread and the pungent barrels of herring did

remind him of a small town in the old country called Dvinsk. He heard more Yiddish than English on the streets. Yet the most disorientating feature was the lack of access to the open countryside; it took a long while for him to be reconciled to Glasgow, mainly by the parks, the trams and the library.

The Gorbals were so tightly packed that the Jews were never numerically dominant – in the peak years there were perhaps ten thousand Jews out of 60 or 70 thousand inhabitants – although since the Catholics went to separate schools, the Jews did form a majority in some of the 'non-denominational' (effectively Protestant) ones. Nonetheless, there were quite enough Jews for a complex system of over a hundred small friendly societies and many other welfare, social and educational institutions to grow up. The most famous of these was probably the Jewish Institute. Quite apart from Avrom Greenbaum's politically committed Players, the Institute was a major social centre, with a Literary Society, distinguished bridge and billiards teams and Sunday night dances. 'Many folk in Glasgow,' one old-timer recalled, 'can thank the Institute (or otherwise) for the fact that their romances were sealed there, and mainly in the Isaac Wolfson ballroom.' The atmosphere was so good that many of the jazz stars and bands who topped the bill at the Empire would drop by for impromptu performances, while bearded East European Jews would mingle among the dancers trying, with scant success, to collect money for the local *yeshiva*. There was also the annual boat trip up the Clyde: a specially chartered steamer left the Broomielaw, whence many other Jews set off for America, for an afternoon of eating, music and dancing. People of every age went along, again with the best entertainment star who happened to be in town.

Equally famous was Geneens, a splendid hotel where many of the entertainers would stay. Yet Mrs Sophie Geneen was far more than a successful businesswoman; the old, the poor and injured soldiers on leave could always be sure of a warm room for the afternoon and a meal. Food parcels were prepared for those who needed them anywhere in Scotland as well as for Allied soldiers. The restaurant closed in 1965, but a Sophie Geneen Forest was planted in Israel in honour of 'The Mother of Glasgow'.

Memoirs of Gorbals days come in two kinds. There are touching but rather sentimental accounts, such as those by Evelyn Cowan, and there is Ralph Glaser's *Growing up in the Gorbals*. This gives a deeply moving account of a very unhappy family and presents the district

in the grimmest possible way – unbelievable squalor, incest, rats'
excrement . . . Nearly everybody in Glasgow thought this portrait
grossly distorted, including the remarkable Dr Ezra Golombok,
editor of the *Jewish Echo* which was once based in the heart of the
Gorbals and is now located at its periphery on Eglinton Street.
He fondly recalled the neighbours and the fellow-feeling from his
tenement childhood, stressed that 'from the Gorbals came some of the
very considerable intellectual and business achievement of Glasgow
Jewry' and summed up as follows: 'The fact is that the Gorbals *was* a
warm and vibrant community – and it was great to get out of it.' The
evidence indeed suggests that people *did* leave the Gorbals as soon as
they could afford it, often soon after arrival. By the end of the 1960s,
the exodus was almost complete.

Dr Golombok is a highly entertaining character with refreshingly
honest views on every subject. His newspaper was founded by his
father in 1928 and combines local news with some of the most
detailed reporting on the Israeli (and international Jewish) scene
available anywhere in English. I asked him about the *Echo*'s rationale.
'Oh, there isn't one!' he replied with a laugh. 'And furthermore it's
commercially insane! Two people spend about half their time on the
typesetting. The rest of the week we're busy making a living – the
paper could never pay for itself.'

Commercial or not, the *Echo* provides a key to Jewish life in
Glasgow. The community is deeply committed to Israel and provides
a good deal of money, yet it is also very well informed on the issues
and not at all shy about voicing criticisms of particular policies. The
paper reflects the wide variety of views about the way forward for
Israel today. There is, for example, a small but significant Glasgow
Friends of Peace Now group which has taken out advertisements
calling for Israel to negotiate with the PLO and even organized a
controversial meeting with a PLO speaker on the site of the local
Representative Council in Copelaw Street. Other people take quite
different lines, although there has traditionally been strong support
for the ideals of 'labour Zionism'.

In 1990, Glasgow was officially designated European City of
Culture, and the Jewish community used the opportunity to show
their support for Israel in a series of events designed to present the
Jewish Contribution to Art, Music and Literature. All involved either
Jewish performers or works by Jewish artists and many, such as a
concert by the Israel Philharmonic, had an Israeli link. The organizer,

Louise Naftalin, said she hoped it would be 'a soft way of selling Judaism. It's *nice* propaganda, showing that Israel is a cultured place, has antiquities, puts on exhibitions, has contact with other countries. People assume that Jews are different. When I give talks to church groups, people assume I'll look different, dress differently.'

If 1990 was proof that Glasgow is successfully generating a new 'post-industrial' economy, the dress rehearsal was the Glasgow Garden Festival. At a time when the newspapers were printing nothing but bad news from Israel, the Israeli garden helped remind people that 'Israel is also part of the normal world'. Even more successful – indeed the hit of the whole festival – was the display of Israeli swimwear.

Dr Golombok also talked at length about Glasgow Jewish life in general. As editor of the *Echo*, he is certainly in a position to know. 'If you're Jewish in Glasgow, you buy it. It's almost a definition of the community,' he suggested controversially. 'You might even say that the last thing a Jew in Glasgow would do is read the *Echo*.'

I must have looked puzzled because he hastened to explain this enigmatic remark. 'There are many Jews in the city who take little interest in welfare organizations, ignore the dietary laws and don't go to the synagogue. The last thing they do before completely severing contact with the community is read the *Echo*.'

Even his views on statistics were trenchant. One estimate is that the community has declined from a peak of 14,500 to 7,000, but Dr Golombok's circulation figures (which he would not reveal) suggested that the peak was an overestimate and today's figure was too low: 'There are so many interested parties. You know about the Lubavitch – there are many people like that who have a vested interest in doom. They complain all the time about people who marry out and never mention the people who marry *into* the community.'

The *Echo* naturally also reflects changing mores. Recent issues have included advertisements from a local pizzeria – which would have been inconceivable fifteen years ago – because many local Jews, at least when eating out, pay far less attention than they used to to the dietary laws. The same applied to driving on the Sabbath. 'What is the difference,' Dr Golombok asked me, 'between an Orthodox and a Reform synagogue? At a Reform synagogue the congregation park in the car park, at an Orthodox they park round the corner!' Since Giffnock synagogue has a large congregation and a perfectly adequate car park, this causes understandable irritation among local residents.

The community, in other words, combines a tolerant and easy-going attitude with a desire not to give offence to the more deeply observant. The same attractive pragmatism led the Jews, when some of the more snooty golf clubs were unwilling to admit them, simply to found their own. Although Glasgow is firmly Orthodox in outlook, one also senses a note of impatience with the ultra-religious who draw attention to every instance of mild hypocrisy. Cantor Levi of Giffnock synagogue, a most impressive man who survived several concentration camps, clearly loves Glasgow: 'People here are strongly committed to values and traditions but blend in beautifully with their surroundings. They're not so over-sophisticated, which is good – they know what matters.' Yet he did express some concerns about a rise in 'a kind of narrow-minded ghetto Judaism': 'The ultra-Orthodox still have reservations about Israel, because it's too secular and they're waiting for the real Redemption. Let them wait! I've no objection. I don't know what they're waiting for, but it's the easiest thing in the world just to wait and pray and hope, not to recognize when something good happens to you – oh no! We're not used to that.'

My final discussion in Glasgow was at the offices of the Jewish Representative Council in Copelaw Street. The exodus out of the Gorbals to the south proceeded small step by step, and the first point of call was in this area. There are still the usual communal facilities nearby, although the residential centre of gravity has moved much further south.

Mrs Judith Tankel, a woman of immense energy, is the Vice President of the Council. Despite smaller families these days, she believed that the numerical decline in the community had now steadied and enthusiastically set out the advantages of being Jewish in Glasgow: 'It's like living a village life in a city . . . The Church of Scotland has always respected us as the People of the Book and we have absorbed the Calvinist work ethic and become very much independent Scottish free-thinkers ourselves.' She quoted the recent case of a lecturer from Israel who had come to talk on *gemetria* (a form of Biblical interpretation based on number symbolism); ideas which had gone down very well with Jewish communities everywhere else were apparently treated with open scepticism in Glasgow.

Glasgow has a Jewish primary school, although no secondary school, so most children get a good grounding in the tradition. Perhaps inevitably in a community of 'independent free-thinkers', most of the adolescents rebel for a time, although many return to the community when they have children of their own. Interestingly enough, a few Asian children attend the Calderwood Lodge School; more generally, the Asian community has followed the Jews out of the Gorbals into the southern suburbs and now has exactly the same problems with rebellious teenagers ('When we have our joint meetings, we have our joint sighings together.')

The Jewish Representative Council acts as the umbrella body for different Jewish groups in Glasgow. It had recently been necessary to disaffiliate the surviving rump of the famous Jewish Institute, which had just become a haunt for elderly gamblers. Yet the range of welfare organizations remains extremely impressive – so impressive, according to Mrs Tankel, that people who are not eligible sometimes apply: 'The prison chaplain gets a steady stream of people who fancy being Jewish – either because they are bored or because they think there'll be the odd perk. Some of them even try to convert in prison. . . . '

9

MARSEILLES

CITIES AND TOWNS ALL over Europe had large Jewish populations which were decimated by the Nazis. Marseilles was one of them. Most have recovered, if at all, only very slowly. Marseilles is *the* shining exception. For here is a city whose Jews have been completely transformed since the War and are now flourishing as never before. Think of Italy, Spain and Austria – centres of extraordinary Jewish achievement over centuries. The total number of Jews today in the three countries may not reach 60,000. Marseilles alone has a population of 70,000.

Although there is no Jewish quarter as such, clear signs of the community – precarious, improvised and temporary though many of them seem – can be found almost everywhere. In the Cours Julien, for example, a former fruit-and-vegetable market which was one of the first parts of Marseilles to be 'done up' and is now among the most fashionable areas in town. With a car park tucked away below ground, it forms an oasis of calm for pedestrians only, paved over and 'landscaped' with ponds, benches, a wooden shelter and a rather unexpected memorial to the cellist Pablo Casals. Adolescents lounge around and look cool amid brightly painted up-market shops – a de luxe publisher, something called Misty Eagle Création, sellers of grand antiques and even a sauna – and a wide variety of restaurants. Among them are two impressive kosher restaurants licensed by the rabbinate: Le Dizengoff and Le Lotus de Nissane, which serves Chinese food.

Altogether less glamorous are the small improvised synagogues scattered throughout Marseilles. The Chevet Ha'him in the Rue Beaumont (close to the railway station) is just a ground-floor room, opening on to the street like a shop, behind frosted glass in an

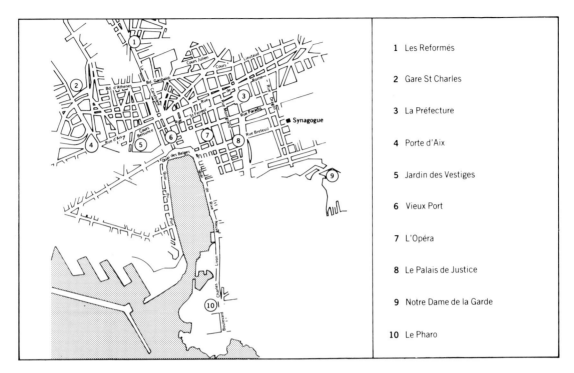

1 Les Reformés

2 Gare St Charles

3 La Préfecture

4 Porte d'Aix

5 Jardin des Vestiges

6 Vieux Port

7 L'Opéra

8 Le Palais de Justice

9 Notre Dame de la Garde

10 Le Pharo

apartment building. Even stranger is the Keter Torah synagogue on the Rue Tapis Vert which, unlikely as it sounds, is virtually part of a Catholic church. An imposing façade contains a main entrance for Christian worshippers and two flanking doors which seem to lead to flats; only the name Rabbin Demri on one of the bells indicates the beautiful little synagogue within.

On the Rue Montgrand, a cavernous and dirty internal courtyard gives access to piano teachers, lawyers' offices and an unfortunately situated Marseille Acceuil ('Welcome to Marseilles'). A grand double door in deep-brown wood at the back forms the entrance to the Temple Beth-Chalom (1965). The synagogue receives about 200 people for *shabbat*, but the room is far wider than it is deep and, with functional straight-backed chairs in wood and brown plastic, a board of switch-on candle-shaped orange eternal flames and small overhanging women's gallery emerging from the wall on the left, resembles nothing so much as a school hall. The donated Ark in white marble with a *menorah* picked out in gold on the door looks over-grand and quite out of place. The platform in front, with a *bimah* like a table covered by a tablecloth and charmless cream plastic chairs standing around, could almost be a bridge club.

Yet it is far too easy to make fun of such a building; its slight absurdity should not detract from its poignant significance. For here are small and often poor congregations with their own particular traditions and rituals, transplanted from North Africa under very difficult circumstances, which have rebuilt themselves on French soil. This post-war rebirth is almost unparalleled in Europe.

To form a clear picture of Jewish Marseilles you should start at the main railway station, the Gare St Charles, and descend the monumental staircase to the Boulevard d'Athènes. Sculptures of two exotic giantesses, said to represent the former French Colonies of Africa and Asia, lounge languorously at the bottom. The Boulevard leads down to the Canabière, the most famous street in Marseilles, known to generations of sailors as the Can o' Beer. This eventually reaches the head of the finger-shaped port, surveyed from far above by Notre Dame de la Garde, the church and statue of the Virgin Mary which form one of the most evocative symbols of Marseilles. Yet before the port, on the right, is the former Bourse (or Stock Exchange), now the Chamber of Commerce, built like a nineteenth-century palace of seafaring and containing a charming little naval museum. Giant anchors and statues of Navigation and Commerce stand outside, prows of boats burst from the walls above the main entrance, and 'badges' commemorate the great explorers along the top.

Behind the Bourse is Marseilles' main shopping centre, the Centre Bourse, which contains everything from a garden of Roman remains to a huge ultra-modern hotel. It extends over several blocks up to the Cours Belsunce, where two immense Vs of concrete provide the support for a tower block. This has no visible name; the only sign of any kind, rather surprisingly, is for the Chez Simon kosher butcher in the covered market below. An illuminated neon cow's head can be seen by the entrance.

In so far as a Jewish quarter exists in Marseilles at all, it can be reached from the Place Charles de Gaulle, opposite the Bourse on the Canabière, where a lovely eighteenth-century Venetian merry-go-round with seats like stylized gondolas can be seen during the holidays. Behind is the Rue Paradis, which soon starts climbing and eventually reaches the Israeli Consulate-General, guarded by a solitary French policeman. Parallel to it are the prostitute-infested Rue Beauvau, which leads to the opera house, and the Rue Breteuil.

One of the roads which links the Rue Paradis and the Rue Breteuil is the Rue Dragon, and it was there that I spoke to Monsieur Amsellem, the owner of the Librairie Kodesh, who took a few minutes off from checking *mezuzah* texts to tell me his personal story. An elderly, faintly melancholy man with a mischievous smile and straggly white beard, he looked back on hard times. In Algeria he had owned three businesses selling cloth and provisions for the French settlers. 'When I arrived here I had to live in a single hotel room with three children. I could only earn a tenth – no, I mustn't exaggerate, a *fifth* – of what I used to pay the lorry drivers back in Algeria. Most of the family went to Israel, but I got a bit delayed – and now I've been delayed here for almost thirty years! I had only planned to come for a month or so, but the news from Algeria was so bad I decided to stay on.'

This is a typical story. Marseilles, like Glasgow, was for many years the second city of a great empire. But there was also a crucial difference. Glasgow is nowhere near Aden, India and Nigeria, but Marseilles is just across the Mediterranean from the French North African colonies. When they gained their independence in the late 1950s and early 1960s, most of the Jews decided to leave. At the end of the savage Algerian War (1962), in particular, well over 100,000 Jews came to take up residence in France. After Paris, the most popular destination was Marseilles, although there were smaller influxes into the towns all along the Riviera from Toulon to Nice.

Monsieur Ansellem managed to find work first as a salesman for a Jewish company (which respected his desire not to work on the Sabbath or festivals), then for one of the network of local Jewish charities, and had finally opened his bookshop two or three years before. I asked about his initial impressions of Marseilles. 'The whole place was a desert for Jews! There was no kosher food available, the synagogue round the corner was empty and there were only a few Ashkenazis left. And everything was so black! People like me were used to the bright sunshine of Oran, so the first thing we wanted to do in Marseilles was to clean up the places we lived in and let in the light!' (Even today *specialités Oranaises* remain a major attraction in the Jewish shops and street markets of France.)

Close to the Librairie Kodesh in the Impasse Dragon is the Edmond Fleg community and resource centre, whose top floor is taken up by Radio JM, the local Jewish radio station. On the air 24 hours a day, the Radio both provides support for the State of Israel and defends the interests of the Jewish community. One possible threat comes from Monsieur Le Pen and his extreme right-wing Front National, but nobody I spoke to in Marseilles seemed particularly anxious.

Monsieur Yama, the President of Radio JM, had illuminating things to say about the Jews of Marseilles today. The old community from before the War, he told me, had been made up largely of immigrants from Greece, Turkey and the Comtat. When French North Africa became independent, the Moroccan Jews mainly went to Israel, but the Tunisians and Algerians, who were largely French-speaking and French-educated, had come to France. Furthermore, the Algerian Jews had a right to the full range of allowances and social security payments, since most of them had been granted French citizenship in 1870. (The decree was far from universally welcomed: at the time of the Dreyfus Affair, for example, the antisemitic Comtesse Sibylle Martel de Janville, who worked as a cartoonist under the name of Bob, produced a repulsive print which depicts the Algerian Jews as locusts invading *la belle France*.)

But why, I wanted to know, had these Jews chosen France instead of Israel? Monsieur Yama suggested two reasons. There were fed up with the problems of living among Arabs and they believed in the great republican traditions of France, 'the land of the Rights of Man'. There is a good deal of irony in the first explanation since Marseilles, of course, is a city notorious for the racial tensions caused by its large Arab minority – tensions which have led many people to embrace the racist inanities of the Front National. (There were even a certain number of Jewish supporters, until Le Pen made his infamous remark about the Holocaust being just a 'detail' in the Second World War. Other members of his party have followed up with a series of grossly offensive 'jokes' aimed at Jewish politicians.)

There is also a certain irony in the fact that the Jews of Algeria looked to France, rather than Israel, as 'a light unto the nations'. France, of course, *does* have great republican traditions, it *is* the land of the Rights of Man where Jews received full civil rights in 1791. But what, I asked Monsieur Yama, about the persecution and antisemitic legislation of the collaborationist government in Vichy? 'The North African Jews,' he replied, 'didn't live through Vichy. They were largely untouched by Nazi persecution, at least until the very end of the War.'

The post-war period marked the beginning of a new chapter for the surviving Jews of Marseilles and the many newcomers to the city, but the Jewish presence in Provence stretches back through many centuries. Marseilles is the oldest city in France, and there is a good deal of evidence that they were already playing a significant role, for example in the trade between Provence and the Middle East, as early as the sixth century. The city was also visited by Benjamin of Tudela, the famous mediaeval Jewish traveller, in the twelfth century. The career of a particular major moneylender called Bondavid has been reconstructed in detail from a lawsuit of 1317; far from being simply despised as a 'Shylock', he was widely admired for his generosity, charity and necessary role in the local economy. When he came to trial, a string of witnesses appeared in court to sing his praises.

When Provence was incorporated into the Kingdom of France in 1481, the Provençal Jews obviously became French – until they were expelled in 1501. (The rest of French Jewry had already been expelled in 1394.) Many then took refuge in the Comtat Venaissin, the area around Avignon (roughly equivalent to the modern *département* of the Vaucluse), which formed a separate papal state from 1274 to 1791. Although the Jews were confined to *carrières* or ghettos, they were subject to fewer restrictions than in many other parts of Europe and came to play an important role in both finance and commerce.

The history of the Comtat includes the extraordinary period when there were rival Popes in Rome and Avignon; but what brings Comtat Jewish history to life today are the marvellous eighteenth-century synagogues which survive in Carpentras and Cavaillon. (It was also in Carpentras that Jewish graves were desecrated in 1990, but the response to this ghastly incident was a huge procession in Paris and a spontaneous outburst of solidarity and sympathy from a large proportion of the French public.)

At Cavaillon, for example, the elegant panelling and delicate pastel shades – yellows, peaches and pale blue – create the effect of a salon. Thin white Corinthian columns support a balcony with an elaborate pulpit surmounted by a baldequin. A Chair of Elijah is supported in a corner high above the floor on a special little platform decorated with blue wave motifs. Fine ironwork embellishes the exterior gateway, the staircase up to the balcony, the rail of the balcony and a sort of fender which protects the Ark. The Ark itself

View towards the balcony and remarkable pulpit in the Cavaillon synagogue (Ancient Art and Architecture/Ronald Sheridan)

is like a grand doorway, with details picked out in gold on white, with gilded columns on each side, a overhanging canopy above and a brightly coloured stucco decoration of an overflowing basket of fruit at the very top. There are no longer any Jews in Cavaillon (although there is a small community in Avignon), yet this splendid synagogue is undoubtedly one of the great Jewish monuments of France.

A similar view of the sister synagogue in Carpentras, where there has been a Jewish presence since the fourteenth century. Building started in 1741, but was long delayed by the local bishop's claim that the dimensions and high walls would give offence to Christians. The synagogue was taken over as a meeting hall by the Revolutionaries in 1793, repossessed in 1800 and is now a Historic Monument, restored to its eighteenth-century glory (Ancient Art and Architecture/Ronald Sheridan)

The Comtat became part of France in 1791, the same year as the Emancipation decree. Many Jews naturally took up residence in Marseilles, the major city in the area. Yet we are talking about a comparatively small community. In the nineteenth century, despite talk of a minor 'golden age' during Napoleon III's Second Empire (1852–70), there were never more than 3,000 Jews in the city. Only with the collapse of the Ottoman Empire at the end of the First World War did large numbers of Jews, from former Ottoman territories (Turkey and the Balkans), move to Marseilles.

It was in the nineteenth century, however, that the central secular and religious organs of local Jewry – the Consistoire and the Grand Temple (or main synagogue) – were established on the Rue Breteuil. Indeed, when the synagogue was built in 1864, its façade incorporated two porches, one of them labelled Concierge and the other Consistoire. The rabbinic team, about 60 in all, have their offices on the floor above.

Monsieur Rolland Draï, the Director of the Consistoire, explained how the system works. The hierarchy of consistories (very loosely modelled on the Catholic Church) was established by Napoleon in 1806 to represent the secular interests of French Jewry. Members are elected every six years and were originally required to be men of substance, a tradition which has inevitably continued – on the governing board of the Paris Consistory, for example, it is only very recently (for the first time in over a century) that the name Rothschild ceased to appear.

The Ministère des Cultes (or Ministry of Religion) has direct contact with the Central Consistory and Chief Rabbi at the top of the tree, so orders can be passed down easily. The aim was both efficiency and control. In exchange for certain rights, French Jews were in effect incorporated into the French state. (Rabbis were required, for example, to preach sermons praising Napoleon and his family and encouraging young men to enlist.) The traditional system of virtually independent individual rabbis was considered inappropriate in a modern state administered by a centralized bureaucracy.

Today, the consistories deal with education, finances and PR and are responsible for the Jewish sections of municipal cemeteries and the provision of kosher meat. It is they who make contracts with the suppliers – there are currently no abattoirs in or near Marseilles, since it is not a cattle-raising area – and the butchers pay a commission on every kilo they buy up. At the Leon and Marco butcher on the Rue d'Aubagne, for example, a series of six-monthly certificates signed by the Chief Rabbi of Marseilles, each a different colour from the last, hang suspended from the wall, although someone had rather incongruously put a baby's dummy on the top.

Among more obvious functions, the Marseilles rabbinate has set up a 'Jewish European Marriage Centre', where the young, the widowed and the divorced are provided with advice 'discreet, free and personalized' about how to establish a Jewish household. It is safe to assume that such an organization is a reaction to a fair amount of intermarriage and religious laxity, so I asked Monsieur Draï about the current scene.

There were about 2,000 children in Jewish schools in the city, he replied, but only about a quarter of the community was seriously observant. He spelled this out with an elaborate classification system: together, *les Juifs de tous les jours* and *les Juifs de shabbat* made up his 25 per cent, but there were also many *Juifs des fêtes* (or major festivals) and *Juifs de kippour*. His final category – *les Juifs de shofar* – only spent about an hour in the synagogue each year!

When Napoleon created the consistories, there were a mere 440 Jews in the city. By 1864, when the main synagogue was erected, it was designed to hold 1,500 people. The influence of Arab and Byzantine architecture was remarked on at the time, but today it seems very obviously nineteenth-century, an elegant monument to a complacent bourgeois era. The façade is impressive, with a dominant fanlight window and clock, and steps leading up to the main wooden double door, which is surrounded by a stone arch with elaborately carved columns on either side. Wings link up with the porches to form a charming courtyard. The vestibule contains a list of donors, who were almost exclusively Ashkenazi; today, of course, sheer pressure of numbers demands the use of Sephardi ritual. The current Chief Rabbi, a Sephardi by birth, served for many years as Grand Rabbin de la Moselle in Metz, Alsace, where there has been a large Ashkenazi community since before the Revolution. He has now reverted to the Sephardi traditions he grew up with.

The interior is also compelling. There is an organ in the baroque style above the door, but one's eye is at once drawn to the Ark in white marble set back up six steps in a domed niche with a sky-blue ceiling. Double columns support an elaborate white stone arch with gold lettering around the Ark. Indeed, white is the dominant colour of the synagogue, until it is replaced by a yellowish brown for the

The Consistoire porch attached to Marseilles's main synagogue on the rue Breteuil (Joelle Sintes)

upper levels and ceiling, and arches are the dominant motif. Huge arches above plain wooden barriers create the women's galleries; above, a number of religious sayings adorn the walls in Hebrew and French; and above them are a series of far smaller arches on an upper floor used for a Talmud Torah. They are echoed in the simply decorated stained-glass windows above the Ark. Mediterranean light floods in from all sides, and the overall effect is grand, airy and faintly impersonal.

There is also a side door to the synagogue, which leads down to a courtyard close to the Centre Fleg which contains no fewer than three more synagogues. The Chalom Rav, low and whitewashed, links the adjacent house with the two others, the Ozer Dalim and the replacement Temple Ashkenazi, which together seem to form a building rather like a squat romanesque church. On 24 January 1944, the terrible day when Jews were rounded up in the main synagogue (an event commemorated in a plaque on the Consistoire porch), a certain number managed to escape through the back entrance.

There were perhaps 15,000 Jews in Marseilles at the beginning of the Second World War and something like 12,000 at the end, yet these figures are deceptive. After the Fall of France in 1940, Marseilles formed part of the so-called Zone Libre or Free Zone. It was, therefore, a natural refuge for Jews and others fleeing Nazi oppression. In 1942, there were probably as many as 40,000 Jews in the city; most of the survivors come from the new arrivals rather than the old community.

France was divided into two parts for much of the war. Yet when the Allies reached Algeria and were obviously planning to invade Provence, Hitler decided to take over the Zone Libre and defend the Mediterranean coastline. The Germans moved into Marseilles on 12 November 1942 and made their headquarters at 425 Rue Paradis, in a building which has now been replaced by a row of shops just opposite the present Israeli Consulate-General. Almost at once, there was talk about Marseilles being 'a nest of international bandits' or 'the cancer of Europe'; the new authorities thought the time had now come 'to clean all the undesirables out of the old districts'. What happened next has left scars ever since, although the details remain controversial. I was lucky enough to see a temporary exhibition in the Musée du Vieux Marseille, which normally houses in a beautiful sixteenth-century mansion a charming permanent collection of objects dealing with fishing, Christmas crèches, the great plague of 1720 and the role of the city in the manufacture of playing cards. Yet the building was one of the very few which survived the destruction of the Vieux Port; nowhere could be better suited to an exhibition of wartime German photographs.

Long before *The French Connection* and similar films established the stereotyped (and very unfair) image of Marseilles as 'sleeze city' and 'the drugs capital of Europe', the famous trilogy of films by Marcel Pagnol – *Marius* (1931), *Fanny* (1932) and *César* – presented an equally one-sided picture, drenched in local colour, of the denizens of the Vieux Port. Down-on-their-luck but plucky, resilient and resourceful, the café owners, sailors and their sweethearts provide the classic image of 1930s' Marseilles.

The world of Pagnol, no doubt, never really existed, but his films have a real poignancy now because the whole locale was utterly destroyed. Once the Germans had decided to blow up the Vieux Port, French police started rounding up people on 22 January 1943; out of the total 2,000, the majority were Jewish refugees from Eastern Europe. As the cries of the Levi family being led away echoed through the streets, German soldiers surrounded the port area. At six o'clock in the morning on 24 January 1943, radios woke up the 25,000 residents with instructions to collect up their belongings and evacuate their homes. Hand carts were bought up at exorbitant prices, furniture thrown from windows by desperate old men lay in shattered heaps on the pavements, and people of all ages were forced to assemble on the Quai Maréchal Pétain. As they trundled by with their little cartfuls of worldly goods, the rest of the town looked the other way or rushed to join cinema queues.

The densely packed port area was now deserted, except for a few pillagers with false papers; pipes, food and anything else of value were stripped out; and French police were posted outside to stop anyone returning to their homes. It was now time for the next stage. Explosives were placed on 1 February and for sixteen days they went off, destroying 1,500 buildings and leaving rubble over fourteen hectares of land. Having destroyed the heart of Marseilles, the Germans had to justify their savagery by a search for the 'guilty'. Most of the real resistance, naturally, managed to escape, so adolescents were arbitrarily accused of sabotage and deported.

What was the rationale for this terrible atrocity? The Germans clearly hoped to root out hidden arms caches and black marketeers; they were taking revenge for a few isolated attacks on their soldiers; perhaps they feared the sheer anti-authoritarian cussedness of the Marseillais and wanted to destroy the warren of alleys which would have been perfect for street fighting in the event of an Allied landing. Furthermore, the clearance of the Vieux Port was something that had been actively discussed the year before by French town planners. This is either a remarkable coincidence or evidence that occupiers and collaborators were hand in glove in an attempt to rid the city of 'undesirables' and share the proceeds of an ambitious redevelopment scheme. The episode, in other words, was *not* inspired by solely antisemitic motives, nor were Jews the only people to suffer: one of the most poignant pictures in the exhibition I saw showed two Senegalese soldiers with a dog, cut off from Africa, looking vaguely in different directions and totally bewildered. Yet the Vieux Port *was* a very Jewish area and many of the Jews certainly ended up in concentration camps.

While the Germans occupied one section of southern France in November 1942, the Italians took over most of the Riviera. The French had not been slack in rounding up Jews; but then, suddenly, most arrests stopped. Those who were arrested were transferred to safe houses in the village of Saint Martin, where communal facilities included a synagogue and a cantor from Antwerp, or even accommodated in luxury hotels! Both the Germans and the authorities of Vichy France were livid, but the Italians were determined to behave humanely and soon devised a range of ingenious stratagems. For example, an official called Lospinoso revealed a great talent for never turning up to a meeting with the Germans when plans to co-ordinate deportation were on the agenda! Others claimed that it was their job to determine the fate of all foreign Jews (although only a small minority were Italian citizens). This put the French in an impossible position: if they decided to arrest the French Jews anyway, it would mean that foreign Jews on French soil were receiving better treatment than French citizens. An even more ambitious project involved shipping 30,000 Jews across the Mediterranean to Free French territory in North Africa.

This plan, tragically, came to nothing as the Italians made peace with the Allies in the autumn of 1943 and withdrew from France. For a brief period they retained control of a small area around Nice and allowed Jews sheltering there to follow their army back to Italy. Others reached safety in Switzerland or among the *maquis*. It was not until 9 September that the Germans finally entered Nice and conducted an unbelievably savage manhunt. Although considerable numbers were trapped, the ten-month Italian occupation had undoubtedly saved lives – perhaps as many as 15,000. One was the eight-year-old Serge Klarsfeld, France's most famous post-war Nazi-hunter, whose father was led away without revealing where the rest of the family was hiding. The whole episode forms a startling contrast with what was happening simultaneously in Marseilles.

At the end of the war, things could only get better. The razed section of the city was cleared and, like a strange omen, ruins of one of the oldest known Greek temples were found beneath the ruins of the

Vieux Port. It was there, 25 centuries before, that the city had been founded!

And here we reach one of the strangest and most stirring aspects of French Jewish life. The roads which make up the *quartier Juif* in Paris were completely cleared out by the Germans and their French collaborators during the War and still bear plaques attesting to individual atrocities. The Vieux Port was physically destroyed by the Germans, partly, it seems, for the benefit of their French friends. And yet, not twenty years later, a completely fresh wave of Jewish immigrants moved into the very same districts, sometimes into the very same streets and houses. Out of the ashes of the past, something new and inspiring has been born.

Astonishingly, Marseilles now contains the third largest Jewish community in Western Europe, after Paris and London. And if one wants a specific symbol of today's community, one could do far worse than the little synagogue in the Rue Saint Férreol. The street itself is an elegant pedestrian precinct off the Canabière, at the end of which stands the great nineteenth-century mass of the Préfecture. Posh shops reveal the affluence of post-war Marseilles. At number 73 is a grand jewellers called Morabito, dating from 1880 and with a lovely façade created from a cream awning above, great sweeping curves of cream glass which open to reveal the stock and a thick gold border below following the line of windows. Yet behind this façade are flats, the Association of French Dog Owners and a synagogue for the strictly observant, the Neve Itzhak.

Like the Beth-Chalom around the corner, this synagogue is about thirty years old and largely faced in dark brown wood. The *bimah* is in the centre of the room, with columns supporting the women's gallery at the back and an unexpected staircase leading down to a room for aperitifs. The Ark is set back on what looks like a slightly raised stage, which seems to be decorated in white marble; the curtain has a beautiful *menorah* design in deep purple. Doors on either side lead to offices and a *sukkah*.

When I passed by one evening, prayers had just finished. The rabbi was smart, urbane and spoke perfect French. The congregation, on the other hand, were Moroccans, wearing hats rather than *kippot*, working-class and at least middle-aged; the language they were using was presumably a form of Judeo-Arabic. And there they all were, on an ordinary weekday evening, emerging from their little synagogue hidden away among shops, offices and apartments. The individual units of Marseilles Jewry may be small, the perches they have created for themselves may still seem precarious; yet together they form something miraculous.

10

Antwerp

THERE CAN BE few railway stations more impressive than the Antwerp Centraal. From a distance, with the great metal arches of the deep red engine shed silhouetted against the night sky, it could almost be a mosque on the Istanbul skyline. The main hall below, at the bottom of a monumental staircase, is even more imposing. Naïve tourists, apparently, sometimes think they have reached the cathedral. It is easy to see why. One's eye is

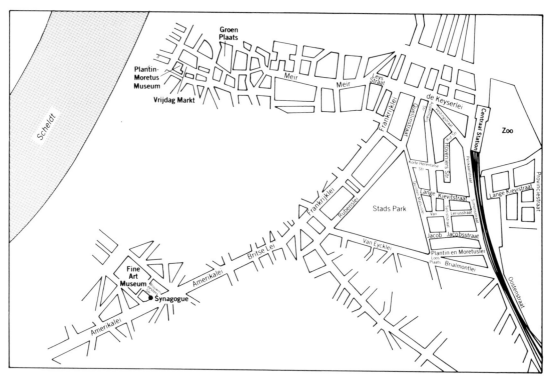

drawn irresistibly upwards past the classical columns, inset galleries and huge fanlight windows to the immense dome and tiny skylight at the top. One goes in to buy tickets or a sandwich and immediately feels overawed, as if in a religious edifice, a grandiose temple to some strange cult.

Yet it is somehow appropriate for Antwerp to have a station which looks like a Temple of Transport or a Temple to Free Trade. The city has long been one of the crossroads of Europe and, like Marseilles, one of the world's great ports. When the River Scheldt, which flows through Dutch territory into the city, was closed in the seventeenth century, Antwerp's trade was strangled to benefit Amsterdam. This continued until 1862, when an agreement with the Dutch allowed shipping to pass freely down the river once again – an event commemorated in the striking Scheldt Monument near the Fine Art Museum.

Antwerp has flourished ever since. Although the huge docks have now moved out of the city centre, it is only a few years ago that the riverside quays were the scene of frenzied loading and unloading, and fathers reunited with their families after a year in the Belgian Congo (now Zaire). A Belgian friend of mine still remembers how her grandfather in marine insurance would stand with a telescope at the top-floor window of his office (now a department store) on Meir so he could note down the names and merchandise of ships coming in from all over the world. Yet if Antwerp was the end of many long journeys, it was also one of the stopping-off points used by Jews *en route* from Eastern Europe to America. Many spent their one and only night on Belgian soil by the quay in what is now the Queens restaurant. Others took a look at the opportunities and decided to stay.

Jews have never been very prominent in the activities of Antwerp port, yet the Scheldt has an unusual connection with the community. Dutch territory is only a few miles up-river and Antwerp's Jewish cemetery is located in the first village over the border, Putte (or 'grave'). This is because Belgian graves are remade every 25 years while Jewish burials have to be for all time.

Most tourists arriving at the Centraal station are drawn at once to the famous sights of the old town: Rubens's House, the cathedral, the gabled guild houses on the triangular Grote Markt, the Steen Castle (now a maritime museum) and Butchers' Guildhall by the river.

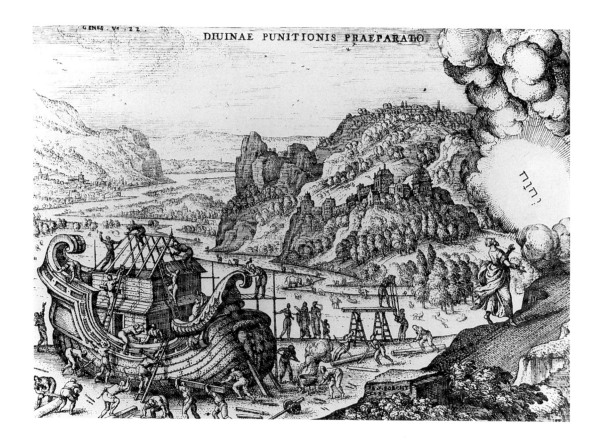

GENES. VI. 22.

DIUINAE PUNITIONIS PRAEPARATO

יהוה

Antwerp's crucial importance as a centre of early printing is made vividly clear at the Plantin-Moretus Museum. Along with his celebrated Polyglot Bible, Plantin also printed Barrefelt's allegorical *Imagines et Figurae Bibliorum* (1582-4), from which this engraving of Noah's Ark is taken

Only the superb Plantin-Moretus Museum has any Jewish link at all. Antwerp was a major centre of early printing, so among the wonders on display are the first known illustrations of the potato, explorers' initial impressions of the Congo, sixteenth-century proofreaders' pages and pioneering works of modern geography. There is also the celebrated Plantin Polyglot Bible (1569–73), with parallel texts in Greek, Latin, Aramaic and Hebrew.

Anyone who wants to explore today's Jewish quarter must resist the magnetic pull of these attractions, and turn instead to the area just around the station. Many of the shops in the arcade under the railway line are cheap jewellers run by recently arrived and not very observant Russian Jews. More interesting, though, are the areas on both sides of the tracks. Just to the right (or East) of the train as it slides into the station, one can catch a brief glimpse of the bulbous domes and *menorah* designs in the windows of the main synagogue on Oostendstraat. Nearby is the Romi Goldmuntz Centre, a kosher butcher and Jewish bookseller on Lange Kievitstraat, which leads from the railway line up to Provinciestraat. This is the site of the Kleinblatt bakery, which stands like a lonely outpost where the eastern limit of the Jewish quarter touches on the Moroccan and Turkish district. Opposite is the Boutique-Zohor selling videos and

Window display in a shop on Pelikaanstraat selling every conceivable form of Judaica; the railway line to the Centraal station is reflected at the top (The Author)

Arab and Indian clothes; nearby, when I was there, a Turkish family was in the process of piling most of their possessions into and on to a Volkswagen minibus for their annual six-week trip back home.

The main Jewish area, however, is on the other side of the railway line. The pelican is a symbol of Antwerp and of Catholic piety, since she was believed in the Middle Ages to feed her children with her own blood, but Pelikaanstraat (and its continuation Simonstraat) is one of the most Jewish streets in Antwerp. Within a few blocks are the town's small Jewish newspaper, the American-style kosher restaurant, another second-hand bookshop and a shop with an extraordinary window display featuring a record of *The Rabbis Sing* and a video of *Eilat, the Red Sea Adventure*, Charles and Diana wedding stamps, old chest watches, a book of barmitzvah speeches, *Hebrew is Easy* and *The Ethics of the Fathers*, as well as a sign assuring customers that 'All foreign currency is accepted'.

Behind Pelikaanstraat is a series of streets leading to the lovely triangular and landscaped Stadspark, which is often full of groups of young Jewish children playing among the war memorials or fathers walking with their sons; the kosher Pizza Park straddles two of the roads which meet at one of its angles. The Lubavitch synagogue and most of the small Hasidic synagogues can be found in this area, along with butchers, bakers, poulterers and *pâtisseries*. On Terliststraat, the Sephardi rabbi lives just next to the central offices of the rabbinate and the Benjamin dry cleaner. On Lange Kievitstraat, the most Jewish street of all, one finds Hoffy's Snack Bar, the Jacob, Kosher King and Moszkowitz as well as a shop offering Zuivelprodukten. On the continuation of the same road, I stopped three women with pushchairs on the scrubland just outside the Seletsky bookshop. They were all from Israel, they told me, and had fallen in love with Antwerpers. But although they stressed that they were fully Orthodox, they were also keen to distinguish themselves from the members of Yiddish-speaking ultra-Orthodox groups whose women wore wigs and received little education. Most men earned so much money – mainly in the diamond trade, a few in the shops serving the community – that wives had no need to work.

Since the merchandise is easily portable and Jews have often been barred from the liberal and other professions, diamond trading has attracted Jewish talent since the Middle Ages. There have been diamond cutters in Antwerp at least since 1485, it became established as the diamond capital of the world in the sixteenth century, and the seventeenth century (until the sources in India began to dry up) was the true golden age. The first major influx of Jews into Antwerp, as into so many other places, came in the aftermath of the Expulsion from Spain in 1492. By the sixteenth century, when the diamond trade was largely in the hands of Italians and Portuguese, a sprinkling of Portuguese Jews were tolerated because of the volume of business they brought in. One of them, a man called Diego Duarte, was involved in a long but unsuccessful struggle to prevent the creation of a diamond guild, since the guilds were strongly Catholic in flavour, with patron saints, an annual mass and so on.

Such Jewish traders set the pattern for the future, but the numbers involved were small. It was only because of the flight westwards of many Jews in response to the pogroms of 1881 that Antwerp became a major Jewish centre. The numbers were around 8,000 at the turn of the century, and their presence in the diamond industry has become ever more evident. Six or seven hundred Jews were involved in the creation of the Beurs von Diamanthandel in 1904 and four-fifths of the community was working in diamonds by 1940. At this stage, there were as many as 50,000 Jews in Antwerp, perhaps a fifth of the population, although the overwhelming majority were refugees and not Belgian citizens. Some survived the War in hiding and others have immigrated since, attracted by both the particular religious climate and the diamond industry. Most are of Polish background and so either Orthodox or ultra-Orthodox.

Mr Friedman of Juwelen Ideal is just one of them. He sits in his shop surrounded by so many mirrors with silvered and gilded stripes that it was hard to find him among the reflections. Discussing Jewish life in Antwerp, he launched into a vivid display of salesmanship and comic banter. 'Don't ask me! I don't know anything about it! It's *him* who knows all about it!' he exclaimed, pointing to my guide from the tourist office.

'Don't listen!' the guide snapped back. 'He's just trying to flatter me because he knows my wife's birthday is coming up!'

'I've no idea when your wife's birthday is, but one thing's for sure – *every* wife has a birthday once a year!'

He continued with an unrepeatable joke about Jesus guaranteed to offend the pious Catholics of Antwerp and then described the man who wanted to buy some herring. There was a whole row of shops, each with a sign in the window offering a better bargain than the one before – 40 Francs a kilo, 35, 30 . . . Finally the man discovers a shop where herring is only five Francs a kilo, so he goes in and orders some. 'Ah, we don't sell herring here!' the shopkeeper tells him. 'I only put that sign up to ruin the competition!' The story seemed only too appropriate, since Mr Friedman's shop is just one of a series of competing jewellers which line both sides of Vestingstraat and the whole area around the diamond bourses. Even the nearest Métro stop is called Diamant – Centraal Station.

His father had been a small-scale dealer in rough diamonds back in Poland. Like many of the Jews in Antwerp, he is part of one of the town's 30 separate communities originating in different Polish towns; many still consult their rabbinical leaders in Israel or the United States about all major life decisions. Those with long-standing family connections with diamonds are often directed towards Antwerp.

The whole story of Antwerp, diamonds and Jews is set out in detail at the Provincial Diamond Museum in Lange Herentalse Straat. The crucial importance of diamonds in drilling for oil and in just about every industry from food to electronics is strongly stressed, together with the central role of Antwerp. It can be no coincidence that two of today's major diamond-exporting countries, along with Australia and Siberia, are Zaire, a former Belgian colony, and South Africa, which more or less shares a language with the Dutch-/Flemish-speaking section of Belgium. On Pelikaanstraat, a map of Africa is picked out in red neon on the Beurs von Diamanthandel next to the large boarded-up office of Frohman Frères.

About four-fifths of world trade is now controlled by de Beers, who try to stabilize the market through the Central Selling Organization in London. The gems are sold off ten times a year to 150 sightholders, a third of them from Antwerp, and they are then sealed up and dispatched to buyers by the Diamond High Council. This is also the body which grades diamonds according to the '4 C's' criteria – carats, colour, clarity and cut – and certifies them accordingly; over 60,000 passed through their hands in 1987. This makes up about half the world's rough diamonds and 70 per cent of cut. It also represents one sixth of Belgium's total exports, with about 35,000 Antwerpers working in the trade.

One can catch a glimpse of the fascinating process which turns rough diamonds into jewels at Diamond Land on Appelmans Straat or one of the smaller diamond factories nearby. After a fierce security check, I descended into a sort of cellar lit by equally fierce artificial light where the stones are loosened with a mixture of diamond dust and olive oil and sawn up, over several days, with bronze blades. Two gems mounted on sticks are used to 'girdle' each other, which removes the corner on the square faces to create the first facets. Then they are polished with diamond powder and copper steel on rotating discs which resemble a gramophone and are hung up against the wall like barbells in a gymnasium. The final stage is the one which really turns the stones into jewels, creating the romantically named princess, *marquise* and radiant cuts, tear-shaped *pendeloques* and, most complex

Signing the marriage contract, the Sephardi synagogue in Hoveniersstraat (The Author)

of all, the *brilliants*. One man is employed to put on the first four facets and another brings the total up to 52 – with a 53rd on a large gem to avoid a sharp point.

At least one of these factories is run by Orthodox Jews (and is not easy to visit), but the vast majority of the town's diamond *workers* are local Flemings. In diamond *trading*, however, the Jewish contingent is probably as high as 80 or 85 per cent, despite substantial numbers of Zaireans, Indians and Lebanese in the bourses.

All four of Antwerp's diamond bourses (out of twenty in the world) and the Diamond High Council are located in Hoveniersstraat, which has a security guard and a Weinberg Travel at each end as well as a take-away kosher sandwich shop for the office workers and a workshop with the unlikely name of Deep Boiling Charlotte where diamonds are boiled up in vitriol to remove grease and an ingenious system of pipes has been rigged up to remove the noxious smells. A huge new office block is being built by an Armenian Lebanese business called Arslanian Frères, and opposite is Antwerp's only Sephardi synagogue, which caters to a community of about 100 families who have almost all arrived since the War from Germany, England, New York, Spain and, particularly, Israel.

A terrorist attack a few years ago inflicted terrible damage on the building, killed three office workers and wounded a hundred more. By a miraculous coincidence, no Jews were in the synagogue at the time since it happened during the festival of *Simhat Torah* and it had been decided the day before that prayers should be put back half an hour to 9.30. A stark photograph of the synagogue just after the attack is displayed inside, although it has been fully restored and Rabbi Abraham Mugrabi kindly invited me to a very lively wedding of a worldly young man from Israel – the only clean-shaven face among dozens of beards – and a local girl. With all the drinks and general high spirits surrounding the signing of the marriage contract and the entry of the bride, I found it hard to disagree with the rabbi and his son that Jewish Antwerp is a most convivial community.

It is also very religious. The proportion of children who receive a traditional Jewish education is very high. There are some twenty rabbis, 40 synagogues and as many as 700–800 large Hasidic families who, of course, never go to the cinema or watch television and tend to be more than sceptical about the value of any non-commercial contact with the *goyim*. Indeed, their interaction with Belgian life in any real sense is minimal. Many of the people I talked to were agreeable and often amusing, yet they were intensely concerned about the dangers of intermarriage – when a whole body of tradition handed down the generations is lost forever. This desire for continuity is expressed visibly in both dress and behaviour. I happened to be in Antwerp on Friday 14 July, 1989, when the television news reports were full of the elephants, performers and general razzamatazz of the French Revolution Bicentennial processions in Paris – at least symbolically, the 200th birthday party for The Modern World. Yet on the streets of Antwerp, at dusk, the rituals of Jewish life unchanged for centuries were continuing. Suddenly one could see everywhere little boys with side-locks, their fathers, elders with the huge cake-shaped *streimel* fur hats, hastening to the synagogues and then back home for the Shabbat meal after the services – and, just as suddenly, the streets were left empty again for the young lovers.

Most Jewish communities in Europe contain strong traditionalist elements, but nowhere else are they so dominant. Few other people have changed less in 200 years, and in few other places are the rituals and spirit of the Polish ghettos kept so alive. A woman who works in a Peace Centre outside Antwerp put it like this: 'The Jewish people of Antwerp live in the centre and don't go out of the centre. It's a little bit like a ghetto. It's different from Brussels, it's different from Paris and I think it's different from London too. In fact, it's unique – I think someone like Chaim Potok could write a very good book about it.' It was equally obvious that she found the atmosphere slightly oppressive: 'If I want to go to some Jewish festivities, then I go to Brussels.'

There is, indeed, nowhere quite like it. In many European cities where Jewish life is flourishing today, the Jews have clearly acquired some of the habits of the host community. External circumstances and pragmatism play a strong part. Jews live as they wish in Paris, Marseilles and other parts of France largely because the situation became impossible in Algeria. In Prague and in the rest of Eastern Europe, Jews have tended to keep a low profile to avoid persecution; more liberal regimes now allow them to come out into the open. Something important is being reborn, but the level of observance and religious commitment tends to be luke-warm. Antwerp feels quite different. An altogether more intense and uncompromising way of life has been transplanted root and branch across Europe, as an act of conscious choice. A pre-Holocaust world has been defiantly recreated, and even people who are unsympathetic to ultra-Orthodoxy cannot fail to be moved. To that extent, whatever one's feelings about Jewish separatism, Antwerp represents one of the great success stories in contemporary Jewish Europe. And, since the families there have many children, demography poses far less of a threat than elsewhere.

Some of Antwerp's kosher shops and restaurants may have an exclusively Jewish clientele, but many do not. There is an oddly named Delika Shop in the shopping centre off Appelmans Straat, and a whole series of kosher as well as Thai and Indian restaurants in the same street. One building displays photographs of girls of a very un-Belgian glamorousness to lure clients into an up-market hairdresser, but it also contains an art gallery, a kosher snack-bar, the King David restaurant and the Antwerp branch of Weight Watchers. Opposite is the Blue Lagoon, a rare kosher Chinese (or 'Chinees') restaurant run by an extremely enthusiastic woman called Régine Suchowolski. The waiters are Flemish, the cooks Chinese and the only Jews involved are the *patronne* and a representative of the rabbinate. Madame Suchowolski stood among the cheap Oriental splendour of the décor, confided in me about the daughter of a friend who had just dropped by ('She's such a brilliant girl, but she dresses like a hippy!'), and effortlessly demolished the claims of all her rivals: 'I've never been there, but it's just the felafel style and I hear it's not too clean . . . They may be kosher, but we're *more* kosher. Look, if you just want to eat out instead of staying at home, they're fine, but if you want somewhere to take your friends, you've got to come *here*. Even the Chinese delegation who came to buy diamonds would all come for lunch. . . . '

As I was eating, oddly enough, the bride and groom from the day before came in with some friends. The bride was wearing a canary-yellow dress and they said not a word to each other all evening. This gave rise to some instant novelettish speculations on my part, but it also throws up some interesting issues about marriage in Antwerp. Weddings across the Ashkenazi–Sephardi divide are common – the new couple usually take on the ritual and traditions of the bride's family, since they have paid for the wedding. What is also common is for men seeking a partner who has been brought up in a reliably religious and traditional background to come looking in Antwerp.

★

How do Antwerp and its Jews fit into the overall Belgian scene? The country as such did not exist as an independent state until the nineteenth century, yet one of the central figures of European history was born in Ghent. This is the Holy Roman Emperor Charles V (1500–58), who for a while controlled territories all the way from Spain (and the Spanish colonies in America) to the Balkans. One of his most famous remarks was that he spoke Spanish to God, Italian to women, French to men – and German to his horse. Belgium today is equally fragmented linguistically, since it is divided into a small German sector, the utterly cosmopolitan city of Brussels, French-speaking Wallonia and Flemish-speaking Flanders, Flemish being a version of Dutch. The Walloons refuse to learn Flemish, the Flemings refuse to speak French, and much needless conflict ensues. The Jews – Yiddish-speakers from Eastern Europe, Hebrew-, Arabic- and English-speakers from Israel – obviously add a further set of linguistic complexities.

Postcard showing the Bouwmeester synagogue around 1908 (Anne Cowen)

Belgium is so prosperous and civilized a country that it is hard to take very seriously the endless feuding between its two communities, although it may help deflect hostility away from minorities like the Jews. What *is* important is that the Flemings entered what is now Flanders with the German invasions of the seventh century. This means that some of the Jews, arriving in Julius Caesar's baggage train, got there first! It also means that the Nazis were inclined to treat the Flemings, far more than the Walloons, as Aryans and potential allies. In the early stages of the German Occupation, the Jews of Antwerp were treated comparatively well, since the Nazis were keen to keep the diamond trade going. What happened afterwards still plays a part in the continuing conflicts within Belgium. Jacques Brel, the wonderful satirical *chanteur* from the French-speaking sector, made a career out of abusing the Flemish; in his last record, when he was already dying, he returned to the attack, complaining about the endless rain in the largely Jewish coastal resort of Knokke-le-Zoute and accusing the Flemish of being 'nothing more than acrobats': '*Nazis durant les guerres et Catholiques entre elles. Vous oscillez sans cesse du fusil au missel.*' ('Nazis during the wars and Catholics in between, Sometimes with a gun in your hands and sometimes with a missal.')

More serious historians put it far less strongly: although there is no doubt that there were more collaborators among the Flemings than Walloons, there was a great deal of principled resistance to Nazis and help to persecuted Jewish families among all groups in society – from the underground and the communists to Church leaders, King Leopold and his mother. The government-in-exile in London was the only one to declare that any expropriation of Jewish property would have no legal validity. The Jewish community itself was far better organized than elsewhere. The result of all these factors was that 20,000 Belgian Jews survived.

Professor (and rabbi) Malinsky provided more revealing details. A self-confessed 'night owl', he came to collect me at eleven p.m. and gave me a whistlestop tour of Antwerp's largest and most imposing Bouwmeester synagogue. This is now used only on special occasions since it is located in a part of southern Antwerp near the Fine Art museum where there has been little Jewish presence since the war. There is a grand turreted entrance which leads into a late-nineteenth-century interior modelled on the main synagogue in what was then St Petersburg. The marvellous Scrolls of the Law, Malinsky told me, had been kept hidden by non-Jewish Antwerpers throughout the occupation and returned to the synagogue afterwards. A less pleasant story concerned the so-called St Gudele cathedral in Brussels, where a sixteenth-century stained-glass window depicts a scene in 1370 when Jews were burnt at the stake for murder and desecration of the Host in a chapel. Decades of lobbying were needed before the church authorities were persuaded to put up a tiny plaque saying that the details of this horrible story were 'not sure'.

Despite this, most of the Jews in Antwerp seemed to feel they were well treated by their fellow Belgians and accepted for what they were – a hard-working, law-abiding and economically significant element of national life. Some thought it had something to do with the traditional tolerance of ports, but few had any complaints about the government, the municipality or the police. Only a few melancholy elderly men in the second-hand bookshops seemed doubtful: 'Outwardly they smile, but in their hearts . . . Who knows what they really feel about the Jews? If there were another Hitler. . . . '

To get the official view of the city, I spoke to the Burgomeister of Antwerp, a charming white-haired and moustached man who reminded me of a colonel in the British Army. He was refreshingly indiscreet. 'The importance economically of the Jewish community is tremendous. We sometimes regret there is less of a cultural influence. In Brussels, there is a lay Jewish centre and we've often tried to establish something similar here, but it doesn't work, which means there is less cultural participation.'

In religious terms, the Burgomeister stressed, Antwerp is unlike anywhere else in Europe: 'There are only three main ultra-Orthodox centres in the world – New York, Jerusalem and Antwerp. Even in Israel they sometimes have problems with the government, but they never have problems here. I think they feel very much at home here.'

He also spoke about his experiences celebrating marriages before he became mayor: 'There was one kind of marriage we'd see time and time again: American chaps coming from the Bronx to pick up a bride here – and away they'd go! That has been going on for years. They obviously wanted to be sure of finding a partner from a strict religious background, although we had to warn the brides sometimes, mind you: "Are you aware of where you're going now – not to Hollywood, but only to the Bronx?"'

11

PRAGUE

A<small>N IMPORTANT DIFFERENCE</small> between Prague and Vienna is the street-lighting. This may sound trivial, yet it helps give the two cities, for so long great centres of the same Empire, utterly different atmospheres. Vienna is impressive, imposing, even beautiful, but utterly unmysterious. As in a stage set, floodlights direct one's line of vision, and one almost swoons at the marvellous collection of architectural pastiches. Everything is controlled, rational and clear-cut. In Prague, by contrast, churches suddenly loom up in the darkness like giant goblins; their outlines only slowly become clear

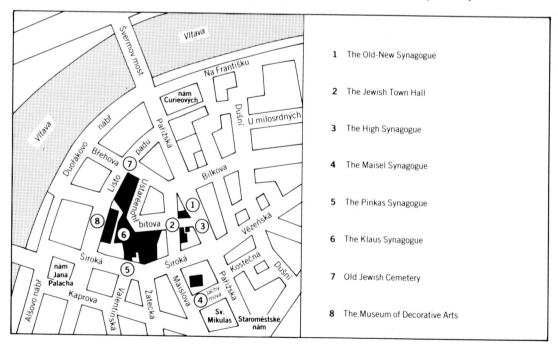

1   The Old-New Synagogue

2   The Jewish Town Hall

3   The High Synagogue

4   The Maisel Synagogue

5   The Pinkas Synagogue

6   The Klaus Synagogue

7   Old Jewish Cemetery

8   The Museum of Decorative Arts

The imposing façade of the Spanish Synagogue, close to the heart of Prague's old Jewish quarter (State Jewish Museum)

as one approaches. Even in the lovely Old Town Square, where all is elegant, pastel-coloured and harmonious by day, the Tyn church is like a spectral presence at night, never quite taking shape. (It also has an intriguing link with Franz Kafka, who once had a study with a strange window, built by a former religious tenant, which opens on to the side altar of the church. His novels chronicle a strange and individual world in which nothing is ever quite what it seems; one of his crucial sources of inspiration was the city of Prague itself.)

The main square also contains the Town Hall, which was partly destroyed by the Germans in 1945. A fragmentary tower has been left as a bleak reminder of Nazi brutality, yet in general Prague's glorious architectural heritage survived the War, and survives today, almost intact. Intact, but still evocative, mysterious. Nothing has been pre-packaged and served up as a tourist attraction. It has just survived. It is this which makes Prague – and particularly the extraordinary ghost ghetto, which is gradually coming back to life – such a wonderful place to explore.

One can start, for example, in Parizska, which sets out from the Old Town Square towards the grim slabs of the Intercontinental Hotel and the bridge beyond. 'Paris Street', very appropriately, is a marvellous example of extravagant, tongue-in-cheek turn-of-the-century elegance. Balconies swoop. Turrets sprout. Faces peer from garlands. Eagles beneath stone canopies on the tops of buildings prepare to soar upwards. Dainty sculptured nymphs without clothes but bearing baskets on their heads turn coyly away. Art nouveau props like ornate fly swatters are attached to the walls, in a mélange of whites, creams and pale orange. One house is conveniently labelled 1902.

Now Parizska is simply but evocatively lit by a set of low, dim and old-fashioned lamps. Although it is a textbook example of a particular architectural style, no attempts have been make to 'present' it to visitors. It is just one of Prague's many architectural gems people have to discover for themselves. As soon as one leaves the major roads, everything becomes even more mysterious and atmospheric. The main Jewish quarter is on either side of Parizska, which was built as a major residential street – and to give a bit of class to a run-down area: a conscious act of urban planning split the old ghetto in two.

It is something to marvel at that Prague's old Jewish quarter has survived at all. Prayers are still heard in the Old-New Synagogue after 700 years. Most of the buildings and artefacts, for a most sinister and grotesque reason, survived the years of Nazi occupation. The

Communist regime was at best indifferent and often hostile, attacking members of the very small community first as 'cosmopolitans' and then as 'Zionists'. Yet today, despite all the odds, the community is being reborn.

Two of Prague's minor synagogues offer unexpected delights. One, the Spanish Synagogue, is just to the east of Parizska on Dusni Street. It is now used as a storeroom for the State Jewish Museum, and only the Moorish façade is visible; the church of the Holy Spirit, just across a narrow road, towers above it. Yet the sheer solidity of the building is impressive. Built in 1868, it was the latest of the synagogues constructed in the old Jewish quarter, not very long after the district – known as Josefov – was incorporated into the city (1850). It is built of light-brown stone with two green baubles, surmounted by Stars of David, at the top. The inverted horseshoe-shaped arches and interlocking tracery outside already give an Islamic flavour, but the inaccessible interior is a veritable treasurehouse of Moorish pastiche, with multi-coloured and gilded arabesques set into the vaults of a huge cupola. Perhaps this daring architectural experiment will eventually be open to the public again, when funds allow the museum to reorganize its stock.

The other Moorish-style synagogue is located in Jerusalem Street, fairly near Wenceslas Square in the New Town at the 'top' of Prague. Built in 1905–6, it is a wonderfully cheerful extravaganza in bright primary colours. The front is decorated with red and yellow stripes, and steps lead up to a small portico by the main entrance. The red and brown stone columns support horseshoe arches, which are echoed in a series of stripy column-and-horseshoe windows all over the façade. Above the entrance is another immense horseshoe arch in pale blue, with a Star of David window on an orange background let into it. The overall effect may be slightly absurd, but utterly irresistible, guaranteed to cheer anyone wandering through this part of Prague on a wet winter evening.

The other crucial point is that this is one of the two functioning synagogues in the city, although out of the tourist season there are not always enough Jews around to form a *minyan*. A special commemorative service is held each year for the 600 children who were killed at Auschwitz as they sang the Czech national anthem. The congregation here is of Czech Jews – Jews, that is, from the lands of Bohemia and Moravia, which were once part of the Austrian half of the Austro-Hungarian Empire. Like other Czechs, they have always had a reputation for lukewarm religious commitments; the terrible losses of the War years, ageing congregations and the difficulties of obtaining an education in Judaism have all had their impact; yet it is heartening that the Jubilee is still a functioning synagogue.

The second synagogue still being used is not just a charming building but something close to a masterpiece – and the oldest functioning synagogue in Europe. This, of course, is the Old-New Synagogue, where visitors and Jews originally from Slovakia usually provide enough people for prayers four days a week. (Slovakia is the poorer, far more religious, traditionally less industrialized half of Czechoslovakia which was once in the Hungarian part of the Austro-Hungarian Empire.) Even so, numbers are often minimal.

One front of the Old-New faces on to Parizska, the other is down below on Maislova Street. It is here that an extraordinary brick decorative façade attached to the steeply pointed roof emerges from the dirty grey walls. The basic shape is triangular, but a series of slots are cut into the triangle, giving the unforgettable organ-pipes effect. Here, without question, is one of the great Jewish sights of Europe.

It is hardly surprising that the synagogue is a tourist attraction and that the notice asking visitors to cover their heads should so often be ignored. (Women wait in the entrance hall during prayers, since there is no separate gallery for them, although there is a back room used for services in the winter.) As one enters the main hall, the immediate impression comes from the elaborate cage round the *bimah* in the centre. Golden balls top every strut of this cage, lamps extend from it, and a great red banner with jagged edges is also attached. (This was a treasured gift to the Jewish community in 1648, a reward for their help when the Swedes laid siege to the city.) Two huge octagonal columns breaking into gothic ribs support the roof; a fifth 'arm' is used to avoid a vault with any suggestion of a cross. And, all around, dark wooden seats cling to the walls, while lamps emerge from bronze shields above. Slot windows with rounded arches enhance the sense of mediaeval solidity.

Just opposite the Old-New synagogue, at the end of Maislova Street, is a far more frivolous monument to the Jewish presence in Prague. This is a residential building which now houses the offices of the Cedok tourist agency but once belonged to a popular Jewish doctor. Two huge seated stone Greek maidens, of almost Egyptian severity, flank the entrance. Above is a decorative freize with a row of green medallions containing silhouettes of the owl of wisdom, tennis racquets, a coffee pot, a knight's head and a basket of doves. Because his patients wanted to pay homage to a Jewish doctor, however, they also included some rabbinic sages and Stars of David among this mélange of ill-assorted motifs. Like the houses on Parizska, the result is a wonderfully exuberant piece of architectural indulgence.

Maislova Street is the main thoroughfare through the surviving buildings of the old Jewish quarter. Jewish sights include the Golem restaurant and the Maisel synagogue, which dates from the late sixteenth century but was restored in neo-Gothic style, thus acquiring a three-sided tent-shaped porch. (Restoration is now likely to be speeded up in the freer political climate.) Running roughly parallel to Parizska, the street eventually abuts a little square called U Radnice, a sort of annexe to the Old Town Square. On the corner is a mask commemorating Franz Kafka, erected after the 'Velvet Revolution' in 1989 since Kafka was always considered 'decadent' and suspect by the Communist authorities. (In reality, Kafka offers a startlingly accurate prophecy of the atmosphere in a totalitarian society. When an academic conference which attempted to rehabilitate him was held in 1963, it provided a major impetus to the reform movement and the Prague Spring of 1968.)

A central Kafkaesque image, of course, is the sinister castle looming over the city. One gets a sudden glimpse of it by turning off Maislova Street into Siroka Street. This leads to the Pinkas Synagogue and the river, but high above on the opposite bank, the brooding presence of the castle – St Guy's Cathedral surrounded by the sleek faceless barracks built in the age of Maria Theresa – springs into view. It makes a perfect symbol of aloof, enigmatic, inaccessible government, though it became in 1989 the official residence of the very approachable President Havel.

Siroka Street skirts the edge of Prague's famous Jewish cemetery; the Pinkas Synagogue used to form a moving memorial to the Jews who were killed in the Holocaust, since the names of the 77,297 victims from Bohemia and Moravia were all inscribed on the walls. Damp, unfortunately, is said to have destroyed them (not impossible, since the synagogue is situated well below ground level, although it sounds like an excuse for a political decision). In the new political climate, however, the memorial is being recreated, using the services of students in the art college across the cemetery.

The synagogue too, closed to the public in 1968, can again become part of the State Jewish Museum. It was apparently built for a single family and has rather the flavour of a modest country villa, where an orange outer wall leads into a courtyard with a venerable old tree. An inscription inside gives the year of construction – 1535 – and the style is therefore a combination of Gothic and Early Renaissance. The overall impression is lighter than in the Old-New Synagogue, but there is a similarly intricate metal cage surrounding a *bimah* like a well-head in the centre of the room. The ceiling is again made up of Gothic ribs, charmingly picked out in green and gold, which descend to form columns in semi-relief between the upper section of the arched balcony; four decorative rosettes emerge from square frames on the ceiling. A fifteenth- or perhaps even fourteenth-century *mikveh* was discovered behind the synagogue during restoration.

Many important areas of Jewish history and culture, which were almost taboo during the post-war period of Communist rule, can be examined in exhibitions now that the State Jewish Museum has restored contacts with major museums in Israel and elsewhere. Instead of drawing mainly on its own stock for a single temporary exhibition each year, travelling displays dealing with topics like modern Jewish painters and Simon Wiesenthal should be seen in Prague. Even more exciting will be the opportunity to explore Kafka, Zionist movements and other aspects of the Jewish heritage of the inter-war First Republic. Martin Buber – whose famous *Three Addresses on Judaism* were delivered in Prague – has recently re-appeared in Czech for the first time in decades.

The most important building in the ghetto is the large complex consisting of part of the State Jewish Museum and the Town Hall. The latter, the only surviving such building in the Diaspora, is pink on the outside and contains a marvellous restaurant within. There is dark wooden panelling along the walls, but above the room is decorated in shades of grey, white, cream and light orange. Fruit reliefs picked out in gold emerge from shields on the walls at the point where they reach the ceiling. There are galleries at the back and along one side, and a stage at the front; an interlocking crown and Star of David, of almost calligraphic exuberance, appear above. Twin waiters dash around wearing white and sharp light blue skullcaps flecked with silver dots like party or baseball caps. Every lunchtime, one can get an excellent and very cheap Czech-Jewish three-course meal, and the place is always full of local residents and tourists.

The Town Hall links up with the State Jewish Museum, which incorporates the former High Synagogue. On the roof is the famous clock with a Hebrew face; the hands, of course, move counter-clockwise. The museum, one of the most remarkable in Europe, brings together almost all the surviving Judaica of Bohemia and Moravia. The basis of the collection comes from the first Prague Jewish Museum, which was opened in the Ceremonial Hall in 1906. The Nazis added to it by assembling all the objects they had confiscated, hoping to establish a museum of the defunct Jewish race; it is largely because of this ghastly project that so many wonderful art objects and synagogue textiles can now be examined in the same place.

In terms of immediate propaganda the Nazis failed: far from wanting to gloat at Jewish suffering, the Czechs were moved by their plight. Since the War, new acquisitions have been concentrated on Holocaust material such as drawings and paintings. The result is paradoxical: the Nazis destroyed many traditional Jewish communities in the towns and villages of Czechoslovakia, but they also largely created this remarkable monument to them. It is hard not to feel a burning anger and sorrow as one looks round the museum, yet the beauty of the exhibits is quite exceptional.

The main hall once formed the High Synagogue (1568), probably so-called because of its first-floor location. Some of the main features still remain. Most striking is the elevated Ark with white wooden doors in an elaborate setting of brown stone; capitals and mouldings are picked out in gold while jutting niches on each side support candlesticks. The gold star on top almost touches the ceiling. This is painted in cream with grey moulding and gold rosettes; a huge gold lamp descends from a decorative moulded star in the ceiling. It makes a lovely space for a display of splendid textiles, while retaining the flavour of its original function. Unlike the Jewish Museum in Amsterdam, it does not feel like a synagogue which has been modernized and scrubbed clean to form an antiseptic, generalized environment. The very shabbiness and haphazardness are moving, conveying not the Jewish mission to mankind but the particularity of a few small provincial communities.

Foremost among the items on display are Torah mantles, curtains and draperies. Deep red is the predominant colour, although thick crowns encrusted with jewels emerge in high relief from some of them. There are also some lovely silver Chanukah lamps and Torah

The first-floor High Synagogue, now part of the poignant State Jewish Museum, houses a superb display of religious objects from Bohemia and Moravia (Cedok)

shields decorated with overflowing baskets of flowers, a deer in relief, lions and crowns, and columns embraced by vines. More homely objects like simple folk table settings embroidered with images of candles, food and bread, typically Bohemian glassware decorated in red and elaborate bridal bonnets are on display in the cramped rooms downstairs. The bulk of the Museum's collection is in storage at any one time, but what can be seen gives a vivid picture of pre-war Czech-Jewish life. More modern and rational display techniques – and faster restoration of the other synagogues in the ghetto – should allow future visitors to see a larger sample of the superb collection.

The past is a constant presence in Jewish Prague. The most obvious place is the famous old cemetery, closed in 1787, where so many graves were crammed into a small area that they are as many as twelve

The old Jewish cemetery; in the background are the Memorial Hall, on the left, and the Klaus Synagogue (Cedok)

layers deep. The atmosphere is poignant and hauntingly mysterious, with children taking a perfect opportunity to play hide-and-seek among graves set at every angle, graves half-hidden in the earth, graves lost among the weeds and graves whose tips alone emerge timidly from the soil. The tomb stones are chipped, collapsed or shaggy with centuries of wear, and quite beyond restoration to their original pristine state. In fact, only about 100 or 150 of the eleven or twelve thousand graves are repaired each year.

Since Kafka is buried elsewhere, in the new Jewish cemetery to the west of Prague, the most famous grave belongs to Rabbi Loew (also known as the Maharal). This celebrated sage preached at the Old-New Synagogue, where one can still see his chair, founded an important *yeshiva* and played a key role in the Golden Age of Prague Jewry in the sixteenth century. After his death, petitioners would bring slips of paper with their prayers and throw them into the rabbi's grave. Yet if his achievements were genuine, his role in folklore has proved even more lasting, since legend relates that it was Rabbi Loew who created a golem out of clay. A sort of Jewish Frankenstein, the golem represents the ultimate revenge fantasy for the powerless victims of antisemitism. Utterly vulnerable in real life, they sought satisfaction in a dream of a monster strong enough to defend the community against all its enemies. His remains are said to rest in the attic in the Old-New Synagogue. The Gothic setting and general atmosphere of Prague are perfectly in keeping with this eerie but moving story.

The buildings on either side of the entrance to Prague's old Jewish cemetery are also monuments to earlier times. The Klaus Synagogue, the largest in Prague, was founded by Rabbi Loew himself towards the close of the sixteenth century; its name derives from the Latin word *claustra* or 'cloister' since pupils at the rabbinic school had to live cut off from the world, as in a monastery. The current building dates from 1694 and is notable for its tapering triple-tiered Ark which rises up out of a low marble 'stage' and its charming lunettes and stucco floral decorations on the vault of the cream ceiling. The square *bimah* which once had pride of place in the centre of the hall, as in Prague's other main synagogues, is now missing. It is used today as an exhibition space, with marriage certificates and samples of early printing, for example, used to illustrate the history of Jewish life in Bohemia.

On the other side of the entrance to the cemetery is the Memorial Hall, built in pseudo-Romanesque style in 1907 for the Funeral Bretheren. It later housed the original Jewish Museum. Today, it contains some of the most affecting of all Holocaust images: the children's paintings from Terezín. They are displayed very simply, with just a few strands of barbed wire to evoke the ghetto. Some of the scenes are harrowing representations of everyday life in the barracks: hangings, cramped bunk beds, tightly shut gates, soldiers herding crowds of tiny children away while others look down from a window above. Almost more moving are the utterly normal pictures of forests, butterflies, bouquets, Christmas trees, princesses and dragons, all painted by children destined for deportation to the East.

Terezín itself is both a strange and haunting site of wartime Jewish suffering and a particularly blatant example of a successor regime's attempt to distort the past. It is located not far from Prague and consists largely of a macabre tourist attraction known as the Little Fortress and the barracks, established in the 1780s as a defence against Prussia. The star-shaped fortress was never required to hold back an enemy attack and instead became a prison. Its most famous inmate was Gavrilo Princip, the assassin who sparked off the First World War when he shot Franz Ferdinand.

As you approach Terezín from Prague, there is a turn-off to the right just before one reaches the modern town. The road leads through a cemetery like a vegetable patch, the miniature tombs often marked only with numbers, over the moat and into a tunnel which pierces the thick stone walls. The whole building might have the ghoulish fascination of the Tower of London, if the crimes had been committed in the safely distant past. Yet it was re-opened and used by the Nazis in the 1940s – to hold politicians (the ex-Foreign Minister was shown off to visitors!), officers of the former Czech Army, relatives of those who fled abroad, the 'work-shy', British parachutists and a few genuine criminals. One can visit the cells; a reasonably comfortable bathroom (shown to concerned visitors, although rarely used by the inmates); the assembly point for prisoners setting off to duties in the fields, on the railway tracks or in underground factories; and a scaffold and shooting range in a quiet back yard. All the signs are in German, and the famous slogan used on the concentration camps – *Arbeit macht Frei* ('Work will make you free') – appears above the entrance.

Any site so vividly evocative of Nazi brutality leaves a very unpleasant taste, but there are some almost equally distressing signs of Nazis at leisure. The café near the entrance retains the original dark furniture, modernist lamps and *chambres séparées* where the soldiers came to have fun. The SS cinema with its uncomfortable wooden seats is also unaltered; until recently, visitors were shown an unpalatably one-sided film about Terezín stressing the glorious Russian role in its liberation and the bright Communist future.

There are also several exhibitions on the site of the fortress, one dealing with Soviet suffering in the Second World War and another with safe humanitarian anti-war and anti-Fascist themes. The persistence of Fascism used to be illustrated with images of British skinheads, German neo-Nazis – and Israeli soldiers attacking Palestinians. Such vicious propaganda was only too common in Czechoslovakia, although some members of staff have always tried to get round the official restrictions. Since the rules of the museum required them to purchase works of art dealing with the theme of imprisonment, they often bought high-quality statues of saints or Jesus (renamed 'Prisoner'!) instead of the expected tawdry pieces of Communist propaganda.

Most tasteless of all was the plan to erect a huge – and hugely expensive – sculptural monument depicting six heroes returning from imprisonment. Similar socialist realist 'masterpieces' of quite staggering ugliness were not unusual in Czechoslovakia, but here, in the moving cemetery in front of the fortress or on the mass grave at the back, the effect would have been particularly offensive. The change of regime, fortunately, means that visitors will be spared the sight of the completed work – one suggestion was to ship it off to Cuba!

All of this, however, might be defensible – the Little Fortress *is* a monument to Fascist brutality, however partially the information is presented – but what is truly disgraceful is the treatment of the rest of the garrison town. The comparative figures are revealing. About 250 prisoners were executed in the Little Fortress, although many more were tortured or badly treated. In Terezín proper, however, there is now a population of about 2,500 people living in charmless rows of houses which were once a barracks; from 1941, 140,000 Jews from all over Europe – up to 50,000 at any one time – were crammed and confined in the notorious ghetto. Conditions were so bad that 34,000 died there; another 87,000 were deported to the death camps. A bright and greatly enlarged child's picture of a cat has recently appeared as a huge mural on the former ghetto school, the site of a planned Ghetto Museum. (The cost of this, it is estimated, will probably be no more

than the cost of the huge – and now discarded – heroic monument
I mentioned.) For many decades, however, it was a Police Museum
and there was virtually no acknowledgement of the appalling history
of Terezín itself.

It is a piece of history which remains extraordinarily difficult to
grasp. Within the boundaries of the ghetto there was much stress on
Jewish self-government, since Hitler hoped to score a propaganda
coup by 'giving a town to the Jews'. Intense efforts were made to
keep inmates ignorant of their likely long-term fate – there was
even a family camp attached to Auschwitz where Jews were briefly
kept in almost tolerable conditions so they could send letters back
to Terezín saying that all was well. A Red Cross team produced a
remarkably favourable report after a visit to the ghetto, when shops
were specially stocked up with goods confiscated from deportees,
although some historians believe that they *must* have seen what was
really going on.

Even today, evidence of what happened has to be searched out
from a remote spot tucked away behind the town. Here are the railway
tracks used to deport the inmates, small ceremonial halls for laying
out the Catholic, Protestant and Jewish dead, and the four ovens of
the crematorium used for those who died of disease. Their ashes were
normally dumped in the river, but a symbolic cemetery, tiny columns
marked with Stars of David, has been built as a memorial round a tree
the children of the ghetto planted. There are also a huge stone *menorah*
like a darts-board split in half and a completely austere concrete path
divided up by walls into sections as an alley commemorating the
different nations who died there.

Nothing even begins to convey the realities of life in Terezín. It
is a drab, depressing town where ghastly things happened, but there
are few visible links between present and past. For anyone who, like
myself, goes there to mourn lost family members or relatives they
never met, a visit is more numbing than poignant. We can only hope
that a proper museum will give visitors a deeper understanding of
what life in Terezín was like.

Prosperous and assimilated old Jews deported there from
German-speaking countries sometimes died of shock. And yet,
despite the appalling death-rate and daily humiliations – the Jews
were required to walk on the roads, only the SS along the pavements
– Terezín was not just an 'ante-chamber to Hell'. Concerts were held in
the park at the centre of town. A certain measure of self-government
was a reality, the ghetto issued its own currency (bearing the head of

Moses) and stamps, and there was such an incredible range of cultural, intellectual and educational activities that some survivors felt a kind of nostalgia for it in later years. (There are no similar signs of life in the dull provincial town of the post-war years.) When liberation came, there were 30,000 Jews left; those from Polish or German backgrounds wanted to stay in Terezín rather than return home.

Prague has a magnificent Jewish heritage in terms of buildings, but what sort of political tradition is likely to re-emerge now that Communism has collapsed? In the chapter on Vienna I mentioned how much of Viennese Jewry, particularly the intellectual élite, was of Bohemian origin. The city offered not only the obvious opportunities of an imperial capital but was often regarded as the heart of the German liberal culture which assimilated Jews identified with. Since the Jews of the Empire had finally received complete equality with their fellow citizens in 1867, many were also supporters of the imperial dynasty. Some were the so-called 'Four-Day Jews' who attended synagogue only on the High Holy Days – and the Emperor's birthday!

In Czechoslovakia, unfortunately, the later nineteenth century saw a clash of nationalisms which left the Jews caught in the middle. While the pan-German enthusiasts were openly antisemitic, Czech nationalists tended to distrust Jewish commitment to German liberalism. The assimilationist road became a very ambiguous one, since nobody could be sure whether a separate Czech nation would ever emerge from the Habsburg realm; some Jews took refuge in Zionism. (In Slovakia, where the population was far more rural and intensely Catholic and where there was a far larger Jewish presence, parallel – but far more serious – problems arose. Since the Jews tended to be pro-Hungarian, there was constant and intense conflict with the local nationalists.)

If the 1890s were a most difficult decade for the Jews of Europe – with the Dreyfus Affair in France and an openly antisemitic mayor, Karl Lueger, in Vienna – the Czech lands were no exception. When a nineteen-year-old girl was found murdered in the town of Polna, suspicion immediately fastened on a Jew called Leopold Hilsner. Now Hilsner was undoubtedly a lazy lout, but there was no real evidence against him; two unknown Jewish accomplices and a 'motive' – that he hoped to obtain the blood of a Christian virgin – were invented out of thin air; the court and antisemitic press harped repeatedly on the theme of ritual murder.

This, however, was not the end of the story. The main counter-attack was led by Professor Thomas Masaryk, in scholarly books and articles which not only argued for Hilsner's innocence but turned a sharply sceptical eye on the 'evidence' for other such murders. Masaryk, of course, went on to become a much loved President of Czechoslovakia when the First Republic was established after World War One. In no other country in Eastern Europe would the defence of a feckless Jewish youth have been a likely step on the road to power. Indeed, few politicians in any country have started their career with such a noble stand against injustice!

The Constitution of 1919 reflects this background. All nation-alities were granted equal status and the right to use their own languages in subsidised primary schools; individuals were granted the option of registering their nationality as 'Jewish' for census purposes. (In 1930, over 57 per cent of them did so.) Both religious observance and Zionism were considered perfectly legitimate. In 1920, about half the Jewish vote went to a specifically Jewish Party, founded by Zionists but transformed into a broader grouping which campaigned on a wide variety of Jewish issues. Nor were they an insignificant presence politically: there were some 350,000 Jews in Czechoslovakia in the 1920s, about two and a half per cent of the population. The distribution, however, was uneven: about one per cent in most of Bohemia and Moravia, four per cent in the capital cities of Prague and Brno, and far more in Slovakia. By the mid-1930s, almost twelve per cent of university students were Jewish.

Despite the attitudes of the Sudeten Germans, in terms of democracy and any normal standards of human decency inter-war Czechoslovakia was among the very best of the new states established at the end of the First World War. Since the new post-1989 order draws partly on the traditions of the First Republic, this is obviously a very good omen. (Indigenous traditions of antisemitism in Poland, Hungary and what was East Germany are, alas, a very different matter.) Even during the German occupation, the record of Czech assistance to Jews was often laudable. Besides, the whole machinery of administration and deportation was in German hands, so the Jews who survived were not left with a strong sense of betrayal by their fellow citizens.

In Slovakia, however, things were very different. The Germans, it is sometimes said, put the hyphen back into Czecho-Slovakia, taking direct control of Bohemia and Moravia but setting up a nominally independent state in Slovakia. Although this regime was corrupt and therefore bribable, it inflicted savage restrictions and worse on the Jews. Nuremberg-style laws such as one which prohibited Jews from owning flats overlooking main roads were only the start. A Federation of Jewish Communities was founded, consisting of wealthy but unsavoury characters who were then required to take all the major decisions about their poorer co-religionists.

Many were deported, although a present-day official of the Prague Jewish community described to me a rather different experience: he was first conscripted into the national 'Labour Army' to work in a stone quarry, then sold off to a private firm. This was probably an example of Slovak humanity rather than savagery: while the Catholic majority were sometimes willing to deport Jews, the Protestants in government often used such means to protect them. Yet when news about the real meaning of deportation to Auschwitz was transmitted from the Papal *nuncio* via the Pope to the Slovak clergy, even this clerico-'Fascist' puppet regime protested to the Germans.

Needless to say, the direct German occupation of the country in 1944 put an end to the possibility of making deals with the authorities. The basic pattern, however, remains clear: Slovak Jews feel a certain amount of justified paranoia about their fellow citizens; Czech Jews can feel much more at home. Indeed, it was emphasized to me, they are Czechs and have taken part as Czechs in post-war politics and dissident movements, including the Prague Spring of 1968. They are far too small in number to revive the separate Jewish political parties of the First Republic.

Today, there are about 1,200 registered Jews in Prague, some 80 per cent of them over 70. (The estimated total Jewish figure for the whole of Czechoslovakia is around 15,000.) This tiny number reflects both the devastations of the Nazi period and the generally hostile attitudes of the Communist authorities. Such hostility regularly took the form of quotas, and sometimes of outright persecution: in 1951, Rudolf Slansky (Secretary General of the Party) and ten colleagues were arrested on Stalin's orders, found guilty of being 'enemies of the Republic' and sentenced to death. Officially they were 'Trotskyist-Titoist bourgeois-nationalist traitors'; but far more significant was their common Jewish origin.

Even in very recent times KGB informers were always to be seen at the back of every synagogue, eager to note signs of people with Zionist sympathies. The 1960s saw a slight cultural liberalization, but also the expulsion of the remaining Jews from the Politburo. Leading posts in the Jewish community were given to people the Party controlled or considered 'reliable'. The single Czech rabbi was essentially an agent, who even attacked recent plans to change the name of Red Army Square to Jan Palach Square after the martyr-hero of the Prague Spring, claiming the Red Army deserved their eternal gratitude for liberating the camps. He was also foolish enough to form his own party and stand for election; when Civic Forum investigated the political past of opposing candidates, his shady background was revealed. He obviously retains his rabbinic title (and now has a job in the cemeteries department), but he no longer functions as rabbi to the community.

In addition to its non-functioning rabbi, the Prague community has two elderly cantors (with another in Brno) and an official to

The greatest surviving masterpiece of Jewish Prague: inside the Old-New Synagogue in 1881, showing the extraordinary *bimah* and a congregation which today is often supplemented by tourists (Anne Cowen/*Graphic*)

oversee the kosher restaurant but no *mohel* to perform circumcisions or *shochet* for the slaughter house. Insufficient funds are available to buy in suitable rabbis or cantors from abroad, and even brief visits by a qualified *shochet* from Budapest or Vienna are a major expense. Furthermore, there are considerable difficulties in repossessing land owned by the community before the War and subsequently confiscated. For example, a building which housed the burial society was taken over by a trade union, which later gave it to the Academy of Sciences; since they in turn spent large sums of money renovating it, there is endless room for disputes about ownership and compensation.

All of this rightly suggests that the Prague Jewish community faces some major problems; yet there are also many reasons for optimism. As a suspect minority, Jews have even more cause than most Czechs to welcome a freer press which no longer hesitates to refer to the Jewish origins of famous men and women. Who can regret the passing of an era of bugged phones and flats – and the ring on the doorbell from the State Security? Far greater opportunities for travel in and out of Czechoslovakia include an opening up to Israel. (Before 1989, Israelis were unable to visit Czechoslovakia, unless they were pensioners with family there or were willing to book expensive trips to a spa town as a cover story.) After President Havel's journey to Israel, a Federation of Czech Jews was established there. Even the rise of ultra-nationalist parties seems unlikely. There was a nasty moment when Slovak separatists in America funded the setting up of a memorial to Father Jozef Tiso, who founded the Slovak 'Fascist' state, under Nazi auspices, in 1939. (It was later removed.) In general, though, Czech Jews are so few and so assimilated that antisemitism is much less significant than the continuing rivalry between Czechs and Slovaks.

In a more liberal regime, people who were afraid to identify themselves as Jews (many of whom changed their names) have now come forward to register; some of those in their 40s or younger, even if they received a minimal Jewish education, have become religiously observant. A further strong contingent is derived from the gentiles, usually from mixed marriages, who converted to Judaism in the late 1970s and 1980s. Although they were often motivated partly by political factors or a rather naïve enthusiasm for the Jewish way of life, such people have added vital numbers and commitment to a small and ageing community.

All this is only a start, but a Jewish revival is unquestionably taking place. Marseilles and, to a lesser extent, Paris are the Jewish 'miracles' of Western Europe, towns in which a stronger Jewish presence than ever has emerged from the terrible war years. No other European countries have seen mass immigration on anything like the same scale, but Eastern Europe as a whole is witnessing a different form of Jewish rebirth. As state restrictions are swept away, many people are recovering their roots.

In Czechoslovakia (and particularly in Prague), a tradition of democracy and tolerance makes serious outbursts of popular antisemitism unlikely. Jewish numbers may be small, but the atmosphere may well prove less hostile than in Austria, Hungary or a reunited Germany. Until the Holocaust, Germany and the famous triad of Habsburg cities – Vienna, Budapest and Prague – were all home to a distinct and exceptionally fruitful Central European branch of Jewish life. If, as seems very possible, something similar develops once again, no environment could be more apt than the great Jewish architectural heritage of Prague.

12

PARIS

ONE OF THE great sights of Paris is the Père Lachaise cemetery. Many of the memorials look like booths, huts or houses, and occasional cars glide around 'streets' marked with road signs and sometimes even No Entry signs. Casual visitors curl up on stone benches with novels. Bare-chested men lounge around the main statue in the centre. Young lovers share sandwiches, kisses and more on conveniently shaped tombs. Teachers bring parties of schoolchildren to look at the graves of Oscar Wilde, Jim Morrison, Edith Piaf and many of the leading figures in French history. And there is always a throb of activity all round, as attendants fill in holes, spray down pathways and bang at tombs. Mourners wash down gravestones and replace bouquets. Truly it is a city within the city.

Marcel Proust is buried under a very simple and fairly small black slab of marble a little way down the path which cuts into the 85th division. The main Jewish interest of the cemetery, however, lies in two contrasting sections which encapsulate the Jewish history of France. The first commemorates the tragedies of the Second World War in a whole series of monuments just inside the Avenue Circulaire in the 97th division. The spot itself, as it happens, has tragic associations, since it was just here that some of the Paris Communards were lined up against a wall and shot in 1871. Today, the sun blazes down on monuments to leading resisters, Communists and those who died in the concentration camps: there is no avoiding politics, even in a graveyard.

A huge pair of bound hands emerges from the Ravensbruck memorial, one striving upwards in hope, the other collapsing in despair; a small garden of Resurrection roses from the camp is planted nearby. Three emaciated figures intertwined commemorate Buchenwald, where the RAF Escaping Society had left a bouquet of plastic poppies. Another emaciated figure in bronze is suspended by the waist by a tormented twisting flame or spiky stylized tree in the monument to the dead of Orianenbourg-Sachsenhausen. A brown marble slab bearing the word DACHAU is held aloft by two austere columns of grey stone. A human figure, as simplified as a doll, issues from the rock on the memorial to Auschwitz, where 80,000 French citizens were exterminated. And a steep flight of stairs which a prisoner, bent double under the weight of rocks, attempts to climb recalls the 'Calvary' of the 186 steps leading to the quarry at Mauthausen.

The other interesting section of the cemetery could hardly be more different. A striking feature of Jewish Paris is the monuments which evoke the optimism, and sometimes the complacency, of nineteenth-century France, after the upheavals of the Revolutionary and Napoleonic years had given the Jews the right to play a much fuller role in national life. (There are some extraordinary pre-nineteenth-century synagogues in France – in Cavaillon, Carpentras and Lunéville, to name three of the finest – but none in Paris.) The seventh division of Père Lachaise is a good example.

Made over to the Jewish community in 1809, it is located near the Rue du Repos entrance and overlooked by austere grey flats. It is not entirely Jewish. A special Chemin Abelard et Héloïse leads to a sort of Gothic bandstand commemorating the great lover-logicians of the Middle Ages. Two solid fortress tombs with prominent crosses stand vigil at the start of the Avenue Rachel. Yet the avenue is a lovely pathway shaded by horse-chestnut trees and one is soon transported into a Jewish world.

Here are the tombs of the early Rothschilds, a shelter-like memorial with a bench for a female Rothschild who married into the Leonino barony and a joint grave for the family of the painter Pissarro, born in St Thomas (then in the 'Danish Antilles') in 1830. Brightly coloured military medals are engraved into the side of soldiers' tombs, the ill-omened name of Dreyfus can be spotted (although Alfred Dreyfus is buried in the Montparnasse Cemetery), an obelisk for David Sintzheim (1745–1812), the first Grand Rabbin of France, was rediscovered under weeds in 1974, and families of the recently deceased still come to tend their graves.

Just next to the Dreyfus tomb is the memorial to Rachel herself.

Born Elisa Félix in 1820, she was one of the greatest tragic actresses of the nineteenth century and lived for many years in the aristocratic Place des Vosges. Troughs for flowers like windowboxes create a space in front of her memorial, which is slightly set back from the path. As befits the queen of the French stage, this is regal in appearance, a tall, thin booth a bit like a palace guard house. The floor is collapsing within, but roses picked out in gold appear on the metal grille outside, and the top of the monument is decorated with an elaborate cornice, stone tiara and her single name.

To dig back deeper into the Jewish history of Paris, visitors should make for the very centre of the city. The landmark used for the purpose of road signs is the *place* in front of Notre Dame; just opposite, on the Left Bank, is the very curious church of St Julien le Pauvre. The nave is truncated, the pediment lopsided and the beautifully austere Romanesque vaulting and forest of columns shelter an unexpected explosion of icons. After centuries of use by Roman Catholics, it was taken over by the Melchites or Greek Catholics in 1889, who gave it this very eastern Christian flavour.

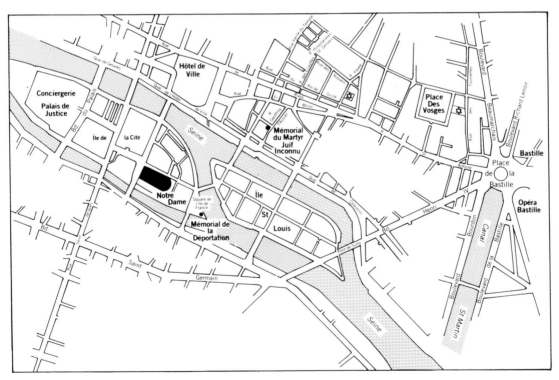

It is also the most ancient church within the old city walls, built in the late-twelfth and early-thirteenth centuries. (Nearby Notre Dame was started earlier but not completed until 1333.) It therefore makes an ideal point of departure for a tour of Christian Paris. Yet, oddly enough, it has also got an intriguing Jewish connection. In the year 585, it is said, a Jewish convert killed a Jew called Priscus, who acted as business agent for the king. The murderer and his friends rushed from the scene of the crime and took refuge on the sacred soil of a church which stood on the site of the present-day St Julien le Pauvre. If we assume that Priscus lived close-by, his home must have been either on the Left Bank or the Ile de la Cité.

Now the Left Bank was the earliest part of Paris to be inhabited – by the tribe of Gauls called the Parisii – since the ground rises rapidly away from the Seine up towards the Sorbonne. Their position was quite secure from attack, protected not only by the river but also by the marshy land on the other side which was to become the Marais (or 'swamp'). When we reach the Middle Ages, there is a good deal of evidence for a Jewish presence there, in the area close to the Petit Pont and Pont St Michel. A particular centre was the Rue de la Harpe, named after a once prominent street sign which featured King David and his harp. Thirteenth-century tombstones from a nearby cemetery can still be seen in the Musée de Cluny.

There were two main reasons for this concentration. The market which was held in front of Notre Dame in the Middle Ages over-flowed on to the nearby bridges, where Jewish and Syrian merchants would offer for sale spices and other goods from the Middle East. And the roads which cross the Petit Pont and Pont St Michel continue across the Ile to the Pont Notre Dame and Pont au Change; they thus formed part not only of major routes across Paris but of important arteries to the south; indeed, the Rue du Petit Pont soon becomes the Rue St Jacques precisely because it was used by pilgrims *en route* to Sandiego de Compostela on the Atlantic coast of Spain.

Before leaving the Left Bank, it is worth mentioning two unusual businesses. Just opposite St Julien le Pauvre is the Tea Caddy, an English-style tea room complete with dark wooden panelling and sombre brown chairs. It was once the stables of the grand mansion next door but was converted into a tea room in 1928, a retirement gift from the Paris Rothschilds to an English governess called Miss Kinklin. Not very far away in the Rue de la Bûcherie is an extraordinary shop called the Galerie Urubamba with a dark-green

'Homage to Paris' by Mané-Katz. Like Chagall, Mané-Katz was a leading member of the 'Paris School' of painters, who combined celebration of the city with motifs drawn from his Jewish background (Mané-Katz Museum, Haifa)

façade sliding round the corner on a little *place*. It now specializes in American Indian crafts: marvellous orange and yellow tiger masks with great rows of gaping teeth snarl at passers-by. Above, on the façade, is an equally menacing row of hooks which were used for hanging up meat when this was a kosher butcher.

On the Ile de la Cité are the Palais de Justice and the Memorial to the Deported. The former adjoins the Conciergerie, where Marie Antoinette was kept prisoner. It was there that a 'disputation' was held in 1240, when the Talmud was put on trial. As in the far more famous show-trials in Spain, a Jewish convert acted as the prosecution and a rabbi put the opposing case to a courtroom which made no attempt to be impartial. Needless to say, the Jews were defeated and every copy of the Talmud in Paris was publicly burnt.

Catholic triumphalism: the statue of the Defeated Synagogue on the main façade of Notre Dame (H. Szwarc)

   The Memorial to the Deported, sited in a garden on the very tip of the Ile behind Notre Dame, commemorates the 200,000 people who were deported during the years of German occupation. Yet it is on the very façade of the great cathedral that one can find an unexpected picture of medieval Jewish life. Huge statues appear in recesses on the main buttresses representing the Church Triumphant and the Defeated Synagogue. The latter is a female figure, eyes blinded by a serpent which coils around her head, her crown crushed under foot and her sceptre broken. Such a theme was popular in the Middle Ages, but the French Revolutionaries disliked Christian triumphalism and destroyed the sculptures. The present copies date from the nineteenth century. Above, a row of 28 Kings of Judah depicts those who were considered ancestors of Jesus.

When it comes to individual scenes from the New Testament, however, the sculptors made a sensitive effort to get the details right. The obvious models to use were the Jews of Paris they lived among. In the centre of the Saint Anne portal is the familiar image of the Angel Gabriel's Annunciation to the Virgin Mary. On either side are scenes from the life of Saint Anne, her mother. One shows her wedding with Saint Joachim, the other the bringing of offerings to the synagogue. The costumes of flowing robes and pointed hats show the garb of mediaeval Parisian Jews, and all the other details of the synagogue seem equally authentic and well observed: the prayer shawl, the eternal flame, the Scrolls, the piles of books, the two men chatting in a corner, one with a pedlar's bundle over his shoulder. It is all quite simple but totally unsatirical, a rare acknowledgement at the very heart of Christian Europe that the key figures in the Gospels were in fact Jews, with their own traditions and ways of life. As we have seen in the chapter on Amsterdam, Rembrandt is equally unusual among leading Christian painters in his acute awareness of this crucial fact.

A short distance from the bridges on the Right Bank of the Seine is the Marais, home to what is perhaps the liveliest Jewish quarter in Europe. It also contains the Place des Vosges and Place de la Bastille, two of the most evocative symbols of royal and revolutionary France. Both have their own Jewish interest. The former was once the Place Royale, built early in the seventeenth century. The harmonious *hôtels particuliers* are all in various shades of red, the overall effect of symmetry set off by subtle differences in each building. The small garden in the middle is always full of tourists and locals speaking many different languages, and even the shrill whistles of the park keeper cannot keep everybody off the grass or spoil the enchanted effect.

Almost every residence has intriguing historical links, but

although it is possible to visit Victor Hugo's house, most of the charming interior courtyards are inaccessible behind plush art galleries, hotels and restaurants. It is difficult, for example, to get a good look at the Hôtel de Chaulnes, where Rachel lived, although it is all too easy to miss the discreet synagogue or Temple Vosges at no. 14. From the outside, it is impressive: the building has the one and only campanile in the *place* and the elaborate balconies on the first floor have been beautifully restored. These form arabesques around the attractive abstract stained glass windows of the synagogue, along with the metal grilles which have been added as protection against terrorists. Inside is a small functional hall, long and narrow, where prayers are held on Friday evenings and Saturday mornings. On the back wall is a decorative metal screen created of Stars of David, a motif which also appears on the criss-crossed square lights overhead. The central section is for women, while notables sit in more comfortable seats to the left of the pulpit.

The Temple Vosges may be located in a most impressive former *hôtel*, complete with a panelled entrance hall, plants, carpets and a grand staircase, yet there is nothing particularly remarkable about it. It uses the Ashkenazi rite and was opened in 1963. The date is significant: in the previous year, Algeria became independent and large numbers of Sephardi Jews moved to France. They therefore took over the famous synagogue on the Rue des Tournelles, and the smaller local Ashkenazi community moved to the Temple Vosges, which backs on to it.

The earlier synagogue is now classified and protected as a *monument historique*, and I was led by the *gardien*'s son – clad in an Africa sweatshirt and Chicago baseball cap – into a superb interior. Above is a cream barrel vault, into which are fitted deep-blue stained-glass windows flecked with stars. At the back, set in a grand arch, there is an intricate golden grille for the Ark and circular golden tracery on a green background above – like a gorgeously ornate lift door and clock in a grand hotel; above that is a huge arch of stained-glass palm branches picked out in cream, green and pale blue. (Stone palm branches also feature prominently on the grand façade.) The lower level of the synagogue has stone pillars, but they support great arching galleries of iron, painted green, with decorative scrolls, elegantly simple wooden railings and a sequence of related pale colours. The result is a building with a slightly Moorish flavour but which also recalls the great days of nineteenth-century engineering. It seats 1,500 and was rebuilt in its present form in 1875; the architect was Gustave Eiffel, in the days before his Tower – a good sign of the wealth and assimilation of French Jews.

Despite the city's immense architectural riches from many different epochs, there is little in Paris that recalls the revolutionary era. The Place de la Bastille, for example, is a wonderful symbol, but the July Column, the sleek curves of the new opera house and the luxury marina on the Canal St Martin make an imposing ensemble quite devoid of echoes of the late-eighteenth century.

There are several reasons, however, for touching here on the events of the revolutionary and Napoleonic periods. In Paris, the most obvious effect was numerical. I have already mentioned the strongly nineteenth-century flavour to the city's Jewish monuments. Until the Revolution, there was a large contingent of Ashkenazi Jews in Alsace, some Sephardim (descendants of those expelled from Spain in 1492) around Bordeaux and a smaller number in the Comtat Venaisson, the papal state centred on Avignon. The Parisian community was much less significant. It was only when revolutionary legislation removed restrictions on residence that large numbers of Jews came to live in the French capital.

It was in Metz, Alsace, that the famous essay contest was held just before the Revolution in which competitors (including a Jewish librarian) had to submit answers to the question: 'How can we make the Jews of France happier and more useful?' One contestant thought there was nothing for it but to ship all the Jews off to South America, others expressed traditional Christian prejudices, while one proposed the still untested solution that all Jews should be forced to take up bee-keeping! The majority view, however, was the enlightened one that Jews were entitled to the full rights of citizenship like everybody else. When these beliefs were put into effect after 1789, it totally transformed Jewish life in Paris, the rest of France and all the European countries where constitutions were imposed by the armies of the Revolution. Even places not directly affected were influenced by the French model.

It should have been very straightforward. The celebrated Declaration of the Rights of Man and the Citizen, issued on 26 August 1789, *seemed* to have settled the issue once and for all. In theory civil rights and complete freedom of conscience had indeed been granted to all adult men, yet right-wing deputies argued that the Assembly could not *really* intend to grant such privileges to Jews, Protestants and members of 'low professions' like actors and public executioners.

Emancipation eventually took place in two stages. The Sephardim of western France, it was pointed out, had traditionally received most of the rights of citizenship in so-called 'Letters Patent' granted by successive Kings when they came to the throne. Did the Revolutionaries really intend to deprive people of legitimate rights they were long accustomed to? As a result of this intervention, one section of French Jewry became citizens in 1790; debate continued about the Ashkenazi. Liberals claimed that the Assembly had created a Jewish aristocracy – which should have been an overwhelming argument to a Revolutionary audience. Opponents replied that the Ashkenazi *were*

The Dreyfus case shattered many of the hopes which French Jews had invested in assimilation. Here Maître Demange makes his final plea to the judges in Rennes, 1899 (Anne Cowen/*Illustrated London News*)

quite different and inferior, and some of the Sephardim echoed these snobbish ideas. It was only when the King tried to flee the country in 1791 that the Right was discredited and full Jewish Emancipation at last became a reality.

Not long afterwards, the revolutionary armies in Italy, led by General Bonaparte, brought liberal constitutions to many parts of Europe; ghetto walls or gates were torn down. Later on, during his Egyptian campaign, Napoleon seems to have toyed with the idea of setting up a Jewish client state in Palestine. Yet once he became Emperor, his firm stress on rational organization, centralization and the overriding duty of military service led him to establish his system of consistories. In return for the basic rights, the Jewish community became part of the French state, controlled hierarchically by the Central Consistory and therefore easily subject to government pressure. The bargain aroused intense controversy at the time, all the way from Warsaw to the United States (would the end of ghetto life, it was asked, also mean the end of independent Jewish spiritual and intellectual traditions?); yet it undoubtedly ushered in an age of great achievement for French Jews.

Something of this can be seen in the huge synagogue on the Rue de la Victoire (not very far from the Louvre). Together with the Central Consistory on the Rue St Georges, the complex seems to take over most of a block; the corner building is marked with a turret and labelled L'Illustration. The synagogue itself was finished in 1874 – with a courtyard which used to provide parking for carriages – and has been nicknamed both the 'cathedral' and 'Rothschild' synagogue. Everything is on the grandest scale, with great stone columns stretching up to a barrel-vaulted ceiling 85 feet high and stained glass representing the twelve tribes of Israel, yet the austere romanesque style is impressive only because of its sheer size.

When this synagogue was built, it was intended to vary its ritual in accordance with the demands of both the Ashkenazi and Sephardi communities (these long-established Sephardim must be distinguished from the recent arrivals from North Africa). This attempt to heal the rifts never really worked out: the Sephardim left to set up their own synagogue (now in the nearby Rue Buffault), although prayers 'in the oriental manner' were continued for fifteen years in the Rue de la Victoire in the hope of reconciliation. Today there are also tiny Egyptian and Tunisian *oratoires* in the grounds of the Central Consistory.

Although the consistories form one of the pivots of French Jewish life, it is an umbrella organization known as the CRIF (Conseil Représentatif des Institutions Juives de France) which speaks for the whole community. It evolved during the first three decades of this century, when there was a large influx of Jewish immigrants from Eastern Europe. Many such people did not feel they were well represented by the Central Consistory, either because they came from secular leftist (Bundist or Zionist) backgrounds or, on the contrary, because they were far *more* religious than the French Jewish establishment. Since they were often poor and did not always feel welcome, they set up their own welfare institutions and burial societies, based on their towns of origin, and these formed the nucleus of the CRIF.

The current President is the first woman, Madame Jacqueline Keller, who welcomed me into an office decorated with a splendid poster of Golda Meir and the caption 'Quand les femmes bougent, l'homme avance' ('When women take action, man makes progress'). Different sections of the CRIF, she explained, dealt with political research, the plight of Soviet Jews, Jews in danger elsewhere in the world, and keeping alive the memory of those who were exterminated by the Nazis. Regional branches had been established in 1981, which had the advantage of giving a larger role to the Sephardim, who dominate in the provinces.

The Chief Rabbi sometimes addresses political issues from a moral point of view, but it is Madame Keller's job to express a consensus position for the whole community. Leading CRIF functionaries have been involved in some bold personal initiatives – a former President, Maître Théo Klein, had a stimulating discussion with a leading Palestinian spokesman in a book called *Deux Vérités en Face* – but official pronouncements have to remain at a safe level of maximum acceptability (i.e. that the democratically elected government of Israel has the right to negotiate with whoever it wishes).

The most obvious danger the Jews of France face is Jean-Marie Le Pen's Front National, even though the party's first target is the Arab immigrants from North Africa (about 800,000 citizens, more than the Jews, and 3,000,000 residents). The CRIF has called for the removal of Le Pen's European parliamentary immunity and has joined forces with Muslims and Christians of many different denominations in protesting. Indeed, despite the many issues that divide them, the

CRIF has reasonably good relations with Islamic organizations, some of which have come to ask advice about establishing lay institutions! During the wars in the Middle East, the Chief Rabbi and the *Recteur* of the Great Mosque walked hand in hand through the Jewish quarter in an attempt to keep down tensions within France.

One of the most inflammatory events, by contrast, takes place every 1 May. Labour Day has long been a national holiday in France, but recently it has been co-opted by the Front National for a celebration of Joan of Arc. Posters are prominent all over Paris for several days beforehand, and attempts have been made to keep the march respectable: thugs wearing neo-Nazi shirts are now told to keep them well hidden. The whole event is unbelievably kitsch, but also rather terrifying; even on best behaviour the Front is disturbing at first hand.

One year I was there the procession set off from the Place St Augustin, in front of a statue of Joan, and made its way slowly – the whole crowd had to adapt to the pace of the contingent of bemedalled veterans, many of them limping or in wheelchairs – towards the Louvre. Much junk was for sale: trinkets, badges saying *Vas-y, Jean-Marie!* ('Go for it!'), books of Le Pen's reflexions and cassettes of genuine French folksongs. Even a *clochard* in a nearby park, draped in a *tricolore* scarf, took time off between swigs to hurl obscenities at every mention of Mitterrand. At the climax of the march, a presidential-style Le Pen awaited his supporters in the Place des Pyramides. Contingents representing almost every town and region of France passed in review before him – from industrial Nancy to suburban Drancy (where the appalling war-time deportation centre must have whetted the locals' appetite for xenophobia). Groups from Brittany, Le Pen's own region, filed past in their traditional costume. Banners proclaimed '*Les Ardennes aux Français!*' and many variations on the theme (some from towns and districts which can seldom have seen a Jew or North African immigrant).

Then came the Cercle Nationale des Femmes d'Europe, acclaimed for their 'grace' and 'fecundity'. Catholic groups distributed leaflets proposing a pilgrimage to Chartres or healthy holidays on Mont-Blanc as an alternative to drugs, AIDS and hard rock. And small children in immaculate white sailor suits represented the Cadets, a sort of ecological and nationalistic scouting movement whose hand-outs spoke of boating excursions where they learned about the 'tears, sweat and blood which have made the French harvest so fertile'.

All this might be described as sub-Fascist trash theatre; but there was a more sinister side to it. Flyers openly advocated throwing the immigrants out. Books by revisionist historians such as Robert Faurisson who deny the existence of the gas chambers were freely on sale. Supporters of the Front National have tried to rehabilitate the collaborationist government in Vichy – or least discourage discussion of its terrible record. Indeed, the whole unhealthy cult of Joan of Arc is very much a throwback to the Vichy years. And Monsieur Le Pen's antisemitic credentials are impeccable – he once referred to the Holocaust as just a 'detail' in the Second World War. There is more than a hint of Fascist rhetoric in his claims to be the one man capable of healing the divisions of France.

It is unnecessary to explore in detail the actions of Marshal Pétain's savage but sanctimonious Vichy government. The French resistance has been deservedly celebrated, but the dark side of the 1940s was very dark indeed. The area of southern France controlled by the nominally independent Vichy regime was the only part of Europe from which native Jewish citizens were deported without a direct German occupation. Indeed, the leaders sometimes tried to win Nazi approval by anticipating their demands. Further north, the German authorities were submerged by hundreds of thousands of letters denouncing Jews, communists, competitors and unpopular neighbours. A militia was formed in 1942, for which potential members had to swear an oath 'against Jewish leprosy and for French purity'.

Functionaries who dabbled in genocide in their youth were never tried after the War but went on to distinguished careers and comfortable retirement. The sheer scale of French involvement in deportations which led to the gas chambers is still acknowledged very inadequately in school textbooks. A particularly harrowing episode involving a group of children from the town of Pithiviers rounded up, interned and sent east without their parents was fully described by *L'Express* magazine for the first time in 1990. The Front National, predictably, complained that they had already heard enough about the crimes committed by French citizens during the War.

Despite the antics of Le Pen, and a number of specific antisemitic incidents, Jews today have an assured place in French society, occupying prominent positions in the law, politics, trade unions, the arts and intellectual life. Just as the Hollywood producers who created 'the American dream' were often immigrants of Jewish origin, two of the most internationally successful films about French rural life – *Jean de Florette* and *Manon des Sources* – were produced and directed by a French Jew from a humble background, Claude Berri.

Paris also has something far more startling, a Jewish archbishop. Monseigneur Lustiger comes from an unequivocally Jewish although not very religious background – his mother was deported and died in Auschwitz – but he was gradually converted to Catholicism in the 1930s and 40s. Despite holidays in Germany just before the War, he claims, in a fascinating extended interview published as *Le Choix de Dieu*, he came across no signs of Christian antisemitism either there or in France during the Occupation. (If so, he was either blinkered or remarkably fortunate.)

Cardinal Lustiger remains Jewish enough to be fiercely critical of Christian missionary activities among the Jews, and supports a post-Holocaust theology which argues that the Jews are already Saved and that only gentiles are required to seek Salvation in Jesus. Despite the fate of his mother, however, he has refused to give historians access to some of the Church's wartime archives – which would presumably provide further evidence of the inglorious role of many Catholic bishops. Today, the Cardinal's rise to such heights within the hierarchy suggests that racial antisemitism, as opposed to remnants of religious anti-Judaism, is not a strong feature of the Catholic establishment. Right-wing extremists, on the other hand, view him with vitriolic hatred.

Jewish archbishops are, no doubt, a case of carrying assimilation too far, but the basic truth remains that Jews have a secure and respected place within mainstream French life. When a ghastly desecration occurred at the Jewish cemetery in Carpentras, many leading French politicians joined in a mass meeting held to express sympathy with the victims; French television screened Alain Resnais's harrowing early documentary about the camps, *Nuit et Brouillard*. Despite an ugly clerical, authoritarian, even mildly Fascist undercurrent in French life, no one would deny the dominance of the republican tradition. France was virtually the first country to emancipate the Jews, and today's community – the largest in western Europe – is still flourishing. Both the Jewish quarter itself and the sheer number and variety of the synagogues scattered round the city stand as uplifting signs of their vibrant presence.

★

One of the most unusual and attractive synagogues in Paris is located
on the Rue Chasseloup-Laubat just opposite an Arab school, although
the caretaker assured me there was no conflict. The interior is square
and made of dark wood. The main wooden columns are made of
single trunks and stretch up to create very high balconies and a
musicians' gallery, used for large weddings. (There is even an organ
now, although it was built in 1913 specifically by Jews keen to get
away from the Sabbath organ music and cathedral-style architecture
and decorum of Paris's main synagogues.) The general impression is
a little like a lofty barn, but yellow, honey-coloured and pale orange
light breaks into the obscurity from stained-glass windows in the
walls and the octagonal bonnet fanlight above. These shafts of soft
light cutting into the gloom create a most striking effect.

Another highly unusual synagogue, also built in 1913, is the
Agoudas Hakehilos on the Rue Pavée, which forms the gateway
into the main Jewish quarter. A side door leads into a surprising
triangular Mediterranean-style tiled courtyard, from where one can
get into the tall thin synagogue. It was echoing with children playing
hide-and-seek when I was there, but the general effect is stark, with a
big plain stained-glass window on the back wall and a colour scheme
dominated by white and pale blues. Again the two tiers of galleries
are very high, and thin columns stretch up to the ceiling. Only the
deep reds of the Ark curtain, the elaborate cloths hung over the lower
balcony and the painted woodwork on the upper balcony produce
dramatic variants in the colour scheme. On the ceiling are restrained
intertwining Art Nouveau floral motifs reminiscent of the ironwork
outside traditional Métro stations. This is not just a coincidence; the
same man, Hector Guimard, designed them both.

The Rue Pavée leads into the Pletzel or Jewish quarter. Few areas
in Europe give such a strong sense of the remarkable continuity of
Jewish life. (The only remotely comparable part of Paris is the area
around the Rue Richer, where rows of kosher grocery shops and little
restaurants stretch away on either side of the Folies Bergères.) It is
only about a quarter of an hour's walk from the original mediaeval
settlements on the Left Bank. Yet the link with particular streets
goes far deeper than that. Officially the Jews were expelled from
France in 1182, 1394 and 1615, but the very fact that such orders
had to be repeated is evidence that they were never wholly effective.
Today's Rue Ferdinand Duval was known as the Rue des Juifs even
in the twelfth century. Sesamé, a booth said to sell the best felafels

in town, stands sentinel at one end, opposite an excellent Jewish *pâtisserie*.

At the far end of the road is Jo Goldenberg's famous restaurant and the Rue des Rosiers. As early as the year 1410, a house sale spoke of the 'Rue des Rosiers, where formerly the Jews lived'. The description was premature: the Rue des Rosiers, Rue Ferdinand Duval and the surrounding network of streets to the West of the Place des

Pâtisserie interior on the rue des Rosiers (*Jewish Chronicle*/Ben Rice)

Vosges today form one of the liveliest Jewish quarters in Europe. Since this can hardly be a coincidence, it is safe to assume that the Jewish presence has been continuous for over 500 years, even if the Jews sometimes had to pretend to live as Christians.

Most of the area in question is to the north of the Rue de Rivoli, which leads from the Louvre to the Bastille, although the Memorial of the Unknown Jewish Martyr is on the Rue Geoffroy-l'Asnier near the Seine. This is in the courtyard of a research institute, with a rather shabby little Holocaust museum and an eternal flame in the basement. An immense bronze cylinder resembling a crematorium urn and labelled with the names of the different camps stands in the centre, while reliefs along the walls depict scenes from the Warsaw ghetto. The windows behind this monument long bore silent witness to a more recent outrage, since the bullet holes were left in the glass after a terrorist attack.

Similar signs of an even more ghastly atrocity can be seen in the window of Goldenberg's. Six people were killed there in 1982, probably by a Palestinian group, a tragedy echoing the horrors of the Occupation years which are recorded in tiny plaques on some of the houses. (The most disturbing is the plaque on the school – once a Jewish primary school – in the rue des Hospitalières-St Gervais, for 165 deported children.) Every year a commemorative vigil is held to mark the occasion, attended by many politicians and media figures. The Rue des Rosiers and those nearby are undoubtedly haunted streets.

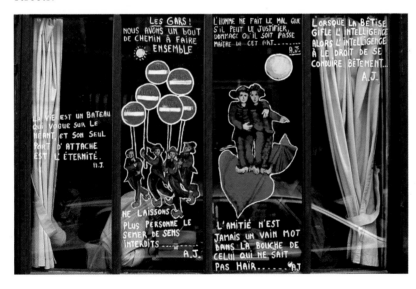

Colourful appeals for tolerance in the window display of a restaurant on the corner of the rue des Hospitalières-St Gervais (*Jewish Chronicle*/ Ben Rice)

Yet this could never be the dominant impression for anyone visiting this exhilarating area. The streets are full of intriguing shops, incongruous contrasts and a wonderful mix of cultures. Goldenberg's is a restaurant-cum-delicatessen, a major Parisian institution with many celebrity clients. It certainly makes its presence felt on the street. A neon sign above the door announces their latest addition to the menu, a forthcoming festival, or a signing session by Baroness Nadine de Rothschild for the publication of her new book. Mountains of aubergine caviar, cakes and other specialities from North Africa and Central Europe are on sale. It is all very *heimisch* and 'kosher-style' (kosher dishes are available for those who want them), although it is not licensed by the rabbinate.

In recent years, chic dress shops have largely replaced the tailoring workshops, but the Jewish butchers, bakers, snack bars and restaurants are still there, displaying certificates either from the Paris Beth Din or the parallel Lubavitch authorities. Food is of a truly Parisian copiousness and variety – from kosher Vietnamese-style *cuisine* to the marvellous Central European cakes described as 'Yiddish specialities' in Sacha Finkelsztajn's elegant *pâtisserie*. Equally elegant are the mosaics on the bath house (Hammam St Paul) long used by North African Jews. The juxtapositions can sometimes be startling: a barber's opposite Goldenberg's displays an appeal from the Lubavitch Rebbe for Jews to return to Torah-true Judaism; next door is a shop selling sexy underwear.

Although the area is small, all of Jewish life seems crammed into a few streets. A plush modern bookshop, jobbing printer and cavernous antiquarian book dealer all sell almost exclusively Judaica. There are souvenir shops, *cafés-théâtres* and ferociously private hidden little synagogues like the Beit Josef on the rue des Ecouffes, whose wooden façade could easily conceal (and perhaps once did conceal) a low-ceilinged little workshop. I once met up with a group of very chic Parisian schoolkids collecting money for the Jewish blind, and one of the restaurants has a colourful painted window display, with cartoon Chagall figures proclaiming the virtues of mutual tolerance and understanding. Many of the shops combine Jewish contents with an understated Parisian elegance. On a good day, the rue des Rosiers seems like a perfect image of the diaspora, bursting with colour and life and an effortless blend of the Jewish and the French.

Best of all are the days when a street market completely chokes up the road with trestle tables, buyers and sellers. I was once there just before *Succot*, when citrons, palm and willow branches suddenly appeared just outside Goldenberg's. A street which had been quiet the day before became dramatically alive and almost impassable. Street traders in traditional garb waved aside photographers who treated them as tourist attractions.

The *Succot* festival, of course, dramatizes, among other things, the eternal homelessness of the Jewish condition. France has not always been the happiest of homes for Jews, and tensions exist to this day. Yet the French tradition of receiving and welcoming victims of persecution is also both genuine and inspiring; Paris remains undeniably *the* Jewish city of Europe. European Jewish history is a terrible catalogue of injustice, persecution and suffering which gives an intense edge of sadness and loss to many otherwise wonderful towns and cities. Yet, despite all the odds, it is also a story of miraculous survival and rebuilding; the rue des Rosiers makes an invigorating symbol of that survival.

BIBLIOGRAPHY

I have not included any general city guides, history or reference books, ephemeral handouts or exhibition catalogues (although those published by the Beth Hatefutsoth/Museum of the Diaspora in Tel Aviv, for example, are often excellent). Although some of the books mentioned have only had a marginal influence on my text, they are all stimulating and informative. Since many are recent publications, they should also be fairly easy to obtain.

BAER, Yitzhak *A History of the Jews in Christian Spain*. Two volumes, Philadelphia, Jewish Publication Society of America, 1961–2

BELLER, Steven *Vienna and the Jews 1867–1938: a cultural history*. Cambridge, Cambridge University Press, 1989

BERMANT, Chaim *Coming Home*. London, Allen and Unwin, 1976

BROOK, Stephen *The Club: The Jews of modern Britain*. London, Constable, 1989

BROOK, Stephen *The Double Eagle: Vienna, Budapest and Prague*. London, Hamish Hamilton, 1988

COLLINS, Dr Kenneth (ed) *Aspects of Scottish Jewry*. Glasgow, Glasgow Jewish Representative Council, 1987

COWEN, Anne and Roger *Victorian Jews through British Eyes*. Oxford, Littmann Library/Oxford University Press, 1986

CURIEL, Roberta and COOPERMAN, Bernard Dov *The Ghetto of Venice*. London, Tauris Parke, 1990

FISHMAN, William J. *East End 1888*. London, Duckworth, 1988

GELLER, Ruth Liliana *Roma Ebraica Jewish Rome*. Rome, Viella, 1984

GLASSER, Ralph *Growing Up in the Gorbals*, London, Chatto & Windus, 1986

JOSEPHS, Jeremy *Swastika Over Paris: The Fate of the French Jews*. London, Bloomsbury, 1989

MACCOBY, Hyam *Judaism on Trial: Jewish–Christian Disputations in the Middle Ages*. Oxford, Littmann Library/Oxford University Press, 1982

RAPHAEL, Chaim *The Road from Babylon: The Story of Sephardi and Oriental Jews*. London, Weidenfeld & Nicolson, 1985

ROTH, Cecil *A History of the Jews in England*. 3rd edition, Oxford, Oxford University Press, 1964

SOCIETY FOR THE HISTORY OF CZECHOSLOVAK JEWS *The Jews of Czechoslovakia*. Volume 1, Philadelphia, Jewish Publication Society of America, 1968

STEINBERG, Jonathan *All or Nothing: The Axis and the Holocaust*. London, Routledge, 1990

STOOUTENBEEK, Jan and VIGEVENO, Paul *A Guide to Jewish Amsterdam*. Amsterdam, De Haan/Jewish Historical Museum, 1985

TOVEY, D'Blossiers *Anglia Judaica or A History of the Jews in England*. New edition, edited and retold by Elizabeth Pearl, London, Weidenfeld & Nicolson, 1990

WEBSTER, Paul *Pétain's Crime: The Full Story of French Collaboration in the Holocaust*. London, Macmillan, 1990

YAHIL, Leni *The Rescue of Danish Jewry*. Philadelphia, Jewish Publication Society of America, 1969

ZUCCOTTI, Susan *The Italians and the Holocaust: Persecution, Rescue and Survival*. London, Peter Halban, 1987